Essays on Kant and Hume

Essays on Kant and Hume

LEWIS WHITE BECK

New Haven and London, Yale University Press, 1978

Published with assistance from the foundation
established in memory of Amasa Stone Mather of
the Class of 1907, Yale College.

Designed by Sally Sullivan Harris
and set in IBM Press Roman type.
Printed in the United States of America by
Halliday Lithograph, West Hanover, Mass.

Published in Great Britain, Europe, Africa, and
Asia (except Japan) by Yale University Press,
Ltd., London. Distributed in Latin America by
Kaiman & Polon, Inc., New York City; in
Australia and New Zealand by Book & Film
Services, Artarmon, N.S.W., Australia; and in
Japan by Harper & Row, Publishers, Tokyo Office.

Library of Congress Cataloging in Publication Data

Beck, Lewis White.
    Essays on Kant and Hume.

    Includes index.
    1. Kant, Immanuel, 1724–1804–Addresses,
essays, lectures. 2. Hume, David, 1711–1776–
Addresses, essays, lectures. I. Title.
B2798.B348   193   77–19999
ISBN 0–300–02170–4

To Karl-Heinz Ilting and Milton Charles Nahm

Contents

Preface

In 1965, thinking that I had said all I had to say about Kant, I published a selection of my papers under the title, *Studies in the Philosophy of Kant*. In the past ten years, however, I have managed to say a bit more, and it is gratifying to be able to publish this second collection of some of my more recent essays. I have properly left some in journals and books where only the diligent scholar would be able to find them. Three of the papers included here have not previously appeared in English, and five have not been published at all. For permission to reprint, I wish to thank the editors and publishers of the journals and books. Full details on the initial publication, and explicit thanks to each editor and publisher, are given at the beginning of each paper.

I have here and there made slight changes, but they are so minor that no worthwhile purpose would be served by indicating every variation from the original.

Works by Kant are cited by giving the pagination in the edition of the Prussian Academy of Sciences, usually indicated by the abbreviation "Ak." Wherever possible I have added a reference to a standard English translation, even when, as was often the case, there was no translation at the time the paper was originally published. The only exception to this rule is citations to the *Critique of Pure Reason* in its two editions, indicated by "A" or "B." Since the Kemp Smith translation gives the A and B pagination in the margin, there is no need to indicate Kemp Smith's own page numbers, though generally I have gladly followed his translation with only occasional modifications. Quotations from my translation of the *Critique of Practical*

Reason give the page numbers in the Bobbs-Merrill edition (1956), not those in the Chicago edition (1949) or its 1976 reprint (Garland Publishing Co.).

PART ONE

Studies in the
Critique of Pure Reason

1 Kant's Strategy

Great strategists are soldiers who win wars, or at least delay defeat, by their genius in efficiently marshalling the forces at hand. Wars are not won just by strategy, but they may be lost by it. For victory, good strategy must be carried out by effective tactics; but good tactics may be wasted by being used in the wrong place, at the wrong time, and against the wrong enemy. While the great strategist will keep in mind the tactical capabilities and weaknesses of his men, so as not to plan battles that cannot be won in the field, the history of warfare recognizes great strategists who did not win, not because their strategy was wrong but because this or that tactical move was not successfully made. Often we discern strategy best in a general who loses, for often we can attribute to his victorious opponent such virtues as stubbornness, single-mindedness, and courage, or ascribe his victory to such gifts of fortune as superior numbers, better weapons, and good luck.

I wish to use these metaphors of strategy and tactics in an exposition of Kant's philosophizing. We know of Kant's keen and learned interest in military matters. Though most of his metaphors which refer to his work are drawn from law and the natural sciences and there are few military metaphors,[1] is it too farfetched to consider

Reprinted from *The Journal of the History of Ideas* 28 (1967), 224–36, by kind permission of the editor, Professor Philip P. Wiener.
1. The richest source of Kant's military metaphors is his late polemic against Schlosser, *Verkündigung des nahen Abschlusses eines Traktats zum ewigen Frieden in der Philosophie* (1796). In this he proposed his theory of freedom as a ground on which dogmatists and skeptics could sign a treaty of peace. Nothing in the present essay is incompatible with that polemic, but I hope

his work as intellectual warfare, and thus to draw on a different set of metaphors? In particular, I see Kant as engaged in a two-front war. Germany has found, twice in this century, and Prussia found, in Kant's lifetime, that to fight a two-front war it must use one army on two fronts and be able to shift this army rapidly from one to the other. In Kant's two-front war, his talent as a strategist was shown by his finding a philosophical argument which could be used effectively against two very different opponents at the same time. I shall try to show the pattern of this strategy by showing how Kant waged one battle before he began writing the *Critique of Pure Reason* and then repeated its plan later and on a larger scale. But before doing that, we must first carefully identify the opponents against whom this strategy was to be used.

At the very end of the *Critique of Pure Reason*, in the chapter entitled "The History of Pure Reason," Kant sets forth three great perennial divisions in metaphysics as the theory of the scope and function of reason. He gives three dichotomies: between intellectualists and sensualists in regard to the object of knowledge, between empiricists and noologists (rationalists) in regard to the origin of knowledge, and between naturalists and scientists (users of the *scientifische Methode*, i.e., systematic, "scholastic" philosophers) in regard to the methods of knowledge. Among the latter, Kant distinguishes two types: those who proceed dogmatically, like Wolff, and those who proceed skeptically, like Hume.

These three ways of dividing possible philosophies are logically independent of one another, but in fact we find certain family affiliations among some of them. The great intellectualists have been noologists and dogmatists; the great sensualists have been empiricists and either naturalists or skeptics. There are, then, two great coalitions opposed to each other, not only in Kant's time but again and again since Socrates and the Sophists met in battle.

that I have come closer to the historical and epistemological citadel of his philosophy than he did in this *Tendenzschrift*. (Titles are given in German when there is no English translation of the work in question.) A sensitive and comprehensive study of Kant's metaphors, "The Fabric of Metaphor in the *Critique of Pure Reason*," by David Tarbet, will be found in the *Journal of the History of Philosophy* 6 (1968), 257–70.

Let us see what were the elements in the two coalitions which were opposed to each other. We may think of Kant as standing isolated between them, looking for future allies in both camps (though of course this is not the whole historical truth because Kant himself was at one time a member in good standing of one of the alliances and, in the later sixties, seems to many historians of philosophy simply to have changed sides for a time). But the mature Kant was never entirely uncritical of the rationalists, and never fully committed to a skepticism based on empiricism. So let us imagine him as standing between, unwilling to commit himself to either; this was perhaps his own conception of his position as when he stirs up trouble between the opposing forces, enticing them into battle with each other so that they will destroy each other.[2]

We shall examine first the composition of the *entente* founded in modern times by Locke. There were three principal allied powers here, all agreeing on one point: that all our knowledge comes from experience. These allied powers were: skepticism in metaphysics, naturalism in ethics, and something I shall call for lack of a better name skepticism tempered with naturalism in the theory of knowledge. Hume is the best example of all three. Kant believed that, though Hume was not a consistent skeptic, he was saved from Pyrrhonism only by his good sense and by a fortunate error he made in the estimation of mathematical knowledge. But Kant believed that a consistently developed empiricism could lead to skepticism not only in metaphysics, which is as far as he thought Hume pushed it, but also in our natural and mathematical knowledge. Since, as Hume put it, "Nature is always too strong for principle,"[3] such a skepticism in metaphysics was quarantined by a recognition that what little knowledge we have suffices for the ordinary affairs of life. As Locke himself saw, "The candle that is set up in us shines bright enough for all our purposes," but does not cast a light into the regions into which we can never venture. Naturalism in ethics, a kind of empiricism in regard to our knowledge of right and wrong

2. *Critique of Pure Reason*, A 422–23 = B 450–51. The same thought with a legal rather than a military metaphor occurs at A 530 = B 558. Hume uses the same imagery in *The Natural History of Religion*, last paragraph.
3. Hume, *Enquiry Concerning Human Understanding*, Sect. XII, Part ii, end.

and a eudaemonism or hedonism in the definition of good and bad, has regularly been associated with metaphysically skeptical but this-worldly naturalistic empiricism. Kant did not equally oppose all the members of this coalition of ideas. He came to share the empiricists' skepticism of metaphysics but always rejected the naturalism of healthy common sense, which he called "mere misology reduced to principle."[4] And he always opposed the naturalistic ethical theory even when praising Shaftesbury, Hutcheson, and Hume for their "beautiful discoveries" in the method of ethical inquiry.[5]

Kant's strategic question in dealing with this coalition must have been: how could he maintain skepticism in metaphysics—to which he was pushed by his study of Hume and his own discovery of the antinomies which he called "the most fortunate perplexity in which human reason could ever have become involved[6]—without falling victim to eudaemonism in ethics and to a jejune appeal to common sense in the conduct of life and the development of science? How could he oppose Hume without falling in with Reid, Beattie, and Oswald, who he thought were very uninspiring company? How could he give up a supernatural metaphysics without making a metaphysics out of naturalism?

Let us now look at the opposing coalition of the rationalists. Here we find dogmatism in metaphysics, to which Kant adhered in the fifties. Opposed to empiricism was the Leibnizian epistemology which proceeded to solve even the simplest problems by an argument *obscurum per obscurius*. It was an epistemology which explained the simplest facts learned through sense experience by an appeal to preestablished harmony, and the theorems of physics by appeal to theodicy. In ethical theory, there was a Scotism making the good depend upon God—another instance of getting the cart before the horse—and a theory of freedom which Kant called a "wretched subterfuge" grounding nothing more than the freedom of

---

4. *Critique of Pure Reason*, A 855 = B 883.
5. *Nachricht von der Einrichtung seiner Vorlesungen, Gesammelte Schriften*, Prussian Academy Edition, II, 311–12.
6. *Critique of Practical Reason* (Ak. V, 107, Beck translation [New York, 1956], p. 111).

a turnspit or marionette.[7] Again we find that Kant was not equally inimical to all these opponents; as I have said, early in life he espoused its dogmatism, and in the sixties he accepted the "wretched subterfuge" in ethics he was later to condemn. Hence his strategic position must have been something like this. Having turned his back upon dogmatism in metaphysics (after 1770), how could he save an ethical theory which required a metaphysical rather than a quasi-physical or hyperphysical foundation? How could he give up metaphysics because it was not empirical? How could he defend our knowledge of nature by giving a theory of synthetic judgments known a priori, without defending metaphysics which consisted of nothing but synthetic judgments known a priori?

Had Kant's strategy been that of *divide et impera*, he would have been an eclectic philosopher drawing a bit from here and a bit from there. His philosophy would itself have been a coalition system of the kind he explicitly condemned,[8] and he would have been as forgotten now as other eclectics and compromisers.

I have been speaking in very broad terms of Kant's attitudes toward a coalition of views into two different *Weltanschauungen*. Kant seldom talked on this synoptic level; he was generally concerned with specific philosophical doctrines, whatever their source. But we have a foretaste of his grand strategy in the tactics of a particular battle he waged in the late sixties and early seventies, so we shall examine this before considering the nature of space and geometry.

It might be thought that empiricism could have no tenable theory of mathematics. If all the material of knowledge comes from experience, all universal statements are inductive and only probable. But since universal mathematical statements are not merely probable, the thesis of empiricism must be false. The empiricist had two ways of dealing with this syllogism. First, he could, with Hume in the *Treatise*,[9] deny the minor premise and make geometry an empirical

7. Ibid., Ak. IV, 96, 97 (Beck, pp. 99, 101).
8. Ibid., §3, Ak. V, 24 (Beck, p. 23).
9. *Treatise of Human Nature*, Book I, Part iii, Section i: "The reason why I impute any defect to geometry is, because its original and fundamental prin-

science which only approximately fits the observed facts of nature. Or, second, he might deny with Hume in the *Enquiry*[10] that mathematics is knowledge of nature and assert that it is only the logical manipulation of symbols. Kant suggests that Hume took the latter point of view in order to keep from giving up mathematical certainty,[11] apparently not knowing that Hume had once committed himself to the former explicitly skeptical conclusion. But given a Newtonian physics and theory of space, the second of Hume's views is in practice as skeptical as the first, because there is no way to justify the application of a merely logically necessary geometry to the space of physics, and, with very few exceptions, the eighteenth century had not yet distinguished between interpreted and uninterpreted axiom system and decided that mathematics belonged among the latter.[12]

---

ciples are derived merely from appearances; and it may perhaps be imagin'd, that this defect must always attend it, and keep it from ever reaching a greater exactness in the comparison of objects or ideas, than what our eye or imagination alone is able to attend" (Selby-Bigge, p. 71).

10. *Enquiry Concerning Human Understanding*, the first paragraph in Section VII, and in Section IV: "If any term be defined in geometry, the mind readily, of itself, substitutes on all occasions, the definition of the term defined . . . " and "Propositions of this kind [geometrical and arithmetical] are discoverable by the mere operation of thought, without dependence on what is anywhere existent in the universe. Though there never were a circle or triangle in nature, the truths demonstrated by Euclid would for ever retain their certainty and evidence" (Yalden-Thomson, pp. 61, 24). But when Hume returns to the subject matter of the *Treatise* in Section XII, Part ii, of the *Enquiry* (Yalden-Thomson, pp. 162–64), i.e., to the application of geometrical concepts to experience, he does so for the purpose of pointing out the discrepancy between geometrical concepts, as commonly (and he believes erroneously) understood, and our spatial perceptions, and thus repeats his *first* answer.

11. *Critique of Practical Reason*, Ak. V, 13 (Beck, p. 13).

12. See E. W. Beth, *The Foundations of Mathematics* (Amsterdam, 1959), on efforts to draw this distinction in the eighteenth century. We may say that Hume's inconsistency, documented in notes 9 and 10 *supra*, arises because in the *Treatise* he is concerned with applied geometry and in the *Enquiry* with pure geometry. But inasmuch as the distinction did not clearly exist, each is mixed up with the other in both the books. Kant recognized the distinction (*Critique of Pure Reason*, B 145; cf. *Thoughts on the True Estimation of Living Forces*, § 115) but did not see how important—perhaps how fatal—it was for his entire position.

Leibniz, on the other hand, never played with an empiricistic theory of mathematics but consistently developed the formalistic theory like that of Hume's later work, and his theory therefore suffered the same infirmity as that in Hume's *Enquiry*—it was hard to see why a system of analytic judgments should have any objective reference to the real disposition of things in space. But whereas Hume could have no theory of how this is possible and, in all probability, thought (as he did in the *Treatise*) that it was not possible, Leibniz did try to show that the propositions of mathematics are necessarily true of space. He did so through two hypotheses. (1) Our perceptions of the physical world are only confused conceptions: hence clear and distinct sense perceptions, of the kind we get through counting and mensuration, must conform to, if they are indeed not identical with, clear and distinct conceptions of numbers and magnitudes. (2) But what we perceive as spatial is not really outside us in an absolute Newtonian space which we could know, if at all, only a posteriori. Rather, space is a *phenomenon bene fundatum*, a phenomenon well founded in the logical relations holding between substances (monads) or states of substances. Geometry is founded on logic; it is a logic which can be mapped spatially as a representation of simultaneously existing incompatibles; space is simply the order in which we perceive compresent possibilities. There is, therefore, no problem as to why the logical relations of concepts fit the intellectual representations we have of space; in a sense, the former generate the latter.[13]

If we compare the outcome of Hume's *Enquiry* with Leibniz's theory of mathematics, we find that these two philosophers agreed on one point and disagreed on another. (a) They agreed, to use Kant's terminology, that mathematical judgments are analytic and logically necessary. (b) They disagreed as to whether mathematics

13. See Kant's very clear statement of Leibniz's problem and solution, *Critique of Pure Reason*, A 275–76 = B 331–32. The flaw in Leibniz's argument is that Leibniz does not distinguish between the sensible appearances and things in themselves, and fails to do so because he makes sensible appearances only confused intellectual representations of things in themselves (substances). But, according to Kant, they are not; hence the problem of the relation of mathematics to the perceptual content is left untouched.

had any necessary objective reference—Leibniz affirming it and Hume denying it.

In 1768 Kant, working from a suggestion made by Euler, formulated the hypothesis that the thesis (a) was false:[14] Mathematical knowledge is not analytic and logically necessary. It is necessary, in the sense that it necessarily applies to our experience of objects in space (here Kant agrees with Leibniz), but it does not apply, even approximately, to anything but objects of experience (and here Kant agrees with the earlier Humean view).

When Kant formulated this view by saying that mathematics contains synthetic judgments, he is disagreeing with both Hume and Leibniz.[15] His answer to it leads directly into the great campaign I have spoken of. Our preliminary study of Kant's treatment of mathematical knowledge from 1768 to 1770 points the way to the larger issue in two respects. First, the answer to the question, "How are synthetic judgments a priori possible?" or "How is pure mathematics possible?" gives the substantive thesis of the *Critique of Pure Reason*, to which I shall turn shortly. But more to my purpose here is the fact that Kant's strategy in this criticism of Hume and Leibniz is in form and pattern exactly the same as his larger strategy in the *Critique of Pure Reason* as a whole.

14. *On the First Grounds of the Distinction of Regions of Space.* The argument is that logically indiscernible entities should be identical, but they are not, as shown by incongruent counterparts in geometry; therefore geometrical figures are not adequately defined by non-intuitive predicates or relations.

15. It is often said that Kant's initial discovery (or claim) from which everything else followed was that there are synthetic judgments known a priori. This is not true. Both Locke and Descartes had admitted judgments which, by the later Kantian criteria, were synthetic and known a priori. It was to explain their apriority that Leibniz and Hume had denied their syntheticity and replaced them with *vérités de raison* and relations of ideas, respectively. But what forced Leibniz and Hume to do so (Hume much more consistently than Leibniz) was the assumption by both Descartes and Locke that we are endowed with an intellectual intuition and that all sense experience is a posteriori. Kant rejected both these assumptions, while Hume denied only the first. Only Kant's denial of the latter permitted him to go beyond Hume and to support the thesis that we have synthetic a priori sensible knowledge. (In this paper I am more concerned with the contribution of sense to the syntheticity of knowledge than to its apriority: but I believe Kant's underlying strategy could be illustrated also in his theory of the latter.)

Kant did not tell us his strategic secrets, and perhaps he was not fully aware of his stratagem. But in our own century, this stratagem has been formulated in what is sometimes called "Ramsey's Maxim." In cases where two opposed arguments seem internally sound but where their conclusions are incompatible and hence a stalemate is created, Frank P. Ramsey wrote: "It is a heuristic maxim that the truth lies not in one of the two disputed views but in some third possibility which has not yet been thought of, which we can only discover by rejecting something assumed as obvious by both the disputants."[16] Two theories, X and non-X, may be reconciled or *both* refuted by finding that they have a common false element. Upon analysis, X may be found to be A + Y, and non-X may be found to be A + non-Y; and A may be found to be false. When the falsity of A is seen, a new theory can be developed without it. Though Y and non-Y are still contradictory, just as X and non-X are still contradictory, these contradictions no longer matter; they are left behind in philosophical debate, because what made them seem frustratingly important was that they seemed to be the only possible corollaries of A, and now A itself has been given up.

We have seen how Kant applied this maxim in the disputes concerning mathematics. Hume and Leibniz disputed whether mathematics applied to experience; and each could give excellent reasons for denying and asserting it, respectively. But they both agreed that mathematical judgments were logically necessary. This agreed upon principle was, according to Kant, false.

We can illustrate this pattern again by referring to Kant's later attempt to resolve the space antimony.[17] Rationalists said the world in space was finite; empiricists said it was infinite. Equally good proofs existed on both sides. The statements are contradictory, but Kant said they were *both* false. What he should have said is that both were statements in compound judgments, "Space is the real form of objects existing intrinsically, and the world is finite," and "Space is the real form of objects existing intrinsically, and the world is in-

16. Frank P. Ramsey, *The Foundations of Mathematics* (London, 1931), pp. 115–16.
17. See the very relevant paper of J. E. Llewelyn, "Dialectical and Analytical Opposites," *Kant-Studien* 55 (1964), 171–74.

finite," and both these compound judgments are false because the first conjunct is false. If we deny the first conjunct, then the dispute about the second no longer matters since the second conjuncts are about something which does not exist in ontological space.

Other illustrations of this strategy could be given. But let us now look at the overall strategic situation. Can Kant find some principle accepted by both coalitions but nevertheless false? If so, rejecting that common principle will defeat both parties simultaneously, or at least break up their internal affiliations and establish a new center of power in Kant's own counter-thesis which will attract allies from both coalitions. Kant's attempt to discover this common, but false, fundamental principle is his strategy in fighting his two-front war; but unlike most two-front wars, here a victory on *either* front will be a victory on *both.* Perhaps we should even change our metaphor, and say that Kant's strategy is to show that a single position which is essential to both sets of opponents is untenable.

The common principle Kant thought he found in both and thought he could show to be false is: *There is but one ultimate source or faculty of knowledge.* The point at issue between the Lockeans and the Leibnizians was: What is this single source of knowledge? That there was such a source was the unexamined dogma of both, and if Kant could show it to be false he would have broken up both coalitions.

Leibniz, he tells us, intellectualized appearances while Locke sensualized all the concepts of intellect.[18] For Leibniz and Wolff, increasing the distinctness of a representation raised it from the level of feeling and sensation to that of thought; sensation and feeling are confused thought. The de facto synthetic connections discovered empirically between representations are to be replaced by logical connections between well-defined concepts resulting from their analysis. Synthetic empirical knowledge is not knowledge but only a pre-stage to rational knowledge of things as they must be. We human beings have to be satisfied with experience, but it is a poor substitute for rational knowledge of necessary connections. Empirical epistem-

18. *Critique of Pure Reason*, A 273 = B 327.

ology as a theory of scientific methodology is at best only an *Interimserkenntnistheorie.*

Locke was too much influenced by Descartes to deny in principle, and too much of a man of good sense to deny in practice, that there is a difference between the experience of seeing the compatibility of two ideas and that of seeing a sequence of logically unrelated ideas. He never formulated one theory that would account for both; but both are there. The differences between him and Leibniz are not as pointed as the rubrics of empiricism versus rationalism make them appear. Even Hume recognized diverse sources for mathematical knowledge and for knowledge of matter of fact; he still sees the difference between thinking and perceiving and, in fact, he insists that there is a gulf between them. How, then, can Kant say Locke sensualized intellectual concepts?

The clue is again found in Hume's theory of mathematics in the *Enquiry.* Precisely because mathematical knowledge is knowledge of the relation of ideas, and thus does not fall under the general rule of empiricism that our knowledge comes from experiences, Hume saw that mathematics has no existential import. By completely intellectualizing our mathematical knowledge, Hume cut it off from reaching the full fruition of knowledge, which is to be knowledge about existing things. The connection with objects, which would be necessary if mathematics were to be full knowledge,[19] was broken by making mathematics logically analytic. Therefore the intellect that had to do with real existence, that is, the intellect that gives knowledge, must be an intellect which *has* been sensualized. It was this sensualized intellect which Kant thought produced the skepticism inherent in empiricism, just as Leibniz's intellectualized senses could produce only dogmatism.

As early as 1762 Kant saw the differences between the methods of mathematics and those of metaphysics. By 1768 he saw the difference between mathematics and logic. Certainly in 1770 he had a theory of two cognitive faculties, the sensibility and the intellect, and of two different worlds, the sensible and the intelligible. No

19. Ibid., B 147.

matter how much clarity we might achieve in our analyses of the content of the empirical or sensible world, we could never raise it to the level of the logically necessary and metaphysically evident; indeed, we have, as a matter of fact, far more clear and distinct ideas of the sensible world than we have of the intelligible. In metaphysics, we have only a few clear and distinct ideas; but our obscure metaphysical notions are not thereby rendered sensible to us.[20]

The *Inaugural Dissertation* of 1770 represents Kant's first strategic coup: he can save geometry from skepticism by showing how it can apply to objects a priori, and he can go on with the dogmatic metaphysics he derived from his rationalist teachers. He thinks that the troubles of the Leibnizians in their metaphysics arose from their mixing concepts which applied only to the senses with those which were produced by pure reason. By a clear separation of the spheres of the two cognitive faculties, therefore, he could save metaphysical dogmatism and, almost as a by-product, avoid skepticism in mathematics. Now this may appear to have been no victory for him at all on a strategic level. For Kant seems to have attacked both Leibniz and Hume on their mathematical theories, but to have drawn a set of conclusions entirely acceptable to the rationalists, viz., the apriority of mathematics and the possibility of an a priori metaphysics. The letter to Marcus Herz of February 1772 is the last manifesto of this rationalism, however, because his "recollection of Hume" soon thereafter awoke him from his dogmatic slumber.

We often speak of what followed as "Kant's reply to Hume," but Kant is replying to both Leibniz and Hume. His question was: How not to be dogmatists in metaphysics without being skeptics in our knowlege of nature. Hume's skepticism was all of one piece: no objective necessary knowledge of matter of fact either in or beyond experience. Leibniz's dogmatism was all of one piece: a priori knowledge of both what is in and what is beyond experience. Kant wanted to break these two continuities; and he saw that each was based on a theory of one source and one kind of knowledge.

20. *On the Form and Principles of the Sensible and Intelligible Worlds* ("Inaugural Dissertation"), § § 7, 8: *On the Distinctness of the Principles of Natural Theology and Morals* ("Prize Essay") I, § 3; Ak. II, 280 (Beck translation, Chicago, 1949, p. 265).

We know little of the history of what went on in Kant's mind between February 1772 and April 1781. But it is clear that two things did happen. One was that Kant, having settled to his own satisfaction the problem of how mathematics is possible, turned his attention to the conditions of our knowledge of existing objects and found that we can know only those given both to thought and sense. Second, Kant continued to think about the book on the "metaphysics of morals" which he had been planning to write for twenty years.[21] We shall see now how his strategy evolved so as to solve both questions at once: how to save the rational features of science from Hume's attack and the irreducibly empirical features from Leibniz's and Wolff's; and how to save the conception of a metaphysics of morals from Hume's naturalism and empiricism and from Leibniz's and Wolff's dogmatism, which did, as he said, "war against it."[22] To show this, I shall quote two passages from the *Critique of Pure Reason* which are absolutely essential to his total philosophy, and I shall show how they are direct consequences of his challenge to the principle agreed upon by all his opponents.

The first is: "Thoughts without content are empty, intuitions without concepts are blind. It is just as necessary to make our concepts sensible, that is, to add the object to them in intuition, as to make our intuitions intelligible, that is to bring them under concepts."[23] The reason for this statement is found in Kant's distinction between analytic and synthetic judgments. Analytic judgments relate concepts to each other by finding one contained in the intension of the other; synthetic judgments are syntheses of concepts which are held together by their common reference to something given, which Kant calls X.[24] In a mathematical judgment, this X is a pure intuition or construction of space; in perceptual knowledge, it is a phenomenal object which is given to me in a set of intuitions which are related by a rule I follow in determining the order in which I entertain them, a rule so formed that they will

21. See my *Commentary on Kant's Critique of Practical Reason* (Chicago, 1960), pp. 5–10.
22. *Critique of Pure Reason*, B xxx.
23. Ibid., A 51 = B 75.
24. Ibid., A 9 = B 13.

conform to a rule of judgment in logic. But when I try to make a synthetic judgment about something not given in intuition, I find that I can only relate my concepts analytically and not bring them into any relation to an object; there is no intuitive X which is, as it were, the glue to hold the concepts together either a priori or a posteriori. If however, there were only one source of knowledge, which Kant calls an intellectual intuition or intuitive intellect, then the act of thinking an object would lead to its representation to me—and dogmatic metaphysics would be possible.

Notice Kant's strategy here. There are two factors involved in knowing: sensibility and understanding. Neither alone can give us knowledge; either alone is blind or empty. (Empiricism is blind;[25] rationalism is empty.) Knowledge comes from the application of one to the other. Dogmatism is the policy of claiming rational knowledge beyond what can be perceived; rationalism is inherently dogmatic; it can best be dogmatic precisely where there is in principle no perceptual source or test for its claims. So that which makes an answer to Hume possible—the rules of relating representations to each other introduce a synthetic element a priori into our empirical knowledge —also makes an answer to Leibniz possible: there is a perceptual or intuitional element in all a priori knowledge that is not merely and emptily logical.

The second sentence is: "I have, therefore, denied knowledge in order to make room for faith."[26] This well-known sentence is the foundation of Kant's ethical theory, because it makes it possible for him to accept the rationalistic thesis of the Third Antinomy without taking also the dogmatism which universally attended it. The thesis of the antinomy states that there is a "causality of freedom" and the antithesis is that there is only a "causality of nature." Both of these statements may be true if the common presupposition is that the sensible world in space and time is the only world to which our concepts apply. But there is no evidence whatsoever that the thesis is

25. "Empiricism is based on touch, but rationalism on a necessity which can be seen." *Critique of Practical Reason*, Ak. V, 14 (Beck, p. 14).
26. *Critique of Pure Reason*, B xxx.

true; all that Kant says he has shown is that it is thinkable, i.e., not self-contradictory, and that it is not even contradictory to the principle of the mechanism of nature if the common presupposition is false. Now this common presupposition is precisely what was challenged by Kant's solution to the Hume-Leibniz controversy over knowledge; it is the presupposition that there is one world of actual objects to be known in only one way (other ways being conveniences or customs of the limited human knower). Had that controversy not been solved as it was, Kant tells us,[27] nothing could have saved the causality of freedom, nothing could have prevented the export into metaphysics of the principle of sufficient reason found essential to physics.

Unless a theory that sharply divides physics from metaphysics can be established, metaphysics can only be an extension of physics and the only metaphysical causality will be mechanical. The theory of the sharp division is the theory that while metaphysics uses only one cognitive faculty and hence is unable to give theoretical knowledge, physics, which does give us knowledge, requires two independent sources, viz., sensibility and reason. Here again we have the negative test on what Kant says about an intellect that would be unitary in its sources of knowledge. If we had an intuitive intellect, the antinomy would not arise,[28] but the antinomy is the most fortunate perplexity into which pure reason could ever have fallen.

I have said that Kant's strategy is to break up the coalitions led by empiricism and rationalism by finding and denying the axiom they agreed upon. Bergson wrote that every great philosopher has said only one thing,[29] and James remarked that any worthwhile system

---

27. *Critique of Practical Reason*, Ak. V, 95 (Beck, p. 98); *Critique of Pure Reason*, B xxix. The Kemp Smith translation of the latter sentence is unclear. The sense is: "Since it is only on the assumption of freedom that its negation [i.e., mechanism] contains any contradiction, while the denial of mechanism contains an obvious contradiction, freedom, and with it morality, would have to yield to the mechanism of nature [on the assumption that speculative reason does not permit freedom except in contradiction to mechanism]."

28. *Critique of Judgment*, § 77; *Critique of Practical Reason*, Ak. V, 100 (Beck, p. 103).

29. *La pensée et le mouvant* (Paris, 1934), p. 141.

of philosophy can be written on a postcard. It is an amusing *jeu d'esprit* to take a philosopher's ten or twenty volumes and try to compress them to postcard length. My proposal for doing this to Kant's will be disappointing, since hardly anyone nowadays will deny the sentence but many will deny that it is the seminal thought in Kant. But it was a highly disputable proposition in his day, and I think that some of the lasting importance of Kant is shown by the fact that it is no longer disputed. The sentence would be: In order to know and to act, it is necessary both to see and to think.

I hesitate, of course, to say that this insipid statement is the sum and substance of Kant's philosophy. But when I see how much of his philosophy depends on it, how much is an elaboration and defense of it, and how many of his polemics are against those whose philosophy was an implicit denial of it, I think there is merit in this as a summary if one insists upon postcard brevity in the history of philosophy.

I have expressed the opinion elsewhere[30] that Kant is too complex a philosopher to be pressed into any single mold, whether that mold be made in Marburg, Heidelberg, Göttingen, or elsewhere. The logistic, metaphysical, positivistic, existential, psychologistic, and axiological interpretations of Kant all have the merit, to be sure, of bringing to the fore what is at most background in the others. It is natural to use any great philosopher of the past as either an arsenal or a target in later philosophical conflicts, and thus Kant has been regarded at one time as a founder of positivism, at another as its opponent; as the destroyer of metaphysics, and as the philosopher who made it "scientific"; as the chief critic of psychologism, and as the man who ruined epistemology by making it psychologistic.[31] It is not likely, therefore, that Kant will appear as a living force in contemporary philosophy if we see him primarily as the arbiter between an empiricism and a rationalism that are themselves no longer living movements in philosophy. Yet if we try to see Kant in

30. *Studies in the Philosophy of Kant* (New York, 1965), p. 52 n.
31. See Max Wundt, "Wandlungen des Kantbildes in der deutschen Geistesgeschichte," *Universitas* (Stuttgart) 14 (1959), 51–58; Wolfgang Ritzel, *Studien zum Wandel der Kantauffassung* (Meisenheim/Glan, 1952).

his own time and try to give full weight to his explicit statements about Hume, Leibniz, and Wolff, we return to the classical[32] picture of Kant which I have been outlining.

32. I call it "classical" because Hegel, the true founder of the history of philosophy, so regarded Kant (*Lectures on the History of Philosophy* [trans. Haldane, London, 1892], III, 429); but it was, until very recently, so naively reproduced that it could equally well be called the "textbook picture."

2   Toward a Meta-Critique of Pure Reason

The *Critique of Pure Reason* explicitly renounced two of the supports of much pre-Kantian epistemology, namely psychology as an empirical science of the structure and operations of the mind, and metaphysics, especially the rational psychology which was an integral part of the Wolffian metaphysics. Against empirical psychology, Kant realized that even if it could exist as a science, it could not be presupposed by a rational science,[1] since a priori knowledge could not be founded on a posteriori knowledge. Against rational psychology as a division of metaphysics, he held that his own work robbed it of all its content except the sole proposition "I think" (A 343 = B 401). The *Critique of Pure Reason* needs to be presuppositionless, and any presuppositions it has must eventually be rendered intelligible and defensible in the body of the work itself, and not remain external and unexamined. "I have to deal with nothing but reason itself and its pure thinking," he says (A xiv), "and to obtain complete knowledge of these there is no need to go far afield, since I come upon them in my own self." He claimed "to

Reprinted from *Proceedings of the Ottawa Congress on Kant in the Anglo-American and Continental Traditions*, ed. Pierre Laberge, François Duchesneau, and Bryan E. Morrissey, University of Ottawa Press, 1976, pp. 182–96, by kind permission of the editors. An earlier version of this paper was presented at a Kant symposium at Rice University, April 18, 1975.

1. *Prolegomena*, §21a, second sentence (Ak. IV, 304). On Kant's attitude to empirical psychology as a science, see *Critique of Pure Reason*, A 848–49 = B 876–77; *Metaphysische Anfangsgründe der Naturwissenschaft*, Ak. IV, 471 (Ellington, p. 8); *Vorlesungen über die Metaphysik* (Pölitz, ed.), p. 128; Theodore Mischel, "Kant and the Possibility of a Science of Psychology," in *Kant Studies Today* (Open Court, 1968; ed. Beck), pp. 432–55, also in *The Monist* 51 (1967), 599–622.

be able to develop a priori from the mere concept of a cognitive faculty (when exactly defined) the objects and everything one can know of them."[2]

In spite of these high claims which seem to be directed toward a rational metaphysics of the human cognitive capacity, a major portion of the *Critique* is devoted to the specific question: how are synthetic judgments a priori possible? Since they are actual, Kant thought, in mathematics and the sciences of nature but are of at least dubious status in speculative metaphysics, a more general statement of his problem is: to determine the foundations of knowledge and to see what superstructure of knowledge they can support. In answering this question, Kant found that all our empirical knowledge presupposes some a priori knowledge, yet the a priori knowledge presupposed is sufficient to support *only* the kind of a posteriori knowledge with which his analysis began; and what makes it capable of giving this support is precisely such as to *limit* that support to knowledge of objects of possible experience, and thus to leave the cognitive claims to metaphysical knowledge going beyond possible experience without support and justification.

In asking how synthetic judgments are possible a priori, and in asking what he thinks is the closely related question of how experience in the sense of an organized body of *rationally* justified knowledge claims is possible, Kant has been accused of begging Hume's question. He was supposed to show that Hume was wrong in denying that our knowledge claims had any rational foundation that could give them certainty; but he seems rather, like Reid, Oswald, and Beattie, to have assumed what Hume had doubted. This is no way to deal with a skeptic. One does not answer a skeptic by making his problems into postulates. But the very table of contents of the *Prolegomena* is enough to convince many readers that Kant begged Hume's question

This is inevitable since the *Prolegomena* follows the analytic or regressive method; it can show what are the sufficient conditions of

2. To Garve, August 7, 1783 (Ak. X, 340; A. Zweig, *Kant's Philosophical Correspondence* [Chicago, 1966], p. 102.)

an unproblematic empirical proposition's being true, but it cannot
show that these conditions obtain and hence that the proposition
with which it began is indeed true. Kant was aware of this and saw
the need for the synthetic method, which began with *unproblematic*
propositions which are self-evident or at least of a kind to which
everyone, including Hume, will agree. The synthetic method shows
that these are sufficient to warrant the certitude of the problematic
propositions either left uncertain or denied by Hume. Thus he tells
us that the *Critique* follows the synthetic method. But he does not
say this for the reasons I have just given, or at least they are not the
reasons he mentions; he says rather that the *Critique* follows the
synthetic method "in order that the science may present all its
articulations, as the structure of a peculiar cognitive faculty, in their
natural combination."[3]

When one turns to the *Critique*, one does find "all its articulations . . . in their natural combination," but one does not readily
discern a synthetic argument in its classical form, moving from what
is self-evident or certain, or at least assumed, to what would otherwise be dubious. Rather, one finds that Kant has heeded his warning
remarks in the *Prize Essay* of 1764 against the use of synthetic
proofs in philosophy. In the *Critique* he calls the method which
mimics that of the mathematician "the dogmatic method" and
denies its validity in philosophy (A 713 = B 741; A 725 = B 753). So
what is the genuine method of the *Critique of Pure Reason* remains a
point of dispute to the present day. There have been many discussions of "the transcendental method" which Kant is reputed to have
invented. Yet the name "the transcendental method" is never used
by Kant; in only one section (A 786 ff. = B 814 ff.) does he employ
the term "transcendental proof" and what he says about it is singularly uninstructive.[4]

As I see it, the logical structure of the *Critique* is a threefold
argument involving an analytical step (largely in the Analytic), a

3. *Prolegomena*, Introduction (Ak. IV, 263).
4. There he is, apparently, exclusively concerned with "transcendental
proofs" which claim speculative value, i.e., he is laying down rules which
proofs in *dogmatic* metaphysics would have to conform to.

direct synthetical step (largely in the Aesthetic and Analytic), and an indirect synthetical step (largely in the Dialectic). The first makes a regression upon the conditions of knowledge from judgments which Hume never thought of doubting and which hence stand in no polemical need for proof. These are such judgments as: our senses are passive recipients of impressions; our empirical ideas are not created by reason or understanding but are abstracted from or are traces left by the senses; the understanding, or at least the imagination, connects these representations together into judgments and beliefs; we are aware of the temporal order of our representations and, indeed, of the temporal order of the events they signify; and we are aware of our selves, though not of a substantial self as a permanent mental substratum of our experiences. At least we are aware of the infirmities of our experiential organization of representations in comparison with what would be true knowledge of the organization of objects meant by our representations, even if we do not know what the objective ontological organization in fact really is. All of these are assumed without question by Hume, and the man who attempts to "answer" Hume does not have to prove them.

Upon analysis of the conditions under which these can be known, as they are admittedly known by Hume, Kant tries to show that there are other propositions which are necessary, in the absence of knowledge of which we could not know even these Humean presuppositions to be true. Among these propositions there are those about the a priori forms of intuition, the pure concepts functioning as rules of judgment, and the necessary synthetic unity of apperception—not merely the tautology that the "I think" must be capable of accompanying all of my representations, but the synthetic unity of consciousness whereby all representations are under specific forms of the "I think," which are the judgments made possible only by categorial concepts. Hume knew nothing of a priori forms of intuition, pure concepts of the understanding, and the transcendental unity of apperception; yet, if Kant is correct, he could not have known what little he did profess to know without surreptitiously making use of them.

With this much done, Kant is finally ready to turn to the synthetic method of showing that these presuppositions are sufficient also to

prove propositions which Hume *doubted*—most notably the permanence of substance and the principle of causality—and (in the Dialectic) that they are better reasons than Hume himself had had for
rejecting arguments purporting to go beyond possible experience.
Kant's answer to Hume is: the *necessary conditions of what Hume
knows are sufficient conditions for what Kant knows.*[5]

We Anglo-Saxons tend to read the *Critique* as if its whole purpose
were to give an "answer to Hume."[6] But what is a good answer to
Hume may be a very inadequate system of philosophy. It is all very
well to say that Hume's philosophy could never have been formulated without some propositions more appropriate to Kant's than to
Hume's own explicit philosophy; but one may ask how successful
Kant is in giving a rational account of these and other presuppositions of the philosophy of both of them.

There are knowledge claims *made* and *used* in the arguments of the
Critique of Pure Reason; there are others that are *mentioned* and
demonstrated, and what is said in support of the latter depends
upon, but because of the implicative direction of the analytical
method does not itself support, the knowledge claims *used*. Let us
take a simple example. The sensible forms of space and time are
necessary if even Hume's deracinated mathematics is to be supported; but how do we know that the only intuition available to us is
sensible? No proof of that is attempted anywhere in the *Critique of
Pure Reason*, and is in fact denied by many other philosophers. Not
only is it not proved, it is not even a well-formed judgment under
the rubrics allowed in the *Critique*, for it is neither analytic nor a
posteriori, and if it is synthetic yet known a priori, none of the
arguments so painfully mounted in the *Critique* to show that such
knowledge is possible has anything to do with how we know this (if
indeed we do know it). Here seems to be a contingent fact—contingent because a non-sensible intuition is consistently conceivable—yet,

5. Cf. "Once More unto the Breach: Kant's Answer to Hume, Again," in
this volume.
6. Continental studies, on the contrary, see the relation to Leibniz as decisive; see Joachim Kopper, "Die Kantliteratur 1965–69," *Proceedings of the
Third International Kant Congress* (1970), p. 10.

unlike other contingent facts, not discovered by anything comparable to the observations by which we know the contingent fact that men with two eyes are better at seeing depth than men with one eye. Such judgments are brutely factual yet in some not well defined sense self-evident; they are factual but not empirical.[7] As to their brute factuality there is no doubt, for Kant repeatedly admits that he cannot tell why there are only two forms of human intuition and why our intuition is sensible and our understanding discursive, why the human will is free.[8] We can at most comprehend their incomprehensibility.[9] But that is not sufficient, for we can comprehend the incomprehensibility of false judgments too. The doubt is about their self-evidence, or whatever the mode of knowledge in which they are known.

What is needed is an investigation of the nature and justification (if there can be one) of the knowledge claims *used* in the *Critique of Pure Reason.* Such an investigation I call a "meta-critique" of pure reason. I do not profess to be able to perfect a meta-critique, and I join most other writers in complaining at the lack of help from Kant in attempting to provide one; but I only call attention to the problem and suggest a possible approach to its solution.

There have been many attempts since Herder's *Metakritik*[10] of 1799 to deal with this problem. Meta-critique has been developed in terms of psychology, biology, the sociology of knowledge, phenom-

7. See Nicholas Rescher, "The 'Special Constitution' of Man's Mind; The Ultimately Factual Basis of the Necessity and Universality of A Priori Synthetic Truths in Kant's Critical Philosophy," *Akten des IV. Internationalen Kant-Kongresses* (1974), Part II.1, pp. 318–28, at 327. Since Kant says (B 423 n.; A 848 = B 876; *Vorlesungen über die Metaphysik* [Pölitz, ed.], p. 130) that "I think" is an empirical proposition he might also not wish to deny that "our intuition is sensible" is also empirical; but it certainly is no normal empirical proposition about what we have learned *from* experience; and though "I think" is an empirical proposition, the "I" is not an empirical representation, he says.

8. *Critique of Pure Reason*, B 145–46.

9. *Foundations of the Metaphysics of Morals*, end.

10. See T. M. Seebohm, "Der systematische Ort der Herderschen Metakritik," *Kant-Studien* 63 (1972), 59–73. In spite of its title, W. Weier's "A

enology, Marxism, metaphysics, and the hypothetico-deductive model. Any meta-critique has to be constructed in non-Kantian terms, since Kant did not furnish us with the lexical apparatus needed in this analysis; and frequently meta-critique has made use of principles and assumptions that are antithetical to critique itself and are in fact borrowed from some other system of philosophy. It is natural, therefore, that some of the most recent efforts in this direction should have been made by linguistic philosophers.[11] What is not always realized, however, is that the underlying metaphor for this kind of meta-critique was suggested by Kant himself.

There is an analogy between a language and its meta-language and critique and its meta-critique. Without using the former technical distinction, which was unknown in his day, Kant points to an analogy that I would like to develop. He compares his procedure to that of the grammarian "who studies a language in order to detect the rules for the actual use of words and to collect elements for a grammar."[12] He calls the resulting system of transcendental concepts a "transcendental grammar,"[13] and he says the categories "serve, as it were, only to spell appearances that we may read them as experience."[14]

But the student of a natural language and the transcendental grammarian do not proceed in the same manner. Kant criticizes Aristotle for trying to discover categories in the way the grammarian discovers grammatical forms, and hence for failing to achieve completeness and exhaustiveness in his collection of categories. The

---

Metacritique of Kant's Pure Reason," *International Philosophical Quarterly* 8 (1968), 317–33, is not very relevant to the problems dealt with in this paper.

11. For example: Hubert Schwyzer, "Thought and Reality: The Metaphysics of Kant and Wittgenstein," *Philosophical Quarterly* 23 (1973), 193–206; Kenton F. Machina, "Kant, Quine, and Human Experience," *Philosophical Review* 81 (1972), 484–97; K. Bagchi, "Kant's Transcendental Problem as a Linguistic Problem," *Philosophy* 46 (1971), 341–45; Josef Simon, "Phenomena and Noumena: On the Use and Meaning of the Categories," *Proceedings of the Third International Kant Congress* (1970), pp. 521–28.

12. *Prolegomena*, § 39.

13. *Vorlesungen über die Metaphysik* (Pölitz, ed.), p. 78.

14. *Prolegomena*, § 30; similarly *Critique of Pure Reason*, A 314 = B 371.

grammarian cannot "give a reason why each language has just this and no other constitution"[15] but Kant professes to be able to show the exhaustiveness and necessity of *his* categorial table. The procedure of the *Critique* must therefore differ from that of every empirical inquiry, which would give, at best, a genetic account but not a justification of our knowledge claims (A 86 = B 119).

Rules of grammar, however, are not found in languages but in grammar books; an inductive generalization about language does not become a rule without an act of institution whereby good usage is distinguished from bad. Rules and generalizations, though they may be in one-to-one correspondence, have different logical behaviors. Rules can be broken but not refuted; generalizations can be refuted but not broken. Rules are incorrigible by observation, and are therefore in this respect like a priori judgments. It is easy to understand, therefore, why many contemporary philosophers, anxious to render some propositions immune to empirical disconfirmation, see them as linguistic rules; and they read back into Kant what was already there as metaphor, viz., concepts and principles are the grammatical rules which enable us to communicate about experience.[16] Even more, since what we can *say* determines to a large extent what we can *see*, the grammatical rules function in articulating the experience to be communicated. Hence the transcendental grammatical rules have a "transcendental content" (B 105) or, in modern language, a semantic as well as a syntactic dimension. This is evident in the metaphysical deduction of the categories, which discovers transcendental concepts by analyzing the rules for the syntax of general logic, and in the transcendental deduction and schematism, which show how these concepts function as rules for the synthesis of intuitions which thereby gain objective semantic reference.

This is the Copernican Revolution in philosophy—the substitution of epistemic for ontological concepts and principles. "The proud

15. *Prolegomena*, § 39.
16. Leah J. Stern, "Empirical Concepts as Rules in the *Critique of Pure Reason*," *Akten des IV. Internationalen Kant-Kongresses*, Part II.1, pp. 158–65, calls them "counting rules" since they determine what is "to count as," e.g., a case of substance.

name of Ontology must give way to the more modest title of an Analytic of pure understanding" (A 247 = B 303). Kant worked in the great tradition of universal grammar of the eighteenth century, but unlike most adherents to that movement he did not give an ontological interpretation of the rules of universal grammar; it was sufficient that the rules be transcendental, and not necessary that they be ontological too.[17]

Kant has been criticized for working as if he were a grammarian with the bizarre idea that there is only one language. The most penetrating criticism of this kind is that of Stephan Körner,[18] who argues that Kant cannot show that the categories he deduces are uniquely a priori, that is, that there are not other (equally good) ways of organizing experience, alternative ways of spelling the appearance so that they may be read as experience.

So far from claiming that experience as he reconstructed it was the only possibility, Kant repeatedly raises alternative experiences as objects of *Gedankenexperimente.* There might be sensible intuitions with other forms than space and time; presumably there might be another logic; we cannot prove that all understanding is discursive. So Körner's criticism of Kant's uniqueness claim is less radical, perhaps, than is warranted by Kant's own words. But Körner's criticisms are significant, because Körner is not thinking, in Schopenhauer's contemptuous epithet, of *die lieben Engeln*; he is thinking of another kind of human geometry and another kind of physics, and asking if the Kantian framework for individuation and reidentification of physical bodies, which is Euclidean and Newtonian, is the only possible one. And his answer, within these constraints, is negative. But just how far does this go toward showing that "transcendental deductions are impossible"? It depends upon what a transcendental deduction is supposed to justify, and for reasons which are well known Kant may have claimed too much.

17. See the detailed comparison of Kant with Chomsky in G. B. Oliver, "Inmate Ideas and Transformational Grammar, A Kantian Interpretation," ibid., Part II, 2, pp. 849–55.
18. Stephan Körner, "The Impossibility of Transcendental Deductions," *Kant Studies Today*, pp. 230–44; also in *The Monist* 51 (1967), 317–31.

I think that this argument designed to show the possibility of alternative categorial schemes takes the wrong *prius* for the application of the analytical method. It takes Kant's problem to be one of justifying a priori a particular scientific language as if it were uniquely necessary. And the problem so formulated is insoluble. But that is not, in my opinion, the place it begins. In opposition to arguments of this sort, Eva Schaper has put the problem into its proper meta-critical position.[19] She rightly sees that while the Newtonian scheme is at best an *example* of articulating possible experience, whether it be the only one or not, the genuine object of Kant's search is "necessary features common to all variants" (if there are variants). Neither the starting point of his analysis nor the proper goal of his synthetic proofs is some *one* scheme of identification and individuation of public objects. Rather, the "unity of consciousness is the fundamental assumption" of all thought about, and all talk about, any, or any alternative, scheme or grammar which can give rise to a possible experience in which we can draw the distinction between the objective and the subjective, the well-grounded and the ill-grounded, the public and the private, and truth and illusion. Because Kant believed, erroneously, that there was one logic, one geometry, and one physics he was prone to confuse sufficient with necessary conditions and necessary with uniquely necessary conditions. But this is an error from which he can be rescued, as Körner in other papers has showed.

For every language there is a meta-language containing its rules. The *Critique of Pure Reason* provides a grammar for science in a meta-language (that is to say, the language of the *Critique* itself) in which Kant talks about stars and atoms in terms of intuitions and concepts. It must, in turn, have a meta-language in which we talk about intuitions and concepts in the language of the cognitive faculties to which they are assigned by what Kant calls "reflection"

19. Eva Schaper, "Arguing Transcendentally," *Kant-Studien* 63 (1972), 101–16. A shorter version under the title "Are Transcendental Deductions Impossible?" can be found in *Proceedings of the Third International Kant Congress*, pp. 486–94.

(A 260 = B 316). The rules for talk and thought about concepts and intuitions are in this meta-language, and the investigation of them constitutes a meta-critique of the works of pure reason which are articulated in the main body of the *Critique of Pure Reason.*

Carnap, in connection with the difference between languages and meta-languages, has distinguished between internal and external questions.[20] The former are questions that can be answered in the object-language, for example, "What is the cause of thunder?" The latter are questions which, if answerable at all, can be answered only in the meta-language, for example, "What is 'cause'?" If we are looking for a complete answer to all our questions, this seems to lead to an infinite regress, the next step of which might perhaps be our meta-critical question, "Why do categories function as rules for the synthesis of representations in time?" Or it may lead to a dead factual stop, because we do not have a language in which the last questions can be answered.

The *Critique*, like any large philosophical work, asks to be judged by its success in answering the questions it itself asks, though we want to evaluate it externally by asking whether its own presuppositions—its meta-critical positions—are true or not.[21] Insofar as the *Critique of Pure Reason* sets the conditions of intelligible questions and answers, however, we have no way of answering this question; and the *Critique* seems to be suspended from nothing in heaven and supported by nothing on earth. It is not unique in this unenviable position, though only one philosopher who has seen this problem has concluded that even his own philosophy is nonsense.[22]

Put in this formal way, we seem to have come to an impasse. It is as if we were looking at another person trying to lift himself by his own bootstraps, or trying to play an impossible game, and it would be wise to persuade him to play another. It is rather different when

20. "Empiricism, Semantics and Ontology," *Revue internationale de Philosophie* 4 (1950), 20–46.

21. This is well argued in Heinz Jansohn, *Kants Lehre von der Subjektivität* (Bonn, 1969), p. 98.

22. Wittgenstein, *Tractatus*, 6.54.

it is we ourselves who are playing a game, even though there might be better games to play. The game we play is rather like the games played by children, who make up rules as they go along, and who do not play by rules they look up in a book and rules whose authority they may not challenge.

The game analogy is, of course, suggested by Wittgenstein's metaphor of language-games; but it is imperfect because knowing is not a game at all. Games are always played in a non-game context which is not play but serious; they always have alternatives. But the whole thing cannot be a game, for it has no alternative, and one cannot opt out of it—for that also is a move in the comprehensive "game" of philosophy.

The philosopher begins where he is. He already knows a lot. He begins with pre-analytic experience and aspirations, some of which he will have to surrender. He holds on to as much as he can, as much as his critic will allow him. Not everything is of equal certitude and weight. What is of most weight is a standard he will not give up, but refine. By reference to it, antecedent conditions or consequences are ratified. For Kant, the antecedent condition of such knowledge is the spontaneity of thought. By it we synthesize only a manifold of givens. Hence two cognitive faculties (abilities) are discerned— sensibility and understanding. And in the awareness of moral obligation there is revealed "a pure spontaneous activity elevated even above the understanding." This spontaneity of thought cannot be made object; awareness of it is called "transcendental consciousness,"[23] but Kant says regrettably little about it. Through it, "man really finds in himself a faculty by which he distinguishes himself from all other things, even from himself [his empirical existence] so far as he is affected by objects [of the senses]."[24] This faculty or ability is reason, and this self-awareness is "the fact of reason"—not

---

23. "Ist es eine Erfahrung, dass wir denken?" Ak. XVIII, 319.
24. *Foundations of the Metaphysics of Morals*, Ak. IV, 452 (Beck translation [New York, 1959], p. 106).

a fact *for* reason, as a kind of object revealed *to* reason, but the fact *that* there is reason.[25]

Kant's "faculty psychology" creates problems by making him talk as if faculties were hidden things, and by making us ask how he knows that the faculties are there and what their characteristic powers are. It would be vain to deny that Kant is a faculty psychologist, but I would remind you that the German word for "faculty," *Vermögen*, is the noun form of the infinitive meaning "to be able." The discovery and assessment of what one is able to do seem to be a much less mysterious process than the discovery and assessment of faculties, and they do not lead so readily to unanswerable questions about "where" the faculties are (in the phenomenal or noumenal world) and the like.[26] One finds out what one is capable of doing by trying and observing successes and failures; on the contrary, one would find, or try to find, "faculties" by processes that are very un-Kantian and mysterious.

The questions, then, of whether it is necessary that our faculties be as they are, and whether other beings have other faculties, and whether we men could use our faculties in another way if our geometry or physics were different, appear in a rather different light if we think not of reason but of reasoning, not of *Verstand* but of *Verstehen*. We are in the process of experiencing (seeking, finding, and communicating meanings) which is sometimes successful and sometimes a failure. If we try to think of other kinds of experience, we necessarily judge them failures unless they are mappable into the

25. This is surely one of the meanings of the term "Faktum der Vernunft," though not the only one. See my "The Fact of Reason," in *Studies in the Philosophy of Kant*, pp. 200–14, esp. p. 210 ff.

26. This procedure of "demythologizing" Kant is persuasively practiced by W. H. Walsh in "Philosophy and Psychology in Kant's Critique," *Kant-Studien* 57 (1966), 186–98, the happy name being introduced on p. 191. Both in terms of questions asked and answers given, Walsh's paper and the present one up to the end of this section are very much alike, though the intervening arguments are different. Somewhat more distant, in terminology at least, but similar in thrust, is Heinz Jansohn, *Kants Lehre von der Subjektivität*, esp. ch. 12. Instead of glossing *Vermögen* as ability, he substitutes *vermögende Bedingung* (p. 274), which he characterizes in terms of epistemic achievements and not existential preconditions.

scheme of our successful experiences.[27] Just as we cannot think of a
series of sounds as a sample of a language unless we believe that it
can be translated into our own language, any behavior has to be
embedded in *our* experience or mappable by *our* standards of
success, or declared a failure, or ruled out of consideration as not
being experience as knowledge of objects at all.

Our abilities are tools we use in knowing, and as tools they can be
criticized. But they are also the measures of knowledge, and as
measures they cannot be measured; we have no Archimedean plat-
form on which to stand while we exercise our meta-critique. If there
is meta-critique, it must be internal.

It is regrettable that Kant did not say more about the peculiarities
of self-knowledge. He was stopped from doing so by the knowledge
that empirical psychology cannot support the weight of knowledge,
and by his own criticism of the pretensions of rational psychology.
*He has no explicit theory of how we come to know of the opera-
tions and faculties or abilities of the mind.* A detailed articulation
of his informal procedure, however, would constitute a meta-
critique of pure reason, but an internal one, continuous with the
critical philosophy itself. I believe it would take the form I have
sketchily outlined and would not be in conflict with any of the
positive teachings of the *Critique of Pure Reason.* Most particularly
it would not require us to have transcendent knowledge which the
Critique teaches we cannot have.

In the beginning of this paper I quoted two sentences from Kant
which seemed to promise a doctrine of reason as a cognitive faculty
from which the scope of all the works of reason (science, morality,
and metaphysics) could be derived. To achieve "the single, supreme,
and inner end" (A 833 = B 861) of reason is to establish "a complete
and certain science"[28] of reason in all its parts and functions. It is
not merely to answer the question, "How are synthetic judgments

27. Schaper, "Arguing Transcendentally," argues this point very effectively
and concludes, "Even if there are [genuinely alternative] schemes, they could
not be intelligibly identified as alternatives" (p. 109).
28. *Prolegomena*, Ak. IV, 262.

possible a priori?", or to answer Hume, or to establish a metaphysics of experience, or to expose the pretensions of speculative metaphysics.[29] Kant's purpose sounds very much like the one Wolff had for his rational psychology, namely, "to give a reason a priori from the essence of the soul why such faculties exist in it rather than others, and why the soul follows these laws in its modifications, rather than others."[30] Yet we know that Kant emptied rational psychology of all its content except "I think" and what can be analytically derived from it. Hence rational psychology, at least as conceived in the *Critique of Pure Reason*, is not the "complete and certain science" of reason which might answer our meta-critical question.

So long as rational and empirical psychology are regarded as opposites, Kant has no systematic way to deal with the problems raised here. Yet he has, in Prauss's words, "penetrated much more deeply into the problem than he himself really held to be possible."[31] What is lacking is not hints about how the meta-critical problem might be solved, but how these hints can be systematized and integrated with the rest of Kant's philosophy and developed within the constraints he placed upon knowledge.

Close to the end of the *Critique* (though perhaps at the beginning of his critical career), Kant seems to have taken a more favorable view of the possibilities open to him than he had held when writing the Paralogisms; and, as so often happens in Kant, a different terminology signals a different level of thought. In the chapter on the Architectonic of Pure Reason he revised the Wolffian fourfold division of metaphysics into ontology, rational physiology, rational cosmology, and rational theology. Rational physiology treats of "nature, that is, the sum of all given objects (whether given to the senses or to some other kind of intuition)" either immanently or transcendentally. Immanent rational physiology "is concerned with

29. George E. Bilek, "The Aim of Kant's 'Critique of Pure Reason,'" *Proceedings of the Third International Kant Congress*, pp. 219–24.
30. Wolff, *Psychologia rationalis*, praefatio.
31. Gerold Prauss, *Kant und das Problem der Dinge an sich* (Bonn, 1974), p. 154, n. 174.

such knowledge of nature as can be applied in experience (*in concreto*)," and one of its divisions is concerned with "the object of inner sense, the soul, and, in accordance with our fundamental concepts, thinking nature." This is *psychologia rationalis*. Its object, that of inner sense, "we obtain through the concept of a thinking being (in the empirical inner representation 'I think') . . . [and we] must dispense with all empirical principles which profess to add to these concepts any more special experience" (A 848 = B 876). This may seem not to go beyond what he had already said of classical *psychologia rationalis*, but I believe it does in two respects. First, the division of the parts of metaphysics is architectonic "in accordance with the essential ends of reason"; and second, there is a perhaps significantly new title, namely the *physiology* of the soul. Taken together they put our question into a new context.

"Physiology," though the term is often used by Kant without any explicit teleological overtones, did have a functional, teleological meaning in Kant's time;[32] physiology dealt with organic wholes and functions of parts within wholes. The proper name for the study of the soul in a part of the *Critique* dealing with the architectonic— another synoptic, teleological consideration—is physiology, since all the actions of mind have a bearing upon the whole and upon the final end of man. Kant does not work out the system of transcendental philosophy which is adumbrated in the Architectonic, and we can only conjecture what its detailed contents and overall organization would be. But I conjecture that "a transcendental physiology of thinking nature" would give *good reasons* for the otherwise brutely factual attributes of mind which are presupposed without argument in the *Critique*. Teleological arguments, of course, prove nothing in Kant; but they do have the effect of reducing what would otherwise

32. François Duchesneau, "Kant et la 'physiologie de l'entendement humain,'" *Akten des IV. Internationalen Kant-Kongresses*, Part II.2, pp. 271–76. M. Duchesneau does not deal with the passages which concern me here; what I say is a conjecture, supported in part by his study of the various meanings of *physiologie* in Kant's time; but if the word *physiology* will not support the weight of my conclusions, I believe that *architectonic* alone will do so.

be a manifold of independent facts to a systematic order. Thus while throughout his work Kant confesses that questions as to why the human cognitive faculty has the form and function it has cannot be answered, it is significant, I think, that he does give *good reasons* for the constitution of our cognitive faculty when theoretical reason is related to practical, and when the constitutive principles of our knowledge of nature are used in the light of regulative principles which provide a transition between knowledge and action, between the metaphysics of nature and the metaphysics of morals.

Two instances of this must suffice here. First, let me call your attention to the section near the end of the second *Critique*, entitled, "Of the Wise Adaptation of Man's Cognitive Faculties to His Practical Vocation." In this section, Kant argues that if the laws of reason (moral laws) had constitutive force so that we could know the existence of God instead of having rational faith in the postulate of his existence, "in so far as our whole nature [as psychological beings] was not changed at the same time," "most actions conforming to law would be done from fear, few from hope, none from duty." Instead, therefore, of having been provided "in a step-motherly fashion" with imperfect cognitive faculties, we discern that "the inscrutable wisdom through which we exist is not less worthy of veneration in respect to what it denies us than in what it has granted." The *Critique of Pure Reason* prescribes limits to what we can know at the precise point where we *ought not to know*. The antinomy, which discovers this limit, so far from being a misfortune, is "the most fortunate perplexity in which human reason could ever have become involved."[33] It is no accident that reason falls into the antinomy; it is a necessary consequence of the specific differences between the proper functions of understanding and reason.

Second, there is §77 of the third *Critique*, "Of the Peculiarity of the Human Understanding by Means of Which the Concept of a Natural Purpose is Possible." The argument is long and complex, but we are here interested only in the conclusion, viz., it is by virtue of

33. *Critique of Practical Reason*, Ak. V, 107 (Beck, [1956] p. 111); cf. *Critique of Pure Reason*, A 464 = B 492.

the fact that our understanding is discursive and not intuitive (that it operates with "analytical universals" instead of "synthetic universals") that the concept of purpose must be employed regulatively by man and can be employed without conflict with the requirements of mechanical causation—a conflict which, were it unavoidable, would inevitably be won by the former (B xxix) at the expense of morality.

I mention these two instances only to show a line of thought which is present in Kant, but not developed systematically into a "transcendental physiology of thinking nature." For morality to be possible, Kant is saying it is necessary that the human intellect have the faculties it has—a sensible intuition, a reflective judgment, a discursive understanding, and a dialectical reason. We can comprehend the incomprehensibility of morality; once comprehending that, we can give good reasons why our cognitive faculties are as they are. We cannot show, as Kant repeatedly confesses, why they must be so and not otherwise; but it is something to show good reasons why they are as they are.

A regress, if not infinite, must stop somewhere, and "the sole fact of pure reason" seems to Kant to be a good place to stop.

3   Did the Sage of Königsberg
Have No Dreams?

This question was asked by C. I. Lewis[1] in order to show that Kant demanded too much of his categories. According to Lewis, Kant required his categories to limit experience to what is categorizable and to prevent us from having non-categorizable experiences. Lewis, on the other hand, wanted to leave experience independent of the categories, and to use categories not as a dam against an otherwise uncontrollable flood of experiences but as nets with which to capture some experiences which, for that very reason, will be taken as referring to objects. "A priori principles of categorial interpretation," he writes, "are required to limit *reality;* they are not

This paper was read at a symposium in honor of Milton C. Nahm, on the occasion of his retirement, at Bryn Mawr College, April 22, 1972. In a revised form and in German it was presented at the Fourth International Kant Congress in Mainz, April 6, 1974, and was published under the title, "Hatte denn der Philosoph von Königsberg keine Träume" in *Akten des IV. Internationalen Kant-Kongresses* (Berlin, Walter de Gruyter, 1975), Part III, pp. 26–43. This translation is published with the permission of the publisher and the editor, Professor Gerhard Funke. A few passages from the first version, omitted from the German, are here retained.

In writing this paper I was helped by extensive discussions with my then doctoral candidate, Dr. Bruce Price. It was another student, Dr. Barbara Levenbook née Baum, then an undergraduate, who first called my attention to the great importance of the passage cited in note 16. I do not remember that anyone had seen how important this passage is, and her insistence upon it produced a substantial change in my understanding of the *Critique of Pure Reason*, for which I am grateful to her.

1. *Mind and the World Order* (New York, 1929), p. 221. I discussed other aspects of Lewis's interpretation of Kant in "Lewis' Kantianism" in *Studies in the Philosophy of Kant*, pp. 108–24.

required to limit *experience.*"[2] Dreams and illusions are experienced, but they are not caught by our normal categorial net; hence they are not taken to be real. But according to Lewis's interpretation of Kant, Kant could not account for even the *awareness* of dreams and illusions, since Kantian categories would keep us from being conscious of them.

My purpose today is to find out how Kant would have defended the obvious answer to Lewis's penetrating question.

In §13 of the *Critique of Pure Reason* Kant points out a "difficulty" in justifying the necessary objective validity of concepts which do not arise by abstraction from intuitions.

> The categories of the understanding ... do not represent conditions under which objects are given in intuition. Objects may, therefore, appear to us without their being under the necessity of being related to the functions of understanding, and understanding, therefore, need not contain their a priori conditions. ... Appearances might very well be so constituted that the understanding should not find them to be in accordance with the principles of its unity. Everything might be in such confusion, for instance, in the series of appearances that nothing presented itself which might yield a rule of synthesis and so answer to the conception of cause and effect.[3]

This famous and puzzling passage has caused "astonishment and even indignation"[4] among commentators. There are two competing interpretations. According to the "patchwork theory," when Kant wrote it he believed that these sentences might be true, and had not yet found an argument to show that they were not.[5] According to the other, this possibility was entertained only pedagogically; Kant

2. Ibid., p. 222. The entire sentence is italicized in the original.
3. *Critique of Pure Reason*, A 89–90 = B 122–23.
4. The quoted words are from H. J. de Vleeschauwer, *La déduction transcendentale dans l'oeuvre de Kant* (1936; New York, 1976), II, 176, who gives a survey of the divergent German-language interpretations.
5. Norman Kemp Smith, *A Commentary on Kant's Critique of Pure Reason* (London, 1923), p. 222.

was asking a question which he imagined his readers would naturally ask and was preparing them for an argument by which this "difficulty" could be averted.[6] Both interpretations agree that Kant finally denied the possibility left open in §13, and only differ about whether he had ever positively affirmed it. If he did really affirm it, at that time he had a simple answer to Lewis's question; and the more the *Critique* moves away from it, the more exposed it is to the scorn of the argument from dreams.

Let us see how Kant removed the "difficulty" of §13, and see if he still left himself a way to admit that he did have dreams. We must draw two distinctions which are implicit in the *Critique* but which are never made explicit.

Two Meanings of "Experience"

Lewis says that Kant used the word "experience" "as if experience and the phenomenally real [i.e., the objectively valid] coincide."[7] Sometimes he did so, sometimes not. The opening sentences of the Introductions to both editions use the word "experience" equivocally. In B we read:

> There can be no doubt that all our knowledge begins with experience. For [otherwise] how should our faculty of knowledge . . . work up the raw material of sensible impressions into that knowledge of objects which is called experience?[8]

In the first sentence, "experience" means "the raw material of sensible impressions," the manifold of apprehensions or Lockean ideas without the conceptual and interpretative activities of the mind. In the second sentence "experience" means "knowledge of objects" and does perhaps, in Lewis's expression, "coincide with the phenomenally real." Let us call these two meanings "Lockean

6. H. J. Paton, *Kant's Metaphysic of Experience* (London, 1936), I, 324–25.
7. Lewis, *Mind and the World Order*, p. 221.
8. *Critique of Pure Reason*, B 1.

experience" and "Kantian experience," or, for short, L-experience and K-experience.

One way of reading the *Critique of Pure Reason* is to see it as an answer to the question: how do we move from L-experience to K-experience? And if this were the whole truth about the *Critique*, Kant would have a simple answer to Lewis's question: we make this move with only partial success. This is, briefly, Lewis's *own* answer.

Two Meanings of "Intuition"

The *Critique* begins with an inspectional conception of intuition and ends with a functional conception. According to the first, an intuition is a passively received inspectable sensory datum giving consciousness of an individual object independently of all categorization. It is given to consciousness as it were ready-made and labeled. The following examples show this usage:

In whatever manner and by whatever means a cognition may be related to objects, intuition is that through which it is in immediate relation to them.[9]

Intuition relates immediately to the object and is single.[10]

Appearances [= representations] are the sole objects which can be given to us immediately, and that in them which relates immediately to the object is called intuition.[11]

The inspectional conception of intuition is presupposed in the "difficulty" raised in §13. Given this conception of intuition, it is obvious that there could be intuitions which would not be tractable to categorial rules.[12]

9. Ibid., A 19 = B 33.
10. Ibid., A 320 = B 377.
11. Ibid., A 108; not in B. Kant often uses "appearances" where he means "representations," i.e., "appearances" often means "appearances to consciousness" and not "phenomena = objects."
12. This is pointed out by R. P. Wolff (*Kant's Theory of Mental Activity*, Harvard Univ. Press, 1963, p. 94), who does not, however, distinguish termi-

The development of the functional conception of intuition is Kant's way of resolving the "difficulty." This development represents the shift from a pre-Copernican to a Copernican conception of the relation of knowledge to object. Kant substitutes for the unknowable relation of representations to ontologically independent objects the rule-governed relation of representations of each other. This brings a new conception of object, and with it a new, a functional conception of intuition.

The new conception of object:

> In so far as our cognitions are to relate to an object, they must necessarily agree with one another, that is, must possess that unity which constitutes the concept of an object.[13]

> Appearance, in contradistinction to the [mere] representations of apprehension, can be represented as an object distinct from them only if it stands under a rule which distinguishes it from every other apprehension and necessitates one particular mode of connection of the manifold [of apprehension]. The object is that in the appearance which contains the condition of this necessary rule of apprehension.[14]

The object is that the concept of which is a rule for the synthesis of representations which, by conformity to that concept, are descriptive of it or serve as evidence for its existence.

And the new conception of intuition:

> The fact that this affection of sensibility [sc. intuition] is in me

---

nologically two meanings of "intuition." Philip Cummins, "Kant on Inner and Outer Intuition," *Nous* 2 (1968), 271–92, distinguishes between two ways in which the relation of intuition to its object may be conceived: the "intentional object" interpretation and the "objective constituent" interpretation. He holds that Kant did not clearly differentiate between them, and there is no suggestion that he moved from one to the other. What makes Cummins's essay relevant to our present concern, however, is that he tacitly indicates (p. 285) that the problem of §13 arises for the *latter* interpretation, which resembles the view that intuition is "inspectable."

13. *Critique of Pure Reason*, A 104–05; not in B.
14. Ibid., A 191 = B 236.

does not amount to a relation of such representation to any object.[15]

Thought is the act which relates given intuition to an object.[16]

Note how radically the second sentence contradicts the inspectional conception. According to this, the pattern was:

concept → intuition → object

According to the last quotation, the pattern now is:

intuition → concept → object.

On the inspectional view, there could be intuitions which relate immediately to objects but do not conform to the categories; representations might not be synthesizable or constructible under the concept of the object and could belong only to L-experience. According to the functional view, representations which do not conform to the concept of the object may be experienced but are not considered intuitions precisely because they fail to conform to the concept of the object.

If this were the whole truth, Kant could easily explain to Lewis how he dreamt. In fact, if this were the whole answer, it would have been so obvious that Lewis would never have raised the question, for Kant would have anticipated Lewis's most original contribution to the theory of categories.

Important as these two distinctions are, they seem nevertheless to be inconsistent with the central line of thought of the *Critique* (which does seem to give Kant difficulties with Lewis's question). This line of thought is the *nervus probandi* of the Transcendental Deduction, which I shall try to compress into four premises and a conclusion.

15. Ibid., A 253 = B 309.
16. Ibid., A 247 = B 304.

1. The "I think" must be able to accompany all of my representations of which I am conscious.[17]
2. To think is to judge.[18]
3. To judge is to relate representations to one another according
to a rule given by a category.[19]
4. Representations synthetically related to each other according
to the rule given by a category as a concept of an object in
general are the same as representations related to objects.[20]
5. Therefore, relation to an object must be ascribed to all representations of which we are conscious.[21]

As a result of this argument, Kemp Smith concluded:

Only in and through relation to an object can sense-representations
be apprehended. . . . Relation to an object is constituted by the
categories, because only thereby is consciousness of any kind
possible at all.[22]

From this it follows for Kemp Smith that L-experience is not conscious experience, that animals are not conscious, and, presumably,
that dreams are not possible. While Kemp Smith does not always
adhere to these shocking conclusions, he describes the position I
have just quoted as the "truly Critical position" to which Kant
moved when he escaped from the "difficulty" pointed out in §13.
What to Kemp Smith appeared "the truly Critical position"

17. Ibid., B 130.
18. Ibid., A 79; B 141.
19. Ibid., B 141. "Judgment is nothing but the manner in which given
Erkenntnisse [intuitions and concepts] are brought to the objective unity of
apperception."
20. Ibid., A 191 = B 236, cited and quoted in part above.
21. Ibid., A 108; not in B: "This transcendental unity of apperception
forms out of all possible appearances, which can stand along side one another
in one experience, a connection of all these representations according to
laws. . . . The original and synthetic unity of the identity of the self is thus at
the same time a consciousness of an equally necessary unity in the synthesis of
all appearances according to concepts, that is, according to rules . . . which
determine an object for their intuition, that is, the concept of something
wherein they are necessarily interconnected."
22. Kemp Smith, *Commentary*, p. 222.

appeared to Lewis, however, to be an absurdity which could be exposed by his flippant question.

Through an exhaustive collection of texts Paton showed that Kant did not draw any of these conclusions from the Transcendental Deduction.[23] But while this was historically interesting, it did not show that Kant *ought not* to have drawn them or how he avoided drawing them. This is what I propose to show.

In one of his private notes Kant added to the first premise another statement which, had it been explicitly stated in the *Critique*, would have made the transcendental deduction less clear. He wrote:

Consciousness can accompany all representations, *and thus also those of imagination*, which, and the play of which, is itself an object of *inner* sense, and of which it must be possible to become conscious as such an object.[24]

We shall work our way slowly to a justification of this addendum; but first of all we need to see whether the radical Kemp Smith–Lewis conclusions truly follow from the statement of the transcendental deduction in its restricted, classical form. I shall argue that they do not, and thus that Kant could, without inconsistency, have made the addendum in the *Critique* itself.

Kant does not anywhere say that the "I think" must accompany all of my representations; he says merely that it must be able to accompany them. While there is no representation, presumably, which cannot be judgingly related to the rest, it does not follow from Kant's statement that every representation is in fact judged to be related to the rest. A perception that *could not* be accompanied by "I think" "would not belong to any experience, consequently would be without an object, merely a blind play of representations, less even than a dream." [25] While the words "without an object"

23. Paton, *Kant's Metaphysic of Experience*, I, 332 ff.
24. Reflexion 6315 (Ak. VIII, 621), italics added. Kant is discussing specifically the imagination "in dreams or in fever." The imaginations in these cases are called *Sinnesanschauungen* but "only in the imagination, to which the object outside the representation is not present." That is, imagination may produce intuitions in the inspectional but not in the functional sense.
25. *Critique of Pure Reason*, A 112; similarly A 111, line 33; neither in B.

suggest that K-experience is meant, the last phrase of the sentence shows that L-experience is meant also. I could not even be aware of a representation of which I could not say "I think it," for such a representation would be "nothing to me,"[26] "nothing at all,"[27] "less even than a dream."[28] It would not only not represent an object; "I would not even be able to know that I have [it]."[29]

This modification weakens the claim made in the conclusion, which should now read:

5'. Relation to an object must be *ascribable* to every representation of which we are conscious.

This conclusion, however, is rejected by Kant because he holds that some representations have no possible objective reference.[30] The conclusion he wants to draw, and which he does draw in the Refutation of Idealism in B, is:

5″. Relation to an object must be *ascribed* to *some* representations of which we are conscious.

The argument of the Refutation of Idealism is that we do not start with an awareness of subjective representations (L-experience) and subsequently infer that some of them have objective reference. Rather, awareness of the subjective stream of consciousness is cognate with the awareness of the non-self or object.[31] Without the representations of outer sense or spatial intuition we have no conception of an inner nonspatial subjective realm of *mere* representations. I cannot say of one representation that it is merely a modifica-

26. Ibid., A 120; not in B.

27. Ibid.

28. Ibid., A 112; not in B.

29. Letter to Marcus Herz, May 26, 1789 (Ak. XI, 52; Zweig, *Kant's Philosophical Correspondence*, p. 153).

30. In the next two sections of this paper we shall take up this claim.

31. *Critique of Pure Reason*, B §18; cf. B xl–xli. See P. F. Strawson, *The Bounds of Sense*, pp. 92, 101, 109. Even closer to the point I am about to make is Eva Schaper, "Kant on Imagination," *The Philosophical Forum* 2 (1971), 430–45: "Imagination must . . . be parasitic upon experience of a real, non-imagined world" (p. 445).

tion of *my mind* unless I can say of some other representations that
they stand for objects; I cannot be conscious of myself except in so
far as I am conscious of what is not-self.

The Refutation of Idealism does not require of any particular
outer experience that it be veridical: I can dream of Paris as well as
see Paris, and

> the difference between truth and dreaming is not ascertained by
> the nature of the representations which are referred to objects (for
> they are the same in the two cases) but by their connection
> according to those rules which determine the coherence of the
> representations in the concept of an object, and by ascertaining
> whether they can subsist together in [K-] experience or not.[32]

Outer representations

> can very well be the product merely of the imagination (as in
> dreams and illusions). Such representation is merely the reproduc-
> tion of previous outer perceptions which . . . are possible only
> through the reality of outer objects.[33]

Kant is here saying that L-experience is possible only if K-experience is possible; but that there is L-experience (such as dreams and
wild sense-data) which is not taken up into K-experience. What is
not so taken up nevertheless belongs to the consciousness which
must contain veridical representations of objects, and may be seen as
modifications of my mind and thus as contributing to knowledge of
the self as phenomenon of the inner sense. The subjective or
empirical unity of apperception, which is my awareness of myself, is
dependent upon the transcendental or objective unity of apperception;[34] but I can synthesize all perceptions "in one consciousness of
my state"[35] even when I cannot synthesize all of them into con-

---

32. *Prolegomena*, § 13, Remark III (Ak. IV, 290).
33. *Critique of Pure Reason*, B 278.
34. Ibid., A 99–100; B 140.
35. *Prolegomena*, § 20 (Ak. IV, 300, line 8; Beck translation, p. 48, line 5).
This content of inner experience (L-experience) is called "empirical self-
knowledge" and is identified with the subject of empirical psychology (Reflexion 5453). Yet to be even knowledge of the self (expressible in judgments) it

sciousness of one world.[36] Thus we reach the justification of the addendum which, we noted, Kant made to the first premise in his private notes, namely the assertion that the "I think" must be able to accompany *all* my representations, whether they be of outer objects or of objects of inner sense.

You may have noticed that the passages which I have been quoting as making it difficult for Kant to explain how we can be aware of what is not conceptualized have been taken largely from the first edition, and the passages quoted as indicating his answer have been taken largely from the second. It is as if someone read the first edition and asked him, "Herr Professor, do you never dream and never have experiences you cannot relate to objects?". In fact, we can date this apocryphal question. It must have been before the *Prolegomena*, and the first answer he gave in §§18–20 of that work was on the level of argument attained in §13 of the *Critique* but

---

must be *categorized* without being *objectified* in the normal sense (viz., ascribed by outer sense to a spatial object); see p. 53 below.

36. The problem which is worrying us here must have been brought to Kant's attention by Kiesewetter, who had many extensive conversations with Kant in 1788–89 and again in 1791. It was Kant's practice then to write brief essays in answer to Kiesewetter's questions. One is entitled: "Beantwortung der Frage: Ist es eine Erfahrung, dass wir denken?", Reflexion 5661 (Ak. XVII, 318–20).

Kant defines *Erfahrung* as "the judgment that expresses an empirical cognition" and asserts that we think something is not, *an sich*, an experience. "Gleichwohl aber bringt dieser Gedanke einen Gegenstand der Erfahrung hervor oder eine Bestimmung des Gemüths, die beobachtet werden kann, sofern es nämlich durch das Denkungsvermögen affircirt wird." My knowledge of that which this thought is *about* is *Erfahrung* but it makes no reference to the time when the thought occurred, whereas the consciousness of the thought (sc. the act of thinking) does so. Kant then quickly develops an infinite regress on the assumption that the awareness of my thought is itself an experience (i.e., has a determinate place in objective time); the objective time under which ("unter der," not "in der") the thinking took place would in turn have to be constituted by an act of mind, "welches ungereimt ist." Hence: "Das Bewusstsein aber, eine Erfahrung anzustellen oder auch überhaupt zu denken, ist ein *transzendentales Bewusstsein, nicht Erfahrung*" (p. 319). In another essay for Kiesewetter (Reflexion 6311, Ak. XVIII, 610), "transcendental consciousness" means merely "the consciousness, I think." (The term "transcendental consciousness" does not occur in the first *Critique*.)

surpassed in the later parts of the *Critique*. For this reason most
Kant scholars regard this part of the *Prolegomena* as inconsistent
with Kant's mature view and cite in support of this the fact that its
teachings are not repeated in the second edition of the *Critique*.[37]
But we shall see, I hope, that the passages in the *Prolegomena* can be
given a sympathetic interpretation which is consistent with what has
been said before.

Kant's distinction between judgments of perception and judgments
of experience is analogous to that between L-experience and
K-experience.[38] Judgments of perception are "only subjectively
valid" and require no category.[39] They obtain "reference to an
object" through "superadding" a category which is a rule that "they
must agree among themselves" and thus have universal, that is to
say, objective, validity. Some judgments of perception, for example,
"When the sun shines on the stone it becomes warm," can be converted into judgments of experience, for example, "The sun warms
the stone," which make no reference to the contingencies of the
matter in which *I* happen to have apprehended the event. But there
are other judgments of perception, for example, "The room is warm,
sugar sweet, wormwood bitter" which "refer only to feeling, which
everyone knows to be merely subjective and can of course never be
attributed to the object and can never become objective."[40]

There are at least three reasons to be suspicious of Kant's account
of judgments of perception, and to regard it more as a statement of a

37. Kemp Smith, *Commentary*, pp. 288–89; Paton, *Kant's Metaphysic of
Experience*, I, 330–31. Only Gerold Prauss (*Erscheinung bei Kant*, [Berlin,
1971], pp. 139–254) and G. Buchdahl (*Metaphysics and the Philosophy of
Science* [Oxford, 1969], p. 636 and passim) have made serious efforts to
salvage the *Prolegomena* teaching. Both de Vleeschauwer (*La déduction transcendentale*, II, 490) and Graham Bird (*Kant's Theory of Knowledge* [London,
1962], pp. 115–16) have given unusually sympathetic accounts of Kant's
reasons for holding the *Prolegomena* doctrine.
38. Even the genetic psychology of the first paragraph of B is repeated in
Prol. §18, where Kant says all our judgments are "at first merely judgments of
perception ... and we do not until afterward give them a new reference to an
object."
39. *Prolegomena*, §18 (Ak. IV, 298, line 3; Beck p. 45, bottom).
40. Ibid., §19 and note.

problem, like the "difficulty" of §13 of the *Critique*, than as a permanent part of the edifice of the critical philosophy.

Judgment Always Makes a Claim to Objectivity

Kant writes in the *Critique:*

> I have never been able to accept the interpretations which logicians give of judgment in general. It is, they declare, the representation of a relation between two concepts.[41]

This does not adequately distinguish between a mere association of ideas and a judgment. A judgment is indeed a representation of the relation between concepts, but this does not tell us "in what the asserted relation consists." Kant finds that

> a judgment is nothing but the manner in which given cognitions [intuitions and concepts] are brought to the objective unity of apperception. This is what is intended by the copula "is." It is employed to distinguish the objective unity of given representations from the subjective. It indicates their relation to the original apperception, and its necessary unity.[42]

But in a judgment of perception "I merely compare perceptions and connect them in a consciousness of my particular state"; the judgment of perception is "merely a connection of perceptions in my mental state, without reference to the object."[43] Since, according to the teaching of the *Critique*, "reference to object" is reduced to "necessary relation of representations among themselves according to a categorial concept," and this necessary relation is what is intended by the objective claim registered by use of the copula, it follows that a judgment of perception as defined in the *Prolegomena* is not a judgment at all as defined in the *Critique*.

41. *Critique of Pure Reason*, B 141.
42. Ibid., B 141–42.
43. *Prolegomena*, §20, para. 1.

It remains to inquire which of the two accounts of judgment is correct, and I suggest that the view of the *Critique* ought to prevail, not only exegetically but also philosophically.

There is a right way and a wrong way to make a judgment of perception. Even a judgment of perception is under rules. While the judgment, "When I see the sun shining on the stone I feel the stone's becoming warm"[44] may be true only *of me*, it is not true merely *for me*. It does not say that if *you* see the one *you* will feel the other; but it does say that *you would be right* if you affirmed that when *I* see the one *I* feel the other, and wrong if you denied it. The judgment is subjective in content (it is perhaps about my subjective L-experience) but objective in its claim to your credence.

In such a judgment I am indeed judging about *my* representations as episodes or states in *my* mental history, and not about what objects these representations may represent. But the *Critique* makes room even for this with the generous scope it allows the term "object": "Everything, every representation even, in so far as we are conscious of it, may be entitled object,"[45] and hence may be judged.

Judgment Always Makes Use of Categorial Concepts

A judgment does not have to mention a categorial concept, but it has to use one. "The cause of the stone's becoming warm is the sun's shining on it" *mentions* the concept of cause; "the sun warms the stone" *uses* it. Kant seems to think that the judgment, "When the sun shines on the stone, it becomes warm," does neither. He is wrong, or at least inconsistent with the teachings of the *Critique* when he thinks this. The knowledge of the objective succession of sun-shining/stone-becoming-warm requires, according to the

44. Kant's example is merely "When the sun shines on the stone it becomes warm." But the sense he must want requires the judgment to be in the autobiographical or even Theaetetan mode, as in Reflexion 3145 (Ak. XVI (2), 678). Accordingly, in the part of the *Critique of Pure Reason* which comes closest to repeating the *Prolegomena* distinction, Kant contrasts, "If I support a body, I feel an impression of weight" with "It, the body, is heavy" (B 142).

45. *Critique of Pure Reason*, A 189 = B 234; cf. A 108, end. The point is well made by Max Apel, *Kommentar zu Kants Prolegomena* (2d ed., 1923), p. 160, and by R. P. Wolff, *Kant's Theory of Mental Activity*, p. 280.

Second Analogy, the causal principle. More obviously, "sun" and "stone" are names of substances which are borrowed from external objective experience to denote mere representations. Most obviously, if all even tacit reference to objects were excluded from the judgment of perception, the mathematical categories would still apply to the intensive magnitude of the brightness I see when I look at the sun and of the warmth I feel when I touch the stone. The Anticipation of Perception applies even to the data of L-experience.[46]

Judgments Predicating Secondary Qualities of Objects Can Be Objectively Valid

Kant denies this when he holds "The room is warm" to be a judgment of perception that can never become a judgment of experience because "it refers only to feeling."[47] Kant's position here is more extreme than Locke's, but it is not as consistently held.[48] We must try to work out a consistent view which Kant did hold at least sometimes.

46. *Critique of Pure Reason*, A 166 = B 208. This was pointed out (so far as I know for the first time) by Prauss (*Erscheinung bei Kant*, p. 163). He states (p. 143) that Kant nowhere speaks of judgments of perception that do not *enthalten* a category. Although I have learned much from this book I disagree with him here. (I do not here discuss the question as to whether *any* judgment can *enthalten* a category unless the name of the category is mentioned. My view is in deeper disagreement with what he means.) Kant clearly says that judgments of perception "bedürfen keines reinen Verstandesbegriffs" (*Prol.*, §18, Ak. IV, 298, lines 3–4). Prauss writes: "Es [ist] auch niemals einfach 'die Kategorie', was Kant den Wahrnehmungsurteilen jeweils abspricht, sondern ebenfalls allein diese *Anwendung* der Kategorie" (p. 162) where "diese Anwendung" means "Deutung von Erscheinungen" presumably in the manner of schematism (see p. 104). This, I argue, is true, but it is not supported by Kant's words cited above.

47. *Prolegomena*, §19 note.

48. Kant seems to have had unusual difficulty in making up his mind, or at least in expressing his ideas, on secondary qualities. In *Vorlesung über Logik*, §40 note, "The stone is warm" is called a judgment of experience; in *Prolegomena*, §19, "The room is warm" is called a judgment of perception! In the *Critique of Pure Reason* he holds that colors "are not properties of the bodies to the intuition of which they are attached." Yet in *Logik*, §40 note, "This

Let us put one of his judgments of perception into the Theaetetan mode: "This room feels warm (to me)." This judgment does not ascribe a one-place predicate to the room. The warmth, grammatically predicated of the room, exists only in me or in relation to me. The judgment is valid (true) *for me* in the sense that it is claimed to be true *of me.* Yet this judgment is objectively valid, for the equivalent judgment, "The room feels warm to Beck," is a judgment of experience about which others can have evidence and on which they must agree if it is true. What just *I* feel is not part of K-experience; but that I feel what no one else may feel, for example, the uncomfortable warmth of my fever, is a part of K-experience.

If my three criticisms of Kant's views in the *Prolegomena* are sound, we can conclude that judgments of perception are not mere associations of ideas without objective validity. They may be about associations of ideas, but if correct they are correct for everyone. They report about subjective episodes or states of mind, and such judgments are made under the rules of the categories. There is no difficulty in showing then how Kant can be conscious of them. Such judgments do not belong in K-experience about objects like the sun, the stone, sugar, and wormwood—what Kant calls objects of the outer sense supposed to be really existent, and what Prauss calls "objective objects." But they may be objective in the genuine Kantian sense of being made according to categorial rules which exact credence from every knowing subject, even if they are about what Kant calls objects of the inner sense or mere feelings, or what Prauss calls "subjective objects."[49]

---

tower is red" is "a judgment of experience i.e., an empirical judgment through which I get a concept of the object." In direct contradiction to the statement quoted in the first sentence of this section, the *Critique of Judgment,* §1, says, "Every reference of representations is capable of being objective, even that of sensations (in which case it signifies the real in an empirical representation)." The view I have constructed in the body of the paper seems to me to be sound and perhaps captures a large part of what Kant meant; it conforms most closely to the views expressed in the *Critique of Judgment,* Introduction VII.

49. Prauss, *Erscheinung bei Kant,* pp. 120, 215–16, 137, 145.

A dream is a subjective object. In a dream I dreamingly-see a three-headed monster. To dreamingly-see it, unlike to-see-it-*sans-phrase*, does not imply that there *is* a three-headed monster. But I say, "Last night I dreamt I saw a three-headed monster," and my judgment about *that* event is as objective as the judgment that I slept in my bed and makes just as valid a claim on your credence. You cannot verify it by inspection, but the occurrence of the dream, unlike the monster in the dream, falls under the Second Postulate of Empirical Thought, fulfilling the criteria of existence. I can verify it by self-observation, and though I get no knowledge of three-headed monsters, I do get knowledge of myself: Inner sense "represents to consciousness even our own self, only as we appear to ourselves, not as we are in ourselves," but in that respect I am in the same epistemological boat as the three-headed monster (if he really exists and I really see him, not dreamingly-see him).

Lewis, it seems to me, would be in agreement with much of what I profess to have found in Kant. "What is not reality of one sort is reality of another," Lewis writes. "What we do not understand in one way, we shall understand in another. The subsumption of the given under the heading 'dream' or 'illusion' is itself a categorial interpretation by which we understand certain experiences."[50] What we do not know as objective objects we can know as subjective objects. Lewis is using the term "categorial interpretation," however, in a much broader sense than Kant would sanction. The difference between seeing Paris and dreaming that one sees Paris is not a categorial difference, but an empirical difference. The "category" *dream* rightly does not appear in Kant's table. The categories Kant is interested in are presupposed in our having and reporting either type of awareness. The categories do not differentiate veridical from nonveridical experience; they make the difference between dumbly facing chaos without even knowing it—"less even than a dream"[51]— and telling a connected story, even if it is false.

50. Lewis, *Mind and the World Order*, p. 225.
51. The representations which may not be accompanied by consciousness (*Critique of Pure Reason*, A 320 = B 376) are like Leibniz's *petites perceptions.* If there were not the understanding, I would not be able to *know* I have

In a lecture on Kant in homage to Milton Nahm I thought it would be inappropriate not to say something about the work of Kant's which Milton Nahm has called "perhaps the most influential writing upon philosophy of art produced in modern times."[52] The *Critique of Judgment*, to the elucidation of which Mr. Nahm has made signal contributions, just had to be referred to for this personal reason. I feared, however, that there was no other reason, and that the artificiality of any device used to make it seem relevant would be obious to all. Imagine my delighted surprise, therefore, when careful re-reading of the third *Critique* made a real contribution to my working out of the problem before us.

Kant tells us in the *Prolegomena* that "the only reason for the judgments of other men necessarily agreeing with mine [is] the unity of the object" of which each man has the same concept no matter how diverse his sensations.[53] Furthermore, Kant tells us repeatedly, pleasure and displeasure are exclusively subjective representations which signify nothing in the object.[54] He tells us that the judgment of aesthetic quality "does not depend upon any present concept of the object"[55] and that the aesthetic quality ascribed to the object is purely and inescapably subjective;[56] yet, despite all this, he teaches that the aesthetic judgment of taste "lays claim . . . to be valid for everyone."[57]

---

even sense data; "consequently for me, *as a knowing being*, they would be absolutely nothing. They could still (*I imagine myself to be an animal*) carry on their play in an orderly fashion, as representations connected according to the empirical laws of association, and thus even have an influence on my feeling and desire, without my being aware of them (assuming even that I am conscious of each individual representation but not of their relation to the unity of representation of their object by means of the synthetic unity of their apperception). This might be so without my knowing the slightest thing thereby, not even what my own condition is." Letter to Marcus Herz, May 26, 1789 (Ak. XI, 52; Zweig, *Correspondence*, pp. 153–54), italics added.

52. Milton C. Nahm, *Aesthetic Experience and its Presuppositions*, p. 119.
53. *Prolegomena*, § 18, end.
54. For instance, *First Introduction to the Critique of Judgment* (Haden translation), p. 28. *Critique of Judgment*, Ak. V, 189 (Meredith, p. 29). On this, unlike secondary qualities, Kant is uniformly consistent.
55. *Critique of Judgment*, Introduction VII, Ak. V, 190 (Meredith, p. 31).
56. Ibid., Ak. V, 189 (Meredith, p. 29).
57. Ibid., Introduction VII, Ak. V, 191 (Meredith, p. 91).

There is, to be sure, no explicit inconsistency between these diverse views since the aesthetic judgment is not cognitive. Yet the disparity between the assertion of the universal validity of the aesthetic judgment of feeling-without-concept and the denial of objective validity to the cognitive judgment of perception (of sensation-without-concept) calls for comment. For the extreme position ascribed to Kant by Kemp Smith and Lewis makes it not only impossible for Kant to dream and to make judgments of perception, but also impossible for him to have aesthetic experience. I feel safe in saying that while Mr. Nahm might not care very much whether the sage of Königsberg could dream or not, he would vehemently reject any suspicion that Kant could not experience beauty.

I will concede that aesthetic judgments do not employ the dynamical categories and principles of substance, causality, and existence—at least I will not now discuss whether they do or not. But the mathematical categories and principles certainly do apply to the qualitites we experience aesthetically. The concepts which Kant holds do *not* play a role in the construction of (pure) aesthetic experience are not categorial concepts but empirical. The quality of the object which is represented in aesthetic judgment "permits of being understood and reduced to concepts," he grants, "but in the aesthetic judgment it is not so reduced."[58] "The judgment of taste does not subsume under a concept at all."[59] How then can it be a judgment? This is comparable to the question asked in the previous section: How can a judgment of perception be a judgment at all?

The third *Critique* distinguishes two types of judgment or rather two ways of judging: the determinant and the reflective.

If the universal (rule, principle, law [concept]) is given, the judgment which subsumes the particular under it is determinant.[60]

The categories are given, and the subsumption of particulars under

58. Ibid., "General Remark on the Exposition of Aesthetic Reflective Judgments," Ak. V, 266 (Meredith, p. 117).
59. Ibid., §35, Ak. V, 286 (Meredith, p. 142).
60. Ibid., Introduction IV, Ak. V, 179 (Meredith, p. 18).

them takes place by schematism.[61] The answer to the "difficulty" of §13 of the first *Critique* can be expressed in the new terminology as follows: the transcendental judgment by which experiences are categorized is determinant judgment. We do not have intuitions (inspectable intuitions) and look around, perhaps in vain, for categorial concepts which apply to them. This is an essential part of the Copernican Revolution with respect to categorial concepts.

"If, however," Kant continues, "only the particular is given and the universal has to be found for it, then the judgment is simply reflective."[62] There is no Copernican Revolution with respect to the concepts used in reflective judgments: "Reflection on the laws of nature adjusts itself to nature, and not nature to the conditions according to which we strive to obtain a concept of it."[63] The subsumability of the more specific concepts of nature (species) under more general concepts (genera) and of special laws under more general laws, and the harmony between what is given to our senses and our psychical apparatus for articulating and mastering it are are *entirely contingent*, not a priori necessary. With respect to these reflective procedures of the mind, therefore, a "difficulty" like that of §13 of the first *Critique* recurs. The manifold of intuition and imagination might be so chaotic and variegated that no empirical concept could be found to apply to its parts; and even if that difficulty were not met with, the manifold of objective perceptions might be so various that no subsumptive arrangement of concepts could be fitted to it.[64] In the latter case, we might have the kind of experience Hegel contemptuously allowed Kant, viz., "a candlestick here and a snuff box there"; but we could not count on having K-experience, viz., nature as phenomena under law and specific laws as specifications of more general laws.

In the third *Critique*, therefore, Kant is impelled to give a "deduc-

61. Ibid., Introduction V, Ak. V, 183 (Meredith, p. 22). See *Critique of Pure Reason*, A 138 = B 177.
62. *Critique of Judgment*, Introduction IV, Ak. V, 179 (Meredith, p. 18).
63. Ibid., Ak. V, 180 (Meredith, p. 19).
64. *First Introduction to the Critique of Judgment* (Haden translation), p. 14.

tion" of the concept or rule of reflective judgment which will do for empirical concepts what the Deduction of the Categories in the first *Critique* did for a priori concepts of determinant judgment. The *Critique of Judgment* proceeds as if there were a Copernican Revolution with respect to empirical imagination and concepts by "prescrib[ing] a law, not to nature (as autonomy) but to itself (as heautonomy) to guide its reflection upon nature,"[65] "making it imperative upon us to proceed on the principle of the conformity of nature to our faculty of cognition."[66] Thus the teleological judgment of reflection is regulative: problematic with regard to the object, imperative with regard to the methodological procedure.

There is, then, a close analogy between the first *Critique* and the *Critique of Teleological Judgment.* This has been known from the beginning, since there is more than analogy; there is an actual overlap of teachings. What has not been recognized (to my knowledge, at least[67]) is the manner in which the *Critique of Aesthetic Judgment* seems to have grown out of the doctrines of the *Prolegomena* which were rejected in the second edition of the *Critique of Pure Reason.* In at least one crucial passage the vocabulary of the *Prolegomena* and *Critique of Aesthetic Judgment* is almost the same;[68] and almost everywhere there is some analogy between their arguments.

65. *Critique of Judgment*, Introduction V, Ak. V, 185 (Meredith, p. 25).

66. Ibid., Introduction VI, Ak. V., 188 (Meredith, pp. 28–29).

67. The analogy between the two types of judgment in the third *Critique* and in the *Prolegomena* has been noticed by Walter Cerf in his introduction to his translation of the "Analytic of the Beautiful" (Bobbs-Merrill, 1963), p. xxxiv; T. E. Uehling, *The Notion of Form in Kant's Critique of Judgment* (Mouton, 1971), p. 52; and Donald Crawford, *Kant's Aesthetic Theory* (University of Wisconsin Press, 1974), p. 34; but they did not exploit the resemblance in the way I here attempt to do.

68. *Critique of Judgment*, §13, talks about *Erfahrungsurteile* (using this word which occurs only three times in the *Critique of Pure Reason*, at B 12 and 13; in passages which are taken verbatim from the *Prolegomena*, and at B 41 where it is simply a synonym for "empirical judgment" in contrast to a judgment of geometry known a priori). I do not find *Wahrnehmungsurteile* in either the first or the third *Critiques*, but in §36 of the *Critique of Judgment* Kant uses *Empfindungsurteil* as a synonym for *Wahrnehmungsurteil.* More usually *logisches Urteil* is used in the *Critique of Judgment.*

The problem of the *Critique of Aesthetic Judgment* is: How can a judgment which is like a judgment of perception in its independence of concepts and its reference exclusively to my own subjective experience of non-objectifiable representations nevertheless "resemble the logical judgment [= judgment of experience] in being presupposed valid for all men"?[69] A judgment of agreeableness is expressed in the Theaetetan mode to show its merely subjective validity: "Canary wine is agreeable to me"[70] is in this respect like a judgment of perception. But in judgments of taste, "One judges not merely for himself but for all men, and then speaks of beauty as if it were a property of things."[71] Judging without a concept,[72] one reaches a judgment of taste which is comparable in some respects to a judgment of experience which is got by "superadding" a categorial concept to a perception:

judgment of agreeableness : judgment of taste =
judgment of perception : judgment of experience.

Something, therefore, must be "superadded" to the judgment of agreeableness to make a judgment of taste. Like the category, it must be a priori if it is to give the judgment a claim to be valid for all men: but it cannot be a concept, for if it were it would convert the subjective judgment of "agreeableness to me" into a determinant cognitive judgment that everyone ought to agree to, namely that the Canary wine *is in fact agreeable to me.* What is needed, however, is some way of making the transition from "The music is agreeable to me" to "The music ought to be judged agreeable *by everyone*, that is to say, is beautiful."

What does this job, for Kant, is an a priori principle of the faculty of judgment, which refers disinterested pleasure to "that subjective factor which we may presuppose in all men (as requisite for a possible experience generally [= K-experience])" and which war-

69. *Critique of Judgment*, §6, Ak. V, 211 (Meredith, p. 51).
70. Ibid., §7, Ak. V, 212 (Meredith, p. 51).
71. Ibid., §7, Ak. V, 212 (Meredith, p. 52).
72. Ibid., §35, Ak. V, 286 (Meredith, p. 142).

rants us "in exacting from everyone the pleasure of the representation in respect of the relation of the cognitive faculties engaged in the estimate of a sensible object in general."[73] Instead of an intuitive image being subsumed under an empirical concept, as in a cognitive judgment of experience, the imagination *itself* is subsumed under the understanding as the *faculty* of concepts in general.[74]

It is thus, I think, that the aesthetic experience, which is not cognitive, gets its place in consciousness under the transcendental unity of apperception. The aesthetic experience and the validity of aesthetic judgments, like illusions and dreams, are preserved without surreptitiously being converted into cognitive experiences and judgments.

73. Ibid., §38, Ak. V, 290 (Meredith, p. 147). Notice also how the objective validity of the judgment of taste depends upon the *Gemeinsinn* (*Critique of Judgment*, §20) just as the objective validity of the judgment of experience depends upon its status for *Bewusstsein überhaupt* (*Prolegomena*, §§20, 22).

74. *Critique of Judgment*, §35, Ak. V, 287 (Meredith, p. 143).

4 *Lovejoy as a Critic of Kant*

I do not know why it is so, but something makes it difficult for most and impossible for many philosophers and students of the history of philosophy to be impartial about Kant and his teachings. A philosopher who excites so much feeling pro and con is subject to philosophical dispute in which veneration is met with abuse, arguments *ad hominem* are replied to with arguments *ad verecundiam*, and more heat than light is generated. I can think of only two other philosophers—Aristotle and Hegel—who have been the object of so much blind vilification and so much blind devotion as Kant.

It has always been so. In his own lifetime the polemics from his opponents reached a degree of acerbity more characteristic of theological debate than of philosophical. His disciples bitterly disputed among themselves the claim to be the "official" spokesman for Kant, and disciples who fell away from orthodoxy were treated with contumely by the others and by the master himself. A hundred years later the violence of controversy between the various schools of Neokantianism in Germany had not abated and, of course, neither had the heat of debate between professional anti-Kantians and professed Kantians.

While I think some of this is attributable to the specifically German academic environment, as I have tried to show in my *Early German Philosophy* and as Fritz Ringer has shown in much greater

This paper was presented as the Lovejoy Lecture to the History of Ideas Club of The Johns Hopkins University, April 23, 1971. It is reprinted from *The Journal of the History of Ideas* 33 (1972), 471–84, by kind permission of the editor, Professor Philip P. Wiener.

detail in his *The Decline of the German Mandarins*, this is not the
full explanation, because we find an emotionalism almost as intense
outside Germany as within. It just seems impossible to take Kant's
works in hand without responding with love or hate—and both states
of mind carry with them the danger of functional blindness.

I must not pretend to stand impartially above the battle; I must
confess that I was powerfully drawn to Kant even as a child long
before I had any comprehension of his philosophy. Fifty years later
I am still unable to explain why, but it is a fact that you should keep
in mind while you listen to my examination of Lovejoy's critique of
Kant.

Though I do not know the details of Lovejoy's intellectual biog-
raphy as a young man, an animus against Kant shows in all his early
writings about him. I knew Lovejoy only when he was an old man,
when he was silent about Kant; he had not even included in his
bibliography attached to his autobiographical essay in *Contemporary
American Philosophy* his articles on Kant. When I knew him, his
erudition, acuteness, and judiciousness were so comprehensive that
there seemed to be no room left for human failings of partiality and
prejudice; he did not even hold it against me that I was a "Kantian."
I cannot guess why his feelings had been so bitter against Kant; I can
only point out some of the evidence that they were.

One of Lovejoy's essays[1] was ostensibly written in part to assess
"the still widely prevalent view that Kant was a singularly penetrating and powerful thinker" (269), and it need hardly be said that the
outcome was negative. Kant's "ability to get lost intellectually on
even the straightest road [was] a perpetual marvel" to Lovejoy (279
n.). In the three essays reprinted by Gram, Lovejoy refers twice to
what he calls "the not uncharacteristic confusion in Kant's thought"
(106, 297) and to "curious" (307), "distressing" (278), "profound"
(282), and "peculiarly inexcusable" (283) confusions. He gently raps
Leibniz's knuckles for things he would have found unpardonable in

1. All the essays I shall refer to, except the one on "Kant and the English
Platonists," were reprinted by Moltke S. Gram in *Kant: Disputed Questions*
(Chicago, 1967). All page references not otherwise identified are to this book.

Kant (e.g., 112). He charges Kant in one place with "a degree of obtuseness rare in history" (121). In an acid paragraph Lovejoy accuses Kant of plagiarism: "Every possibility, I confess, seems to me to favor the hypothesis that Kant was reproducing as a novelty of his own a piece of reasoning with which he had long since become acquainted . . . ," the only exculpation he offers being "the extra-ordinary confusions of memory of which Kant was capable" (292). Lovejoy holds that Kant in his ignorance or forgetfulness of his forebears "usually has very much of the air of a philosophical *nouveau riche*, of a self-made theorist."[2]

Lovejoy quite rightly chides an earlier scholar for arguing from the "reference" due Kant's thought to its correctness (272), and I do not wish to commit the obverse error of arguing for the unsound-ness of a criticism from the animus by which it was inspired or with which it was expressed. But one wants to be very sure whether the enthusiastic distaste with which Lovejoy uttered his judgments is justified by his arguments *ad rem*.

Four essays are important and have been, I believe, influential though seldom cited in later papers with conclusions suspiciously like Lovejoy's. The essay on "Kant's Classification of the Forms of Judgment" (1907) is so good that I will not tangle with it; scholar-ship since then has left its main conclusions unaffected. "Kant's Antithesis of Dogmatism and Criticism" (1906) has anticipated much of the recent disputes over the Kantian theory of synthetic judgments a priori, and specifically the massive attack on this con-cept by C. I. Lewis. "On Kant's Reply to Hume" (1906) is one of the most provocative critical studies of that intractable problem, and in claiming to discern what he calls "one of the most spectacular examples of the *non-sequitur* which are to be found in the history of philosophy" (303). Lovejoy was six decades ahead of Strawson's putative discovery that the Second Analogy contains "a *non sequitur* of numbing grossness." In the essay "Kant and the English Platon-ists" (1908) Lovejoy discussed the ways in which Cudworth, Bur-

2. "Kant and the English Platonists," *Essays Philosophical and Psychologi-cal in Honor of William James* (London, 1908), pp. 265–302, at 302.

thogge, and Collier anticipated some of Kant's views, emphasizing how wrong it is to see Kant as an original critic of English empiricism, since his critique of Hume was anticipated in many details by their critique of Hobbes. While it is not difficult to find precursors for almost every philosophical position without thereby disparaging the philosopher who only subsequently came upon the views, or without accusing him of plagiarism—Lovejoy did not here do that, but could not resist making disparaging remarks—he did raise an interesting historical problem concerning the relation of Arthur Collier's theory of space to Kant's doctrine of the antinomy as proof of the ideality of space. This problem has been reexamined more recently by Lewis Robinson and Herman de Vleeschauwer, who seem to have been ignorant of Lovejoy's explorations in this field.

In this paper I shall examine only the main points of the second of these essays. The thesis of "Kant's Antithesis of Dogmatism and Criticism" is very simple. It is that Kant was historically inaccurate in indicting his predecessors for having practiced metaphysics without first showing how synthetic judgments a priori are possible, and hence that Kant's claim to give a new direction to philosophical criticism is nugatory. Lovejoy attempts to show that Leibniz, Wolff, and their followers had indeed shown how synthetic judgments a priori are possible in a way that Kant could not consistently reject, and that they did so in fact more successfully than Kant himself did because they could dispense with his theory of pure sensible intuition, a "logical chimaera that belongs with other hybrid monsters of antiquity" (127). In this paper I shall not discuss Lovejoy's criticism of Kant's theory of intuition, but will address myself to the historical questions: had the problem of synthetic a priori judgments been recognized? and had it been "answered in a sense to which Kant could not consistently have made objection?" (114).

My answer to the first is less definitely affirmative than Lovejoy's. Lovejoy holds that a distinction identical with that between synthetic and analytic judgments had been made as far back as Leibniz, but he argues that Kant either did not fully understand his *own* distinction or was ignorant of the distinction which Lovejoy uncovers in the pre-Kantian philosophers, or both, and hence did not see the identity which Lovejoy attempts to establish between Leibniz's, Wolff's, and Kant's distinctions. My answer to the second question will disagree with Lovejoy's, being markedly negative, since I think the Kantian distinction is very different from the Leibniz-Wolffian distinction and, per corollary, from the Kantian distinction as Lovejoy conceived it.

It is customary in introductory courses in the history of philosophy to point to two anticipations of the Kantian distinction between analytic and synthetic—namely, Leibniz's distinction between the truths of reason and truths of fact, and Hume's between relations of ideas and matters of fact. We teach our students that the criterion for all three philosophers, Leibniz, Hume, and Kant, is found in the self-contradictoriness of the contradictories of the first member of each of the pairs. From this it follows that all analytical judgments (respectively: relations of ideas, truths of reason) are a priori. It remains an open question whether all a priori judgments are analytic. On this point, Leibniz is equivocal; Hume affirms it in the *Enquiry*, and Kant denies it.

Already at the beginning of the history of the synthetic-analytic distinction, however, there are ambiguities which have been recently brought to light again not only in the continuous debate about the possibility of a priori synthetic judgments but also, and perhaps in a more pointed fashion, about the analytic-synthetic distinction itself. Quine, as you know, holds that a sharp dichotomy between analytic and synthetic cannot be made. To do so would require clear, indeed clearer, concepts of synonymy, self-contradiction, tautology, and logical truth, yet no one of these concepts is so clear that it can be used in the clarification of the concept of the analytic. These concepts form a cluster with which we are so deceptively familiar that we facilely use one to elucidate the others; yet in dubious cases of trying to decide whether some sentence is analytic, we cannot get an unambiguous answer by appealing to any of these other concepts.

Prior to Kant, of course, the terminology of the analytic-synthetic distinction did not exist, but our usual way of introducing students to this distinction in historical courses is to refer to the judgments in Hume and Leibniz which were testable by the law of contradiction and to say that they accordingly had the concept of, but not the name for, analytic judgments. But this presupposes that "contradiction" has a univocal meaning in all three philosophers.

I shall discuss Lovejoy's account of this concept in Leibniz in just a moment; but first let us take a quick look at Hume. Hume in the *Enquiry* explicitly says that the denial of a relation of ideas "implies a contradiction"; and this led Kant to think that Hume interpreted mathematical judgments as analytic.[3] Yet it is clear to us, who (unlike Kant) have read the *Treatise*, that by "contradiction" Hume did not mean merely formal or logical contradiction; his "philosophical relations" which are known with certainty are not analytic in the sense that the denials of them are logically self-contradictory. They are, in fact, at least candidates for the dubious honor of being reported only in synthetic a priori judgments, the criterion of them being not the self-contradictoriness of their contradictories (which would make them analytic) but the inconceivability or unimaginability of their opposites (which might make them a priori). Kant did not read the *Treatise*, thus misread the *Enquiry*, and may have been put on the path to the formulation of his own distinction between the analytic and the synthetic and the discovery of a kind of judgment which he erroneously believed his predecessors had not noticed. For let it be well noted: Kant did not deny that his predecessors had made synthetic a priori judgments; he denied their right to do so since their principles, in contrast to their practice, allowed only of analytic a priori judgments and synthetic a posteriori judgments.

Lovejoy does not consider Hume in this essay but deals only with the continental philosophers. His conclusions would have no doubt been much the same had he dealt with Locke and Hume instead of Leibniz and Wolff, because most of what is ambiguous and problematical for the empiricists is ambiguous and problematical also for the rationalists. But the continental tradition is complicated by an added fact: for Leibniz, all judgments are analytic in the sense that

3. *Critique of Practical Reason*, end of Preface.

every predicate truly attributed to a subject is included in the intension of its concept. So the difference between analytic and ostensibly synthetic judgments lies in the fact that the former are, or can
be reduced to, explicit identities, while the synthetic judgments are
"virtual identities" because the reduction, always in principle
possible, would require an infinite number of steps. Hence Leibniz
acknowledges the existence of judgments not actually demonstrated
to be analytic. Some of these judgments are intuitively necessary and
others are acknowledged or claimed to be necessary by the principle
of sufficient reason. Whether the principle of sufficient reason can
be said to provide a justification for calling a judgment a priori when
we men can know it only a posteriori is dubious, to say the least. It
is necessarily true because is has a sufficient reason, though from its
sufficient reason it cannot be deduced by us; hence we are ineluct-
ably thrown back upon experience to establish it as true.

Lovejoy does not deal extensively with this old question; he con-
siders rather a less metaphysical problem in Leibniz. He deals with
analytical judgments, of which he finds two species which Leibniz
did not clearly distinguish, and these two species, he holds, correspond respectively to the analytical and the synthetical a priori in
Kant. The first type is judgments of explicit identities or tautologies
of the form "A is A," "AB is A," or "A is not non-A." The other
type is acknowledged by Leibniz but not fully explored because he
presumably believed that they could be dealt with under the rubric
of virtually identical judgments.[4] These are judgments of the necessary co-inherence or incompatibility of simple concepts in the constitution of a subject, where the law of formal contradiction is
insufficient to determine the necessary relations of the predicates to
each other. These judgments of "ultimate repugnancies to co-inherence between distinct and positive concepts" and "necessary coexistence" are a priori but neither explicit nor virtual identities
(114). Thus Leibniz, according to Lovejoy, recognized the point of

4. See Margaret D. Wilson, "On Leibniz's Explication of 'Necessary Truth,'"
Studia Leibnitiana Supplementa 3 (1969), 50–63, especially section iii on
"disparates," "almost identities," and "primitive necessary truths," which,
according to Miss Wilson, do not fit Leibniz's analytical theory of judgment.

Kant's distinction between analytic and synthetic judgments and provided an inchoate theory by virtue of which the latter could be known a priori, but he made little of it. Lovejoy raps Leibniz's knuckles for letting it appear that these propositions are strictly established or tested by the law of contradiction; he says, Leibniz "intended no such result" (112) and he gives credit to Bertrand Russell for having pointed out that Leibniz could not have meant literally what he said—overlooking the fact that Kant himself had made this his principal criticism of Leibniz more than a century earlier, as Russell himself, but not Lovejoy, admits.[5]

It was the accomplishment of Wolff to make this distinction between two kinds of judgments explicit. Lovejoy quotes some of the many passages in which Wolff does so, but it must be admitted that Wolff was ineffective in making the distinction stable and well known. For even when making the distinction, Wolff still appeals to the *language* of the law of contradiction just as Leibniz had done and as Hume was to do, and it was not only Kant but Wolff's principal critics, F. A. Hoffmann, C. A. Crusius, and J. H. Lambert,[6] who held it against Wolff that the only a priori knowledge he claimed was that which was established or testable by the law of contradiction. Kant explicitly says, "The only conflict they [the Leibniz-Wolffians] recognize is that of contradiction."[7] The putative inadequacy of that law for testing all a priori knowledge was the main thesis of the men I have named; it was not a criticism which originated with Kant (or a fortiori with Bertrand Russell!).

Wolff had an easier task because he did not consistently adhere to Leibniz's analytic theory of judgment in general, according to which *praedicatum inest subiecto*. (Gram [95] is wrong in attributing this view to Wolff. Wolff may even not have known that this was

5. *A Critical Exposition of the Philosophy of Leibniz*, p. 22. Kant criticized Leibniz in much the same way Russell did; *Critique of Pure Reason*, A 270 = B 326; A 273 = B 329; see B 16 for a clearer statement, though Leibniz is not mentioned here.
6. See my *Early German Philosophy*, pp. 302–03, 379, 399, 406–07, 411–12.
7. *Critique of Pure Reason*, A 274 = B 330.

Leibniz's theory.) Judgment, for Wolff, is the *Verknüpfung* (connection) or *Trennung* (separation) of two concepts.[8] With this definition, Wolff could have inquired into the mode of connection or separation and thus have anticipated Kant's distinction just as he already saw the difference, later pointed out by Kant, between mere association of ideas and a judgmental connection between them.[9] But Wolff did not exploit the benefit he derived from being free of the incubus of the Leibnizian analytical theory of judgment; he rather turned to an examination of possible complex concepts as the *Bedingung* for the *Aussage* (predicate)[10] so that judgment of partial identity ("ABC is A") can be made with complex *notiones foecundae*[11] as subjects. Fecund concepts are "those which contain the determinations of a thing through which other things agree with the subject and are able to be brought together into a whole."

Thus identical propositions with complex subjects are possible, the synthesis taking place not on the level of judgment but on the level of definition or *Begriffsbildung*. The tacit assumption of a priori synthetic *concepts* blocked the way to seeing the problem of a priori synthetic *judgments*.[12] In order that such concepts be made or be recognized when found, it is necessary to establish their real possibility, and this requires real, not arbitrary, definition.[13] Both Leibniz, in his criticism of the ontological argument, and Wolff saw this. "A philosophical concept is certain," says Wolff's faithful disciple Baumgarten, "if we know clearly the compossibility of the *notae*."[14]

8. Wolff, *Vernünftige Gedancken von den Kräften des menschlichen Verstandes*, c. iii, § § 1, 2; *Logica*, § 524; *Ontologica*, § 449.

9. *Psychologia empirica*, § 114. Kant's distinction and his criticism of Wolff are in *Critique of Pure Reason*, B 140–41.

10. *Vernünftige Gedancken von den Kräften des menschlichen Verstandes*, c. iii, § 6.

11. Lovejoy quotes from *Horae subsecivae Marburgensis* (1730), i. 154.

12. As Kant points out in his reply to Eberhard; see also my *Studies in the Philosophy of Kant*, p. 83.

13. *Vernünftige Gedancken von den Kräften des menschlichen Verstandes*, c. i, § 33.

14. *Philosophia generalis* (1769), § 55.

Wolff does not give us a well-organized systematic set of criteria of possibility of a concept, but he does, in various places in his *Ontologia*, provide five or six conditions, one a posteriori ("*ab existentia ad possibilitatem valent consequentia*")[15] and four, or perhaps five, a priori conditions. According to two of them, a concept consisting of the *notae* A and B is a priori possible if A and B presuppose each other[16] or if one follows from the other by demonstration.[17] For meeting these criteria, the law of contradiction presumably provides a sufficient test. Another test is the constructability of the object of the concept,[18] which is at least verbally an anticipation of the test for the possibility of mathematical concepts in Kant, though Wolff does not expand on this and probably did not see the significance of what he had said since he regarded syllogism, not construction, as the paradigm of mathematical proof; certainly Lambert did not see this criterion of possibility functioning in Wolff's mathematical works.[19]

The most interesting of the conditions for establishing the compossibility of *notae* A and B is where they do not determine one another, but "fieri posse constat (sive vi experientiae sive demonstrationis) combinari posse intelliguntur," and this "combinari posse" can be seen by *ratio intuitiva.*[20] But for him the antonym of "agree" is "contradict," and in saying this Wolff falls back into the formalism of Leibniz according to which all impossibility is contradiction and the only acceptable *Grundsätze* are identities.[21] Or else he returns helplessly to the Leibnizian theological justification of judgments of compossibility as virtual identities, as when he says

15. *Ontologica*, §170.
16. Ibid., §89.
17. Ibid., §91.
18. Ibid., §92.
19. See *Early German Philosophy*, p. 404.
20. *Ontologia*, §48.
21. See the quotation from Lovejoy, p. 116 n., and the immediately following passages in *Vernünftige Gedancken von den Kräften des menschlichen Verstandes*, c. iii, §§10 and 13; also ibid., c. iv, §21.

"Something is possible because it is represented by the divine under-standing." [22]

We may summarize Wolff's theory of a priori judgments as it is interpreted by Lovejoy and Eberhard, but not as it was understood by Hoffmann, Crusius, Lambert, and Kant, as follows: [23]

1. There are explicit identities (*leere Sätze*).
2. There are a priori judgments which state a necessary relation of compossibility between simple *notae*, as in "A B is possible," or "A is B," this being seen by *ratio intuitiva.* Wolff calls the test of these judgments the law of contradiction but, Lovejoy adds, "in an enlarged sense" (117); and what Wolff calls the "intui-tive understanding" of these combinations is called by Lovejoy "the subjective necessity of thinking the predicates together" (116) or "*de facto* psychological necessity" (127).
3. There are a priori judgments which are reducible to (2). They are judgments of the form "A is C" where "A is B" and "B is C" are judgments of type (2); or where "A is B" is a definition of A, and C is an attribute of A by virtue of its necessary coexistence with B. Such synthetic a priori judgments are unlike (2) in being demonstrable by the test of contradiction in the normal sense.

I have several brief comments to make about this division. Though there is danger in using Kantian terminology anachronistically, for Wolff, as interpreted by Lovejoy, (1) is analytic and both (2) and (3) are synthetic. When we come to Eberhard, where there is no danger of errors growing out of anachronism, (1) and (2) are analytic and (3) is synthetic. It is not possible, I think, to be sure where Lovejoy himself would draw the line, whether between (1) and (2) or be-tween (2) and (3). Lovejoy sometimes identified (1) with Kant's analytic judgments (120), but Kant did not mean by analytic judg-

22. *Vernünftige Gedancken von Gott, der Welt, der Seele des Menschen auch aller Dinge überhaupt,* §975.
23. Actually Lovejoy (116) merges (1) and (2) together, but it is no in-justice to separate them as, indeed, Lovejoy has to do when he discusses Eberhard.

ments merely formal identities,[24] and inasmuch as Lovejoy later (121) rather grudgingly acknowledges this I will not belabor the point. Hence Lovejoy thinks that Kant ought to have agreed with Eberhard by making both (1) and (2) analytic and only (3) synthetic. There is good reason nowadays, however, to call only (1) analytic.

Second, Kant denies both the Wolffian *ratio intuitiva* and the Lovejoy substitute for it, the "psychological necessity" of seeing the incompossibility of simple representations. Against the former there is his well-known view that our intuition is sensible, not intellectual. Against the latter is his complaint that even Crusius in rejecting Wolff's theory of the adequacy of the law of contradiction had substituted a subjective psychological necessity for an objective necessity.[25] It must be admitted that no one from Leibniz through Kant to Lovejoy had a well worked out theory of such judgments as "Yellow must be brighter than blue" and "Whatever is colored must be extended." But as a matter of fact this kind of judgment was not the kind at issue in Kant's philosophy, and I have no idea what Kant would have said about it. Both Kant and Wolff were interested in propositions like "Every event must have a cause" and "There cannot be a two-sided plane figure." On such judgments as these they are sharply at issue, Wolff holding them to be, in principle at least, reducible by a series of intellectual intuitions to an identity and Kant holding their contradictories to be logically possible but not sensibly intuitable and therefore really impossible. And it is by no means obvious to me that the pure sensible intuition to which Kant appeals is any more a "chimaera that belongs with other hybrid monsters of antiquity" than the pure intellectual intuition used by Wolff.

I must deal more extensively with a third point. In attacking Kant

24. See *Über eine Entdeckung nach der alle neue Kritik der reinen Vernunft durch eine ältere entbehrlich gemacht werden soll*, Ak. VIII, 244 (Allison translation, p. 154); *Fortschritte der Metaphysik*, Ak. XX, 322.

25. *Vorlesung über Logik*, Intro. ii; Ak. IX, 21; Letter to Reinhold, May 19, 1789, in Zweig, *Correspondence*, p. 114; Reflexionen 4275 and 4446, Ak. XVIII, 492, 554.

on the question of whether judgments of the third type are synthetic even if they are reducible (stepwise) to judgments of the second type, Lovejoy undertakes the ungrateful task of defending Eberhard. It was Eberhard who devoted his *Philosophisches Magazin* to attacking Kant on the precise charge raised again by Lovejoy, namely, that the *Critique of Pure Reason* was supererogatory, answering the question, "How are synthetic judgments a priori possible?" when it had already been answered by Wolff. Kant replied to Eberhard in his essay, "On a New Discovery According to which every new *Critique of Pure Reason* is Rendered Unnecessary by an Older One" (1790).

According to Eberhard, in judgments of type (2) the predicate expresses the essence or part of the essence of the subject; such judgments are testable by the law of contradiction in what Lovejoy calls "an enlarged sense," but they are synthetic if we use the criterion of self-contradictoriness of the contradictory in the strict sense. Judgments of type (3) assert in their predictes attributes or properties of the subject and are called synthetic precisely because of that. They likewise are testable by the law of contradiction and are a priori if the predicate has its "sufficient ground in that essence" (122). Hence Eberhard holds, and Lovejoy agrees with him, that the problem to which Kant addressed the *Critique of Pure Reason*, namely, "How are synthetic judgments a priori possible?", had been answered by Wolff.

We must consider two objections of Eberhard's separately. First, a judgment is synthetic, according to Eberhard, if its predicate is an attribute, not the essence (genus and differentia) of the subject-concept. It is well known that Kant has two diverse and often incompatible criteria for analytic judgments: the introspective or phenomenological criterion of discerning what is "actually thought" in the subject-concept, and the logical criterion of the self-contradictoriness of the contradictory. By the first criterion, analytic judgments are merely explicative or noninstructive,[26] while judgments whose predicates are attributes can certainly be ampliative or instructive by any plain interpretation of what is "actually thought"

26. *Prolegomena*, § 2.

in the subject. Hence by the criterion of what is thought in the subject-concept, judgments of type (3) can be synthetic and at the same time a priori. But the point at issue for Kant, Eberhard, and Lovejoy is whether they are synthetic by the *logical* criterion. Kant did not fully confront the problems he ran into by having two criteria for analytic judgments. He erroneously assumed that what was analytic by one would be analytic by the other. Here he is obviously using the logical criterion, while Eberhard and Lovejoy, who faithfully follows Eberhard, are using the phenomenological criterion. But the point at issue is whether the judgments in question are synthetic by the logical criterion, and Eberhard and Lovejoy attempt to show that they are testable by the law of contradiction without drawing the obvious conclusion that if they are they must be analytic.

On the second point, that judgments of type (3) are testable by the law of contradiction, and yet are synthetic because they have attributes as predicates (synthetic by an easy application of the phenomenological explicative-ampliative distinction), Kant draws attention to an equivocation in the terminology of essence and attribute.

The distinction between essence and attribute which underlies the distinction between judgments of type (2), which for Eberhard are analytic, and of type (3), which for Eberhard are synthetic, is a merely logical distinction. The essence Eberhard is concerned with consists of those marks which are jointly necessary and sufficient for the definition of a concept. The attributes for Eberhard are those marks which without exception pertain to the concept of the subject but are not explicitly included among the marks which constitute its definiens. We can be sure that a predicate is an attribute if it is a logical consequence of the essence so that its denial would formally contradict the essence or definition. Thus having more than two sides is an attribute of a triangle. Because such an attribute follows analytically from the definition by the law of contradiction, Kant calls such an attribute "analytical" and holds that a judgment with such an attribute is an analytical judgment, even though it is possible that it is, for someone, ampliative and instructive.

But Kant holds that there is a real and not merely a logical distinction between two kinds of predicates. The analytical attribute follows by the law of contradiction from the logical essence and is the predicate of an analytical judgment. But a synthetic attribute, which Kant also calls a *Bestimmung*, is one which does not analytically follow from the *logical* essence and yet has a sufficient ground in the real essence[27] and hence can be necessarily predicated of a subject. A judgment with such a necessary, but synthetic, predicate is one which Kant calls a synthetic a priori judgment. Thus, to use Kant's example, that space has three dimensions does not follow from the *definition* of space by the law of contradiction, and yet it is known to be necessarily true. His problem is to see how this predicate can be attached synthetically, yet a priori, to a subject the concept of which does not *logically* entail it in such a manner that its contradictory is self-contradictory.

It is at this point where I think Lovejoy fails to be a perspicuous guide in the interpretation of the difficult Kant-Eberhard controversy. He makes, in my opinion, two mistakes.

First, just as he has spoken of the law of contradiction "in an enlarged sense," he now (128, 129) substitutes the much vaguer criterion of the impossibility of the inconceivable for the impossibility of the self-contradictory. "Inconceivability" is a somewhat vague term, including in its meaning unimaginability and counterintuitivity as well as self-contradictoriness. Kant holds that a straight line which is not the shortest distance between two points is unimaginable and counter-intuitive, and hence that a straight line is the shortest distance between two points is a priori. But he holds, with Hume,[28] that "a straight line is not the shortest distance between two points" is *not* self-contradictory; and hence "a straight line is the shortest" is not analytical. I do not here wish to defend Kant's explanation of this or even his exposition of the problem; I do wish to say that "inconceivability" is too vague a term to cover both what

27. Letter to Reinhold, May 12, 1789 (Zweig, *Correspondence*, p. 140).
28. *Treatise of Human Nature*, ed. Selby-Bigge, pp. 49–50.

Kant and what Eberhard are insisting upon because it covers what Kant was careful to separate.

Closely related to the point just mentioned is what I must regard as a serious misinterpretation of a passage from Kant's reply to Eberhard[29] quoted by Lovejoy (123). Lovejoy does not see (in that passage and more particularly in a footnote of Kant's which he does not translate) that Kant is distinguishing two meanings of the word "essence." After quoting Kant's orthodox distinction between *essentialia* and *attributa rationata*, which I have alluded to above, Lovejoy says that for Kant attributes "are yet indispensable to the *interna possibilitas* of it [the concept]" (123) and that this is equivalent to the thesis of the Wolff-Eberhard theory that judgments *per attributa* (judgments of type [3]) are "legitimate sources of *a priori* [synthetic?][30] knowledge" (123). But it seems to me to be evident, in spite of Kant's bad style of exposition, that he is maintaining his distinction between synthetic and analytic attributes precisely by *distinguishing* the *interna possibilitas* of the concept (*die innere Möglichkeit des Begriffes*) from its *logisches Wesen* (logical essence), and not using these terms as synonymous, as Lovejoy would have it. If I am correct in this, then Kant has not contradicted himself (as Lovejoy says on p. 122, n. 10) or unwittingly surrendered to Eberhard on a point of capital importance by inadvertently treating all attributes as if they were analytical of the *logical* essence.

Too much readiness to believe in Kant's awkwardness in philosophical argument has, in my opinion, kept Lovejoy from reading through the textual thicket to see what Kant was getting at. He is ascribing to Kant a blunder of such monumental stupidity that it could be credible only to a critic who had little or no respect for his prey. In spite of what Lovejoy says about the passage in question, it seems to me to be very clear what Kant is saying, and it seems to me to be clearly different from what Lovejoy thinks he is saying.

29. *Über eine Entdeckung*, Ak. VIII, 228–29 (Allison, p. 141).

30. Since Kant has not denied that attributes can be predicates in analytical judgments and the only question between Eberhard and Kant was whether "having an attribute as predicate" is a sufficient condition of syntheticity, it appears necessary to insert the word "synthetic."

Let it be granted that Kant is not at his lucid best in the passage which Lovejoy misunderstands. The very expression "*die innere Möglichkeit des Begriffes* [the internal possibility of the concept] " invites precisely the kind of misinterpretation Lovejoy makes; because what Kant means is the "*innere Möglichkeit des Objektes des Begriffes* [internal possibility of the object of the concept]." This is made clear in the *Vorarbeiten zur Schrift gegen Eberhard*, which Lovejoy cannot have seen, when Kant finds Eberhard's fundamental error to lie in the fact that he did not distinguish the logical essence from the real essence or the "nature" of the thing.[31] But in other works which Lovejoy did read or could have read, the meaning of "internal possibility" as "real essence" is made clear. "A logical essence is the ultimate internal ground of everything that is contained in the concept. A real essence, however, is the ultimate internal ground [*der erste innere Grund*] of everything that pertains to the thing itself," he says in his elementary *Lectures on Metaphysics.*[32] Unfortunately, however, I cannot absolutely clinch the point by citing an unambiguous example of Kant's use of "*innere Möglichkeit des Begriffes,*" because I cannot find that Kant used this expression elsewhere. But the *Critique of Pure Reason* (B 302, 624, 638) makes what I take to be the same distinction by contrasting logical with transcendental possibility, and the very early work, *The Only Possible Premise for a Demonstration of the Existence of God*, distinguishes "*innere Möglichkeit* [internal possibility] " from "*das Logische in der Möglichkeit* [the logical element in the possibility] " and identifies "*innere Möglichkeit*" with the "*Wesen der Dinge* [essence of things]."[33] Still, even if we had only the passage in the published work against Eberhard to guide us, I think it would be captious to interpret the text as Lovejoy does, though the words "*innere Möglichkeit des Begriffes*" certainly would appear, in isola-

31. Ak. XX, 376, first full paragraph; also *Logik*, Intro. VIII, Ak. IX, 61 (Hartmann and Schwartz, p. 67).
32. *Vorlesungen über die Metaphysik*, ed. Pölitz (1821), p. 38. See also *Critique of Pure Reason*, A 676 = B 703, A 816 = B 844 for unambiguous use of "internal possibility (of a thing)."
33. Ak. II, 77–78, 162.

tion, to refer to logical essence. Only if one believes, with Lovejoy, that Kant was singularly obtuse in philosophical argument would one be tempted to put this interpretation upon his words; assuming this interpretation, one could only agree with Lovejoy that Kant was indeed distressingly confused.

I will conclude by putting, mostly in my own words, what I think Kant meant; in so doing, I have the benefit of other writings of Kant which were in all probability not available to my distinguished predecessor and which might otherwise have led him to modify his judgment.

A concept, Kant is saying, is logically possible if it does not contain contradictory predicates. But the concept may be without an object and thus only an *ens rationis.*[34] To be shown to be really and not merely logically possible, the object must "agree with the formal conditions of experience" including the condition of intuition as well as thought.[35] This intuition might be, as it was for Wolff, intellectual, but, for various reasons that I cannot go into here, Kant denies that intellectual intuition is possible for men. Hence, it must be sensible intuition. If the sensible intuition is empirical, the concept is really possible, because whatever is actual must be possible; but sensible intuition, whether pure or empirical, does not reveal the ontologically real essence of a thing, which is as hidden from Kant as it was from Locke. If the intuition is pure, however, being an intuition of the conditions under which alone anything can be an object *for us*, then we know its real possibility a priori as an object of possible experience. Those features of the object which make it really possible as an object of possible experience may be called its real essence (though not in a Lockean sense, which would apply only to the thing in itself, but only in a sense to distinguish it from Locke's nominal essence or Kant's logical essence). Judgments can be both synthetic and known a priori, therefore, only if there is something a priori which is not logically necessary. This is the condition of pure sensible intuitability. Without pure sensible intuition, all

34. *Critique of Pure Reason*, A 292 = B 348.
35. Ibid., A 218 = B 265.

judgments are either analytic and a priori or synthetic and a posteriori.

Now back to Eberhard! Eberhard regards a judgment as synthetic because it contains attributes as predicates and as a priori because the attributes are logically entailed by the logical *essentia.* Kant, accepting as the criterion of analyticity the strict self-contradictoriness of the contradictory, holds that judgments may have attributes as predicates without being synthetic. They are, however, synthetic if and only if the predicates they contain are either *essentialia,* attributes, or properties of the *real* essence. All such judgments can be denied without falling into a logical contradiction with the logical essence, so they are synthetic. But they are a priori if the predicates are *essentialia* or attributes of the real essence of the object considered only as an object of possible sensible intuition.

And now, finally, back to Lovejoy! I think he has failed in his defense of Eberhard and failed to show that the question of how there can be synthetic judgments a priori had been answered by Leibniz and Wolff "in a sense to which Kant could not consistently have made objection" (114). But one of Lovejoy's purposes in these essays was to show that "we need a fuller and far more precise understanding of the relation between Kant's doctrines and those of his German predecessors" (308). Even when I did not follow all of Lovejoy's interpretations, his insistence that the student of Kant be also a student of those to whom Kant himself was a student provided stimulus to my own studies of Kant's predecessors, and I would not like for my differences with Lovejoy, which I have here emphasized, to obscure how much more I agree with him and learned from him.

5 Analytic and Synthetic
Judgments before Kant

> Men who never think independently have nevertheless
> the acuteness to discover everything, after it has been
> once shown them, in what was said long since, though no
> one was ever able to see it there before.
>
> *Prolegomena*, §3

> Es ist auch schon das gewöhnliche Schicksal alles Neuen
> in Wissenschaften, wenn man ihm nichts entgegensetzen
> kann, dass man es doch wenigstens als längst bekannt bei
> Älteren antreffe.
>
> *Über eine Entdeckung nach der alle neue Kritik
> der reinen Vernunft durch eine ältere entbehrlich
> gemacht werden soll* (Ak. VIII, 242).

It is perhaps customary in introductory courses in the history of
philosophy, and it is not unknown in the literature—including some
of my own writings— to introduce Kant's distinction between analytic and synthetic judgments by referring to Leibniz's distinction
between truths of reason and truths of fact and to Hume's distinction between relations of ideas and matters of fact. Some, more
venturesome perhaps, seek the origin of the distinction in Locke's

Presented at a Kant Symposium at the Florida State University, April 20,
1974, and reprinted from *Reflections on Kant's Philosophy*, ed. W. H.
Werkmeister, by kind permission of Professor Werkmeister and the University
Presses of Florida. An earlier version was read at a colloquium held at North-
western University in 1968.

dichotomy of trifling and instructive propositions, in Hobbes's of truths of universal propositions and truths of existential propositions, and even farther back in truths dependent upon the intellect of God and those dependent upon the will of God.

Under the common assumption that pre-Kantian philosophers equated whatever in their terminology is said to be equivalent to "analytic" with a priori and whatever in their terminology is said to be equivalent to "synthetic" with a posteriori, the following summary table is not uncommon:

	a priori	*a posteriori*
analytic	relations of ideas truths of reason	none
synthetic	none	matters of fact truths of fact

The schema just presented is not exactly wrong, but it is woefully incomplete. It was the thesis of a famous paper by Arthur O. Lovejoy[1] that the table was so incomplete and wrong that it created the fiction that Kant had something original to contribute besides a new terminology, and that if the contribution of one other philosopher (Wolff) is put into the table, it will turn out that Kant was either a mere plagiarist or else unpardonably ignorant of the state of the problem.

Indeed one of the most remarkable things, which ought first to strike the eye, is that Kant *seems to have been ignorant of the information summarized in the table.* For he says, "Perhaps even the distinction between analytic and synthetic judgments has never previously been considered,"[2] and, more specifically, "the dogmatic philosophers Wolff and his acute follower Baumgarten altogether neglected this apparently obvious distinction."[3]

1. Lovejoy, "Kant's Antithesis of Dogmatism and Criticism," *Mind*, 1906; reprinted in M. S. Gram, ed., *Kant: Disputed Questions* (Chicago, 1967), pp. 105–30. I have examined Lovejoy's paper in considerable detail in "Lovejoy as a Critic of Kant."
2. *Critique of Pure Reason*, B 19; not in A.
3. *Prolegomena*, §3.

Yet in the same paragraph in the *Prolegomena* he says he finds "an indication of the division" in Locke's *Essay*, Book IV, chapter 3, §§9–10, where Locke draws a distinction between our certainty of identity and diversity (Kant says "identity or contradiction"–a significant slip) and that of coexistence, of which we have little a priori knowledge. But he seems to have overlooked a more obvious source, namely, Book IV, chapters 7 and 8, of the *Essay*, where Locke distinguishes between "a real truth [which] conveys with it instructive real knowledge" by stating "a necessary consequence of a precise complex idea . . . not contained in it," and "trifling propositions" which are either mere identities or affirmations "when any part of a complex idea is predicated of the whole."[4] Thus it seems that Locke had not only distinguished between analytic and synthetic judgments but that he had held, and that Kant knew that he had held, that some of the latter could be known with certainty, that is, that they were a priori.

In the same paragraph, Kant says that Locke was so vague and indefinite in his remarks on a priori synthetic knowledge that he did not stimulate even Hume "to make investigations concerning this sort of propositions." Yet again and again Kant writes as if Hume had distinguished between analytic and synthetic judgments and had categorically denied the possibility of a priori synthetic judgments. He did so, Kant held, because he failed to draw a needed distinction between the synthetic judgments of the understanding, which may be known a priori for objects of possible experience, and those of reason, which profess to be about things which can never be met with in experience. Since Hume agreed with Kant that the latter type of synthetic a priori knowledge is impossible, his failure to make the needed distinction led him to reject the possibility of any synthetic judgments (of possible experience) known a priori, while Kant, precisely by making this distinction, did not have to condemn all a priori synthetic judgments but only those which claim to refer beyond experience.[5]

4. *Essay*, IV, 8, §§8 and 4. In §3 explicit tautologies are counted among trifling propositions; Kant ("Fortschritte der Metaphysik," Ak. XX, 322) denies that they are analytical: they do not analyze and explicate. He thus distinguishes between judgments based on identity and identical judgments. Only the former are analytical.
5. *Critique of Pure Reason*, A 764–65 = B 792–93.

Hence Hume concluded, according to Kant, that all *genuine* a priori knowledge must be analytic. Concerning the judgments which are commonly believed to be a priori but not analytic (such as the causal maxim), Hume went on to give a psychological explanation of the illusion that they are a priori. Since Kant had such insights into Hume's mode of argument, I cannot explain why he did not cite the opening paragraphs of Section IV of the *Enquiry*, a passage known to every schoolboy. Here Hume draws his famous distinction between relations of ideas and matters of fact. Kant must had read there: "The contrary of every matter of fact is still possible because it can never imply a contradiction and is conceived by the mind with the same facility and distinctness as if ever so conformable to reality." In the *Enquiry*, therefore, matter of fact judgments meet one of the criteria of syntheticity. Accordingly, relations of ideas "discoverable by the mere operation of thought without dependence on what is anywhere existent in the universe" seem to be judged in what Kant called analytic judgments.

Yet had Kant read the *Treatise* he would have discovered that perhaps Hume did not mean exactly what he seemed to be saying; and if we, who can read the *Treatise*, do so, we perhaps can find out why Kant was correct in not taking this to mean that relations of ideas, even if (presumably) testable by contradiction, are equivalent to the relation expressed in an analytical judgment. The relations of ideas in the *Enquiry* correspond to the "necessary and unalterable" philosophical relations of the *Treatise*, relations "which depend entirely on the ideas which we compare together."[6] But the necessary and unalterable philosophical relations are not analytical in the sense that one of the relata is included in the other, nor in the sense that the denial of such a relation involves a formal contradiction.[7]

By "contradiction" Hume did not mean merely an assertion like "A is not A." He means also "A is not B" where an A that is not a B is "inconceivable" or "unimaginable."

6. This correspondence has been established, to my satisfaction, by Donald W. Gotterbarn, "Kant, Hume, and Analyticity," *Kant-Studien* 65 (1974), 274–83.

7. Gotterbarn, "Kant, Hume, and Analyticity"; W. A. Suchting, "Hume and Necessary Truth," *Dialogue* (1966–67), 47–60; R. F. Atkinson, "Hume on Mathematics," *Philosophical Quarterly* 10 (1960), 127–37.

Wherein consists the difference betwixt believing and disbelieving any proposition? The answer is easy with regard to propositions, that are prov'd by intuition or demonstration. In that case, the person, who assents, not only conceives the ideas according to the proposition, but is necessarily determin'd to conceive them in that particular manner, either immediately or by the imposition of other ideas. Whatever is absurd is unintelligible; nor is it possible for the imagination to conceive anything contrary to a demonstration.[8]

Thus even before Kant there were ambiguities which have recently been brought to light again in the continuing debate about the criterion of analyticity, though of course Hume is more ambiguous than those whom Quine is criticizing. For Hume did not mean by "contradiction" a formal contradiction alone; "inconceivability" means not merely logical nonsense, but also unimaginability, and even counter-intuitivity. His relations of ideas are not trifling propositions nor are they analytical propositions as Kant understood the term, though this cannot be seen by anyone who, like Kant, reads only the *Enquiry* and not also the *Treatise*. Had Kant read Hume's *Treatise*, he would have found Hume tacitly admitting a class of intuitively and demonstratively necessary relations of ideas which are not testable by the logical law of contradiction.

Hume differed from Locke in holding that the causal relation is neither intuitively nor demonstratively known. Hence he concluded that it is a matter-of-fact relation which can be known, if at all, only a posteriori. It was this inference which awoke Kant from his dogmatic slumber. He "generalized Hume's problem" and saw that if the syntheticity of the causal maxim implied its aposteriority, then all the propositions even of mathematics (as well as metaphysics) can be known only a posteriori. He held that Hume himself had been saved from the absurdity of holding mathematics to be a posteriori only because he had made the mistake of holding its judgments to be analytic.[9] Believing as Kant did that mathematical judgments were both synthetic and a priori, he had to investigate how it is possible

8. *Treatise*, ed. Selby-Bigge, p. 95
9. *Critique of Practical Reason*, Preface, 3d paragraph from end.

for there to be such judgments, and he "solemnly and legally suspended" all metaphysicians from their occupation until they had
answered the question of how this was possible.[10]

Leibniz's distinction between truths of reason and truths of fact is
another obvious source of Kant's distinction which he does not anywhere mention. Its *locus classicus* is the *Monadology:*

31. Our reasonings are grounded on two great principles, that of
    contradiction, in virtue of which we judge false that which
    involves a contradiction, and true that which is opposed or
    contradictory to the false.
33. There are also two kinds of truths, those of reason and those
    of fact. Truths of reason are necessary and their opposite is
    impossible. When a truth is necessary, its reason can be found
    by analysis, resolving it into more simple ideas and truths,
    until we come to those that are primary.
35. There are simple ideas, of which no definition can be given;
    there are also axioms and postulates, in a word, primary prin-
    ciples; and these are identical propositions whose opposite
    involves an express contradiction.

From these well-known passages it is inferred that truths of fact are
synthetic and truths of reason are analytic, and that only the latter
can be known a priori. But we must remember that the *Monadology*
was a book for popular consumption, and the esoteric doctrine of
Leibniz, which we know mostly through his unpublished writings, is
very much more complicated.

According to the esoteric doctrine, in all true affirmative propositions the concept of the predicate is included in the concept of the
subject.[11] Therefore all true affirmative propositions are identities

10. *Prolegomena*, Ak. V, 277 (Beck, p. 25).
11. Leibniz usually writes that the predicate is included in the subject, but
sometimes that the concept of the predicate is included in (or involved in) the
subject concept (*Philosophical Papers and Letters* [trans. Loemker] p. 363; cf.
G. H. R. Parkinson, *Logic and Reality in Leibniz's Metaphysics* [Oxford,
1965], pp. 9, 28). Presumably he did not notice the difference, but it per-

or partial identities (that is, analytic propositions), and all false affirmative propositions are self-contradictory. If the demonstration of the proposition by reduction to an identity through substitution of definientia for definienda can be accomplished in a finite number of steps, the judgment is called an explicit identity even though its form is not "A is A" but rather "A.B is B" or "A is A.B." If the reduction cannot be effected in a finite number of steps, the proposition is only a virtual identity and cannot be known by showing the self-contradictoriness of its contradictory; though intrinsically analytic, it is known to us in other ways than an expressly analytic judgment.[12]

The *Monadology* gives a succinct account of how we know a theorem in geometry, without taking these esoteric complications into account: by substituting definientia we come to axioms, and axioms are explicit identities whose "opposites involve an express contradiction." Earlier (1678) in a letter to Conring Leibniz had written:

Demonstration is a chain of definitions. . . . All truths can be resolved into definitions, identical propositions, and observations—though purely intelligible truths do not need observations.[13]

But there are two places where this program breaks down, at least one of which Leibniz himself admitted.

1. There must be *primae veritates* which are unprovable and therefore not analytic, because explicit identity or contradiction cannot obtain between simple unanalyzable terms. The contradictory of a

---

mitted him to believe (or shows that he did believe), in Kant's words, "that he could obtain knowledge of the inner nature of things by comparing all objects merely with the understanding and with the separated, formal concepts of its thought" (*Critique of Pure Reason*, A 270 = B 326). This was, for Kant, "the fundamental mistake of Leibniz" from which the monadology followed (H. J. Paton, "Kant on the Errors of Leibniz," in *Kant Studies Today* [ed. Beck; Lasalle, 1968, pp. 72–87] at p. 75). See also W. E. Abraham, "Complete Concepts and Leibniz's Distinction Between Necessary and Contingent Truths," *Studia Leibnitiana* 1 (1969), 263–79.

12. But Leibniz nevertheless argued that contingent propositions can be known a priori. See discussions of this in Parkinson, *Logic and Reality*, p. 66, and Beck, *Early German Philosophy* (Cambridge, 1969), pp. 210–11.

13. *Philosophical Papers and Letters*, p. 286.

prima veritas cannot, in spite of §35 of the *Monadology*, be self-contradictory. In Russell's words: "Any relation between simple ideas is necessarily synthetic. For the analytic relation . . . can only hold between ideas of which one at least is complex."[14]

In a work unknown to his contemporaries but known to Kant, Leibniz seems to have seen this difficulty. He substituted "comparison or concurrence (*concours*)" for the stricter "identity and contradiction" between simple ideas.[15] He furthermore distinguished primitive truths known by intuition into two kinds: primitive truths of reason and primitive truths of fact.

Under primitive truths of reason he listed "identical affirmatives," which are trifling, and "identical negatives," which are either under the law of contradiction or are "disparates." "Disparates" are propositions that state that the object of one idea is not the object of another idea, as "that heat is not the same thing as color." Disparates "may be asserted independently of all proof or of reduction to opposition or to the principle of contradiction."[16]

2. A like problem is met with not merely at the end of a reduction to identity, but along the course of the reduction from an apparently synthetic judgment to an identity. Definition must be reached by analyzing complex concepts and then demonstrating the identity of the analysantia. In order to give real definitions (merely nominal definitions trivialize the project[17]), we must be able to show the compossibility and necessary coherence of predicates in a complex concept. If these predicates are simple (conceived per se) it cannot be demonstrated that they must co-inhere in one subject concept by appealing to the law of contradiction, because there is no formal contradiction in the conjunction of two simple predicates.

---

14. B. Russell, *Critical Examination of the Philosophy of Leibniz*, p. 20.

15. *New Essays Concerning Human Understanding*, IV, 1, §7.

16. Ibid., IV, 2, §1 (trans. Langley, pp. 404–05). See Margaret Wilson, "On Leibniz's Explication of 'Necessary Truth,'" *Studia Leibnitiana Supplementa* 3 (1969), 50–63.

17. For Leibniz's criticisms of the Hobbesian theory which permitted nominal definitions to suffice, see *Philosophical Papers and Letters*, pp. 199, 355, 371. Against Locke on trifling propositions, see *New Essays*, II, 6, §27; III, 6, §§24 and 32; IV, 5, §§3–8, and Douglas Odegard, "Locke, Leibniz, and Identical Propositions," *Studia Leibnitiana* 1 (1969), 241–53.

As Russell says, "This compatibility, since it is presupposed by the analytic judgment, cannot itself be analytic;[18] and Leibniz himself says:

As often as I combine several things which are not conceived through themselves, experience is needed, not only of the fact that they are conceived by me at the same time in the same subject ... but also of the fact that they really exist in the same subject.[19]

(Perhaps by "experience" Leibniz here means to include intuition and not merely empirical observation, which he excluded in his letter to Conring cited above.)

From all this it follows that while Leibniz had, in his *exoteric* works, a reasonably clear distinction between analytic and synthetic judgments, he was not able to maintain in his *esoteric* works that all a priori judgments are analytic. It may well be that Kant was thinking of Leibniz when he wrote:

As it was found that the conclusions of mathematicians all proceed according to the law of contradiction ... men persuaded themselves that the fundamental principles were known by the same law. This was a great mistake, for a synthetical proposition can indeed be established by the law of contradiction but only by presupposing another synthetical proposition from which it follows, but never by that law alone.[20]

Wolff had an easier task than Leibniz because he did not adhere to Leibniz's analytical theory of judgment according to which *praedicatum inest subiecto.*[21] For him, judgment is the *Verknüpfung* or

18. Russell, *Critical Examination*, p. 18.
19. *Logical Papers*, trans. Parkinson (Oxford, 1966), pp. 64–65.
20. *Prolegomena*, § 2.
21. See Gottfried Martin, *Kant: Ontologie und Wissenschaftstheorie* (4th ed., Berlin, 1969), p. 293; Winfried Lenders, *Die analytische Begriffs- und Urteilslehre von Leibniz u. Wolff* (Hildesheim: Olms, 1971), p. 158. On this point alone I disagree with Gram in his excellent introduction to the Lovejoy paper in *Kant: Disputed Questions*, p. 95.

Trennung (connection or separation) of two concepts.[22] With this definition he inquired into the ground of the connection or separation of the concepts and found it in the subject as the *Bedingung* of the predicate (*Aussage*) according to the principle of sufficient reason. But the latter principle was for him a logical principle, demonstrable by the law of contradiction; and hence Wolff did not adequately distinguish between the way in which a subject implies a predicate in what we call an analytical proposition and the way in which it is a mere condition in what we call a synthetic judgment.[23] Thus he did not emphasize the difference between identities and other necessary propositions connecting simple ideas, which ought to have kept him from holding that the denials of the latter are self-contradictory as are the denials of the former.[24] He recognizes that the connection of two simple ideas is not "thought through identity" because they do not determine one another, but *"fieri posse constat (sive vi experientiae, sive demonstrationis) combinari posse intelliguntur"*[25] and this *combinari posse* can be seen by *ratio intuitiva.* A concept is *gedenkbar* if one can see the agreement (*consensio, convenientia*) of the components. But he falls back into the old way of thinking when he holds that the *ungedenkbare* combinations are self-contradictory.[26] This is certainly how Kant read him: "The only conflict they [the Leibniz-Wolffians] recognize is that of contradiction."[27] Because he placed so much more emphasis on the self-contradictoriness of the contradictory than on the intuition of the *consensio,* he was vulnerable to attack from mean like Crusius, as we shall see.

We turn now to Wolff's theory of the constitution of complex

22. *Vernünftige Gedanken von den Kräften des menschlichen Verstandes*, chap. 3, §§1, 2. It is this view which Kant criticizes in *Critique of Pure Reason*, B §19.

23. *Logica*, §§262–64; *Psychologia Empirica*, §369.

24. See the quotation from Lovejoy in Gram, ed., *Kant: Disputed Questions*, 116 n. and the immediately following passages in *Vernünftige Gedanken*, chap. 3, §§10 and 13; also, ibid., chap. 4, §21.

25. *Ontologia*, §48.

26. *Vernünftige Gedanken*, chap. 3, §10.

27. *Critique of Pure Reason*, A 274 = B 330.

subjects (*notiones foecundae*[28]). With such a subject, the criterion of the self-contradictoriness of the contradictory of a judgment is more apt. For now he is considering truly analytical judgments; but the whole burden of proof is shifted from synthetic *judgments* to synthetic *subjects*. Lambert criticized him for this, saying that he took nominal definitions "as it were gratis" and "without noticing it, hid all the difficulties in them."[29] This, however, is unfair to Wolff, for he devoted much effort to establishing the real possibility (not merely the logical possibility) of complex concepts.[30] Regrettably, however, Wolff (perhaps not clearly seeing the importance of the distinction) does not give in any systematic order the criteria by which the real possibility of a concept is to be decided, that is, by which the possibility of the co-inherence of independent *essentialia*[31] is to be established. But he does, in various places in the *Ontologia*, provide several conditions. One—"*ab existentia ad possibilitatem valet consequentia*"[32] —is a posteriori, four (or five) others are apparently a priori. A concept consisting of the *notae* A and B is a priori possible if A and B presuppose one another or if one follows from the other by demonstration.[33] (For these, presumably, the law of contradiction suffices.) Another test is the constructability of the concept.[34] This is, at least verbally, an anticipation of the test for the possibility of mathematical concepts in Kant. But Wolff does not expand on this and probably did not see the significance of what he had said, since he regarded the syllogism, not construction, as the paradigm of mathematical proof.[35] Finally there is the "*combinari posse intelliguntur*" to which I have already alluded. The last, and perhaps the next to last, are the only ones

28. Lovejoy, "Kant's Antithesis," p. 115.
29. Lambert to Kant, February 3, 1766 (Ak. X, 64; Zweig, *Correspondence*, p. 51).
30. *Vernünftige Gedanken*, chap. 1, § 33.
31. *Logica*, § 64.
32. *Ontologia*, § 170.
33. Ibid., § § 89 and 91.
34. Ibid., § 92.
35. Lambert certainly did not see this criterion of possibility functioning in Wolff's own mathematics; see Beck, *Early German Philosophy*, p. 404.

which can build synthetic real concepts a priori. The ones about demonstrability are obviously inadequate for the addition of independent predicates, and the first one does so only a posteriori.

In summary, then, Wolff admits two kinds of propositions whose contradictories he holds to be self-contradictory:

1. Empty sentences, *propositio identica* ("A is A"), sometimes [36] called axioms.

2. Judgments *per essentialia, modus praedicandi essentialia* [37] ("A is B" where A is a complex concept in which B is an *essentia*), elsewhere called axioms [38] and identities. [39]

Lovejoy [40] calls (2) synthetical judgments a priori because they have a synthetical or "fecund" subject, but they are clearly analytical by Kant's criterion.

To these must be added a third type of judgment, some of which can be known a priori and others a posteriori:

3. Judgments *per attributum, modus praedicandi attributa* [41] ("A is C" where C is an attribute of A not included in its definition or essence but having its sufficient reason in the essence).

Since it is judgments of this kind that were claimed later, by Eberhard, to be synthetic and known a priori, we might wish that Wolff had given a systematic treatment of them in some one place. His examples, however, are instructive.

a. His first example is meant to be a judgment known a priori: "It is an attribute of a triangle (*Dreyeck*) that it has three angles (*Winkel*). For this is attributed to it (*kommet ihm zu*) because a triangle is a space enclosed in three lines." [42] Presumably this is a logical "because," since the proposition is supposed to be reducible

---

36. *Vernünftige Gedanken*, chap. 3, § 13; *Logica*, § 270.

37. *Logica*, § 223.

38. Ibid., § 273.

39. Ibid., § 223.

40. Lovejoy, "Kant's Antithesis," p. 117.

41. *Logica*, § § 220–21.

42. *Vernünftige Gedanken*, chap. 5, § 6. Oddly enough, Kant regards the proposition "A triangle possesses three sides and three angles" as analytic (A 716 = B 744). See Gottfried Martin, *Kant: Ontologie*, pp. 276–77.

to axioms and definitions which are identities;[43] but elsewhere he says it is evident "by construction."[44]

b. "Hardness is an attribute of stone but not of wax" is obviously a posteriori, and Wolff tells us how to find out by experience which predicates are attributes and which are mere accidents of things.[45]

c. Finally, there are judgments which can be known a priori in the sense that, as Kant says, they cannot "be derived immediately from experience but from a universal rule"; but they are not a priori ("completely a priori," as Kant says) in the sense that they can be known completely independently of all experience, since the "universal rule" is itself based upon experience.[46] Wolff hold that one can "prove" a judgment *per attributum* by syllogism. His example is "Wood can be cut."[47] The proof is given by providing a definition of cutting ("the separation of parts") and of wood ("Made up of fibers"). Such a proof converts "historical" (that is, empirical) knowledge into "philosophical" knowledge or "knowledge of the reason of things."[48]

Crusius, the principal pre-Kantian critic of Wolff, is now largely forgotten, but Kant himself did not forget him. Long before Hume awoke Kant from his dogmatic slumber, Crusius[49] had already pointed out what Kant was later to relearn from Hume at a critical point in his own development when the impact of Hume's discovery

43. *Vernünftige Gedanken*, chap 4, §21, end.
44. *Ontologia*, §143; cf. §546, note.
45. *Vernünftige Gedanken*, chap. 5, §§6, 7.
46. *Critique of Pure Reason*, B 2.
47. *Vernünftige Gedanken*, chap. 5, §8. Other examples are: "Bodies have weight," and "Air is elastic"—examples Kant himself uses.
48. *Preliminary Discourse on Philosophy in General* (trans. R. J. Blackwell, [Indianapolis, 1963]), §6.
49. Crusius developed an idea which was present in the works of Clauberg, von Tschirnhaus, and Friedrich Adolf Hoffmann (see Beck, *Early German Philosophy*, pp. 185, 191–92, 302–03); later the same way of distinguishing two types of relations was followed by Johann Heinrich Lambert and Johann Heinrich Tetens (ibid., pp. 406–07, 421, 425), but Kant had by then already learned the lesson from Crusius.

about causality "gave quite a new direction to [Kant's] investigations."[50]

J. S. Beck[51] in 1793 wrote Kant that Crusius's *Weg zur Gewissheit* (1747) provided a better "indiction" of the analytic-synthetic distinction than the passages Kant had cited from Locke, but Kant knew Crusius's work already in the 1760s. In his *Dissertatio de uso et limitibus principii rationis determinantis, vulgo sufficientis* (1743) Crusius had criticized Wolff's attempted derivation[52] of the principle of sufficient reason from the principle of contradiction. In his *Entwurf der nothwendigen Vernunftwahrheiten* (1745) and *Weg zur Gewissheit* he had criticized Wolff for believing in the sufficiency of the principle of contradiction for the establishment and testing of a priori truth. "The question," he says, "is not whether, upon presupposing [certain] concepts we are required by the law of contradiction to deny the opposite; this is well known. The question is: whether the law of contradiction was, or even could have been, the sufficient reason for the constitution (*Einrichtung*) of the concepts themselves."[53] He answers this question in the negative.

He takes the case of causality.[54] "Every effect has a cause" is clear from the principle of contradiction, but that does not show that the existence of one thing is dependent on that of another. The latter can be denied without contradiction, because the subjects to which existence is attributed are different and exist at different times. Experience, even Wolff saw, must be called upon to discover what *specific* thing is the cause of another; but, unlike Wolff, Crusius believed that the general principle cannot be established merely by a proof from the law of contradiction. That is to say, in Kantian language, Crusius sought a proof of the principle of causality as, or as derived from, a synthetic a priori principle. Real knowledge must be founded on a different principle from the law of contradiction, which suffices for what Crusius calls "hypothetical knowledge."

50. *Prolegomena*, trans. Beck, p. 8.
51. Letter of August 24, 1793 (Ak. XI, 444–45).
52. *Ontologia*, §70.
53. *Weg zur Gewissheit*, §260.
54. *Entwurf der nothwendigen Vernunftwahrheiten*, §31.

We have seen earlier philosophers supplement demonstration with intuition so as to have two bases for certain knowledge. Hume denied that the causal principle is known in either way, and therefore asserted that it is not known a priori. Crusius, on the contrary, supplements demonstrative knowledge with two *Vernunftwahrheiten* (truths of reason) which he calls the "principles of inseparability and uncombinability": "Whatever two things cannot be thought apart from one another cannot exist or be possible apart from one another," and "Whatever two things cannot be thought with and beside one another cannot be possible or exist with and beside one another." [55] These give the ground why contradictories cannot coexist or be compossible, but they go far beyond the realm of the merely logically impossible. The real ground of a predicate or a relation must be distinguished from the logical ground, and the connection of real ground with the predicate can by known a priori; but the real ground itself can be known only through experience.

Not only did Crusius have a clear conception of the difference between analytic and synthetic judgments; he also had a theory as to how synthetic judgments are possible a priori. It was not a theory that Kant could accept, as he accepted the consequences of Crusius's distinction between judgments from logical grounds and judgments from real grounds. After a long period in which he honored Crusius for drawing the right distinction he turned against him for failing to show how synthetic judgments can be known a priori: Crusius, he said, made mere custom and incapacity to think otherwise into an objective necessity, and could get to objective necessity only by accepting a preestablished harmony between innate ideas and their objects. [56] But what Kant did learn from Crusius must not be underestimated; he learned that "the rain never follows the wind because of the law of identity." [57]

55. Ibid., §15.
56. Letter to Reinhold, May 19, 1789 (Ak. XI, 41; Zweig, *Correspondence*, p. 144); Reflexionen 4275 and 4446 (Ak. XVII, 492-554); see also *Vorlesungen über Logik* (Ak. IX, 21).
57. *Versuch den Begriff der negativen Grössen in die Weltweisheit einzuführen*, 1763 (Ak. II, 203).

I shall not attempt to recount the steps by which Kant was led to make his classical distinction between synthetic and analytic judgments. I refrain from this for two reasons: first, we do not actually know what they were or when they were taken; and second, what is known about them has already been adequately presented.[58] Rather than going through this history of the development of the distinction, I wish rather to turn to a defense of the originality of his distinction which Kant made late in his life: *On a Discovery according to which the Whole New Critique of Pure Reason is Rendered Unnecessary by an Earlier One*, published in 1790 against Eberhard.[59] This is an important paper both historically and philosophically—historically because it is Kant's *Auseinandersetzung* with the Wolffian tradition; philosophically, because it shows us how Kant would answer his modern critics who deny that there are synthetic judgments known a priori—for most modern critics have, perhaps unbeknownst to themselves, merely repeated Eberhard's criticisms.[60]

On p. 91 above, I gave Wolff's division of judgments which are not formal identities into judgments *per essentialia* and judgments *per attributum*. Eberhard holds that they are both a priori, and that whatever is valid in Kant's distinction between analytic and synthetic judgments a priori coincides with Wolff's distinction. Eberhard calls judgments *per attributum* synthetic because they affirm attributes which are not included in the essence of the subject

---

58. Dieter Henrich, "Kants Denken 1762–63: Über den Ursprung der Unterscheidung analytischer und synthetischer Urteile," in *Studien zu Kants philosophischer Entwicklung*, ed. Heimsoeth, Henrich, and Tonelli (Hildesheim, 1967), pp. 9–38; Gottfried Martin, *Kant: Ontologie*, Part III; Beck, *Early German Philosophy*, pp. 441–46, 451–55.

59. Since this paper was written, Professor Henry E. Allison has published his translation of *Über eine Entdeckung* with supplementary material and a historical and critical commentary: *The Kant-Eberhard Controversy* (Johns Hopkins University Press, 1973).

60. See Beck, *Studies in the Philosophy of Kant*, pp. 81–84, 118–20, for comparison of Eberhard's strictures on Kant with those of C. I. Lewis. In that essay I deal largely with another problem raised by Maass, Eberhard, and Lewis, that of the variability and arbitrariness of the distinction between analytic and synthetic, which here I must pass over in silence.

concept, and a priori because they have their sufficient ground in the subject concept from which they may be explicated by analysis. Hence Eberhard holds that the problem to which the *Critique of Pure Reason* is addressed—namely, "How are synthetic judgments a priori possible?"—had already been answered by Wolff, and that all Kant contributed was a new (and confusing) terminology. Against the accusation that the distinction was already known and was not invented by Kant, Kant replied:

> Maybe so! But the reason why the importance of the distinction has not been recognized seems to be that all a priori judgments were regarded [by Wolff] as analytic . . . so the whole point of the distinction disappeared.[61]

In modern terminology (which we owe to C. I. Lewis)[62] "synthetic judgments a priori" are sometimes said to be implicitly analytic judgments—ampliative ("synthetic") by the criterion of "what is actually thought in the subject concept, though not so distinctly and with the same (full) consciousness,"[63] but explicative ("analytic") by the criterion of logical deducibility and testability by the law of contradiction.

Kant and Eberhard agree—Kant accusingly, Eberhard proudly[64] — that the distinction between essence and attribute which underlies Eberhard's analytic-synthetic distinction is one drawn in general logic. But, Kant says, "The explanation of the possibility of synthetic judgments is a problem with which general logic has nothing

61. Letter to Reinhold, May 12, 1789 (Ak. XI, 38; Zweig, *Correspondence*, p. 141); Allison, *The Kant-Eberhard Controversy*, p. 164.
62. *Analysis of Knowledge and Valuation*, p. 89. S. G. E. Maass, "Ueber den höchsten Grundsatz der synthetischen Urtheile," writing in Eberhard's *Philosophisches Magazin* (2 [1790], 186–231 at 197) and Eberhard's ally in the battle, distinguishes between immediate and mediate analytic judgments, corresponding exactly to Lewis's distinction. On Maass, see Allison, *The Kant-Eberhard Controversy*, pp. 42–45.
63. *Prolegomena*, § 2, a.
64. *Über eine Entdeckung*, Ak. VIII, 230, 242 (Allison, *The Kant-Eberhard Controversy*, pp. 142, 152); Eberhard, "Ueber die Unterscheidung der Urtheile in Analytische und Synthetische," *Philosophisches Magazin* I (1780), 307–22, at 321.

to do. It need not even so much as know the problem by name."[65]
In short, the problem as Kant sees it is one of epistemology, or what
he calls transcendental logic; hence he feels justified in classifying
judgments according to their *grounds (Wahrheitsgründe)*[66] and not
merely as they are classified in formal logic (*per essentialia, per
attributum*).

The essence with which Eberhard is concerned consists of those
marks (*notae*) that are the necessary and sufficient conditions for
the definition of the concept. The attributes for Eberhard are those
marks that logically follow from the concept of the subject ("belong
to it") but are not explicitly included in the logical essence or its
definiens ("do not lie in it").[67] We can be sure that a predicate
signifies an attribute if it is a logical consequence of the essence or
definition, so that its denial would be self-contradictory. Thus
"having more than two sides" is an attribute of a triangle, since
"having three sides," the essence of triangle, logically entails "having
more than two sides." An attribute which follows analytically from
the definition or logical essence by the law of contradiction, as this
one does, is called by Kant an "analytical predicate." Even though
the judgment containing such a predicate may be ampliative or
instructive for someone who does not know the implications of the

65. *Critique of Pure Reason*, A 154 = B 193.
66. Eberhard, "Über die analytischen und synthetischen Urtheile zur Beantwortung des zweyten Abschnittes von H. Prof. Kants Streitschrift," *Philosophisches Magazin* 3 (1791), 280–303 at 282, complains of this, saying that
the presence or absence of intuition has nothing to do with the division of
judgments. In "Weitere Ausführung der Untersuchung über die Unterscheidung der Urtheile in Analytische und Synthetische," ibid., 2 (1790), 285–315
at 299, Eberhard says that since he is convinced "dass die allgemeinen Prin-
cipien der menschlichen Erkenntnis transcendentale Gültigkeit haben: so halte
ich mich berechtigt, so lange mein Beweis von dieser transcendentalen
Gültigkeit [sc., of the principle of sufficient reason derived from the law of
contradiction] noch nicht widerlegt ist, einen jeden logischen Grund auch für
einen Realgrund zu halten." It is the thesis of Lenders's monograph (*Die
analytische Begriffs- und Urteilslehre*) that also in Wolff the ground of distinction among the kinds of judgment is ontological, not epistemological or logical.
67. *Critique of Pure Reason*, B 40, A 71 = B 96; *Vorlesungen über Logik*,
§8; cf. Vaihinger, *Commentar zu Kants Kritik der reinen Vernunft* I (1881),
258.

definition, Kant is now content to call a judgment analytical if it contains an analytical predicate.[68]

But Kant holds that there is another kind of essence which he calls "real" instead of "logical," and another kind of attribute,[69] which he calls "synthetic" instead of "analytic."

A synthetic attribute, a *Bestimmung*,[70] is one which does not follow from the logical essence and yet has a sufficient ground in the real essence.[71] Hence it can be necessarily predicated of the subject in a synthetic judgment. Such a judgment is a priori synthetic. (To cite Kant's own example, that space has three dimensions is not known by analysis of the definition of space [its logical essence] and yet can be known a priori to be true of space.)

The problem of the *Critique of Pure Reason* is to see how an attribute can be attached synthetically, yet a priori, to an object whose concept does not logically entail it by containing it implicitly.

A concept is logically possible if it does not entail contradictory predicates. But a logically possible concept may be without an object and thus only an *ens rationis*.[72] To be shown to be really and not merely logically possible, the concept must be of an object

68. Kant has often been criticized for holding two criteria of analyticity, the phenomenological or introspective ("actually thought" in the concept of the subject) and the logical (testable by the law that the contradiction of an analytical judgment is self-contradictory). Here we have a clear indication that when these criteria give conflicting answers, Kant accepts the latter as prevailing. On the other hand, it is equally clear from their dispute that, when they conflict, Eberhard must use the former in justifying his considering a judgment *per attributum* to be synthetic.

69. *Über eine Entdeckung*, Ak. VIII, 230 (Allison, *The Kant-Eberhard Controversy*, p. 143). The distinction is (naturally) denied by Eberhard in his reply, "Über die analytischen und synthetischen Urtheile, zur Beantwortung des zweyten Abschnittes von H. Prof. Kants Streitschrift," *Philosophisches Magazin* 3 (1791), 280–303, in particular p. 302.

70. *Critique of Pure Reason*, A 598 = B 626. "Praedicatum logicum kan [*sic*!] analytisch sein; determinatio est praedicatum syntheticum." Reflexion 5701 (Ak. XVIII, 330).

71. *Über eine Entdeckung*, Ak. VIII, 242 (Allison, *The Kant-Eberhard Controversy*, p. 152); letter to Reinhold, May 12, 1789 (Zweig, *Correspondence*, p. 140; Allison, *The Kant-Eberhard Controversy*, pp. 163–64).

72. *Critique of Pure Reason*, A 292 = B 348.

which "agrees with the formal conditions of experience"[73] (First Postulate of Empirical Thought), and this includes the condition of sensible intuitability.

If the sensible intuition is empirical, that is, a real perception, the concept of the perceived object is really possible because whatever is actual is possible. A judgment founded on a perception is synthetic, but a posteriori.

Sensible intuition, whether pure or empirical, cannot reveal the ontologically real essence of a thing, which is even more hidden from Kant than it was from Locke. But if the sensible intuition is pure, it reveals the real essence[74] of the thing since it is an intuition of the condition under which alone a thing can be an object for us. Though Kant calls it the real essence, to avoid confusion between what, for Kant, is known a priori and what, for him and Locke, is not known at all, let us call it the *phenomenal essence*. It consists of all the conditions of an object that are necessary if it is possible for us to experience it.

What follows from the phenomenal essence is a synthetic attribute because it is not contained in, or found by the analysis of, the logical essence. The synthetic attribute follows from the sole condition under which the object can be known, not from its metaphysical (supersensible) real essence. By virtue of the necessity with which the synthetic attribute follows from the phenomenal essence, the judgment containing this attribute is known a priori. Because it does not follow by the law of contradiction from the logical essence, it is

73. Ibid., A 218 = B 265.
74. Kant may perhaps have confused Eberhard by calling real essence "die innere Möglichkeit des Begriffes" or "interna possibilitas" and distinguishing it from the "logisches Wesen" (*Über eine Entdeckung*, Ak. VIII, 229). By "innere Möglichkeit des Begriffes" he actually means "innere Möglichkeit *des Objektes* des Begriffes*." This is made clear in the manuscripts Kant prepared to help Schulz in Schulz's reply to Eberhard (Ak. XX, 376, first full paragraph); similar usage in *Vorlesungen über Logik* (Ak. IX, 61); *Vorlesungen über Metaphysik* (ed. Pölitz, 1821), p. 38; *Critique of Pure Reason*, A 676 = B 703; A 816 = B 844. *Einzig möglicher Beweisgrund* (Ak. II, 77–78, 162) distinguishes "innere Möglichkeit" from "das Logische in der Möglichkeit" and identifies the former with the "Wesen der Dinge." I have examined all these passages in "Lovejoy as a Critic of Kant," above, pp. 76–77.

synthetic. Hence a judgment whose predicate signifies an attribute of the phenomenal essence is a synthetic a priori judgment.

Kant's answer to Eberhard is that judgments may therefore have attributes as predicates without this fact determining whether the judgment is analytic or synthetic, a priori or a posteriori. But:

a. If the predicate signifies an attribute or property of the logical essence, the judgment is analytic and is known a priori.

b. If the predicate signifies a property or accident learned by experience of an object, the judgment is synthetic, but is known a posteriori.[75]

c. If the predicate signifies an attribute or property of the phenomenal essence as the condition of intuitability, the judgment is synthetic (because the predicate does not follow from the logical essence) and known a priori (because it can be known to apply without appeal to actual experience).

75. *Critique of Pure Reason*, A 728 = B 756.

6 *Lambert and Hume in Kant's Development from 1769 to 1772*

Had Kant succeeded in 1768 in achieving his professorship, he would have had to prepare an inaugural dissertation in that year. Presumably it would have been a compounding of teachings that he had published in the foregoing decade, and it would have been notably different from the Inaugural Dissertation which he actually wrote in 1770, for in 1769 Kant revised his teachings in several essential points.

It appears to me that Kant, upon attaining a professorship in 1768, would have been prepared to defend the following theses:

a. Speculative metaphysics, in the sense of a knowledge of things and of powers of substances outside of experience, is impossible.

b. The genuine task of metaphysics is the determination of the limits and foundations of knowledge. Metaphysics is not competent to ground knowledge of a realm lying beyond that of experience.

c. The genuine method of metaphysics is analogous to that of natural science. The model for the method of the latter is Newton's method, which the philosopher should imitate.

A lecture given August 28, 1968, to the Philosophical Seminar of the University of Bonn and published in *Kant-Studien* 60 (1969), 123–30; here published in English for the first time. It was a part of an early draft of material for *Early German Philosophy* (Harvard University Press, 1969) and corresponds roughly to approximately pp. 455–67 of that book. It is published here with the kind permission of the editors of *Kant-Studien* and the Harvard University Press.

d. Through the analysis of our experience we find some unanalyzable concepts and unprovable principles, which will be able, eventually, to serve as the foundation of a philosophical system; but the time is not yet ripe for that.

e. Metaphysics, properly understood, is indispensable for the true and lasting well-being of mankind.[1] But speculative knowledge of God and of the immortality of the soul is not necessary for the practice of virtue.

f. Space is Euclidean and Newtonian. It is absolute and ontologically basic, not relational and ontologically derivative, as it was for Leibniz. It is not an *ens rationis;* it is ontologically real.

g. We do not know space empirically, through sensation, but through a "fundamental concept" or "an intuition of inner senses by an idea of reason."[2]

h. Mathematics commences with these fundamental concepts and intuitions and proceeds by a synthetic method. The method of mathematics is therefore totally different from that of philosophy.

i. Things observed in space are determined by causal laws. But we can know their inner forces only insofar as they are manifested in the relations between their appearances. (With Newton, Kant could have said, *"Hypotheses non fingo."*)

These were theses Kant would have been prepared to defend if called upon to do so in 1768—but he was not promoted. Therefore he did not have to maintain this edifice of thought in public. Since we have the inestimable advantage over Kant himself of already knowing his later works, we can see what he probably did not see in 1768—namely, how much looseness and how many veiled inconsistencies there were in this collection of teachings. At any rate, when Kant finally two years later did receive his professorship and actually wrote an Inaugural Dissertation, he had completely changed some of

1. Letter to Mendelssohn, April 8, 1766 (Ak. X, 70; Zweig, *Correspondence*, p. 55).
2. *On the First Grounds of the Distinctions of Regions in Space*, Ak. II, 383 (John Handyside, *Kant's Inaugural Dissertation and Early Writings on Space* [Chicago, 1929], p. 28).

his opinions. Once again he believed in the possibility of a theoretical, speculative metaphysics, and he gave a completely new account of the ontological status of space. What is responsible for this is the fact that, as he said, "the year '69 brought a great light,"[3] and some of the theses of 1768 were given up. One can, as it were, subtract the explicit theses of 1770 from the conjectural theses of 1768 to discover what change the year 1769 brought.

The essential change consists in his new insight that there is no continuity between natural science (including mathematics) and metaphysics, and yet that both are possible as valid bodies of knowledge. Reasons for this change of view have been said to lie in Kant's occupation with the just published *Nouveaux essais* of Leibniz, in his study of Plato, in his discovery of the antinomy of space, in the influence of Hume, and so on. Only the first two of these seem to me to be at all credible. In the Inaugural Dissertation there is much terminology that springs from Plato and from Leibniz; and certainly the denial of a continuity between experience and metaphysical knowledge and the emphasis upon the possibility of both is genuinely Platonic and genuinely Leibnizian. The dictum: *Nihil est in intellectu quod non fuerit prius in sensu excipe intellectus ipse* Kant could have first learned from Leibniz's *New Essays*, and this Leibnizian thesis was markedly different from that Leibnizianism which he had long known. This, and the Platonic discontinuity between experience and the intelligible, constitute, in my estimation, the principal difference between the conjectural dissertation of 1768 and the actual Dissertation of 1770.

I should like to make this more precise: the essential discovery was that of the difference between the senses and the faculty of thought as a difference between two independent sources of knowledge. The sensible was no longer regarded as merely obscure and diffuse thought, but as not thought at all; it was something fundamentally different from thought. On this radical differentiation depended everything else—the difference between phenomenon and noumenon, between intuition and thought, and the new Kantian inter-

3. Reflexion 5037 (Ak. XVIII, 69).

pretation of the difference between content and form. Form and content now stand on *both* sides of the dividing line between sensing and thinking. Consequently there arose the possibility of taking up and developing Baumgarten's idea of a science of sensible knowledge, namely of aesthetic (in the sense of the first *Critique*). The sensible world no longer offered only the mere content for the logical forms, but had also its own necessary forms in itself—not logically necessary, but intuitively necessary forms. This gave Kant the key to the problem of mathematical knowledge and the intuition of space.

From this discovery in the great light of the year '69 there arose three tasks of the Dissertation: (1) The determination of the forms and principles of the sensible world, the world known through intuition; (2) the determination of the forms and principles of the intelligible world, the world known through pure reason; (3) the description of the manner in which the forms and principles of the one interpenetrated the world of the other—legitimately and necessarily in mathematics and natural science, illegitimately and avoidably in metaphysics. These three tasks determine the structure of the Dissertation: (1) In Section III of the little book there is developed the well-known Kantian theory of space and of mathematical knowledge, which become a constitutive part of the mature Kantian system. (2) Section IV contains a typical metaphysics of the eighteenth century, in which the existence of God, etc., is proved. In my opinion, this section is interesting only because it is the last expression of Kant's propensity to theoretical metaphysical knowledge. Whereas Kant could take over Section III with little change into the *Critique of Pure Reason*, almost nothing from Section IV was saved—it was, rather, the object of the *Critique* to show how impossible such a metaphysics was. (3) Section V will have to be discussed in more detail, for it is in it that the seed of mature Kantianism is buried.

Metaphysics contains the fundamental principles of the *usus reale* of reason, but prior to it there is a propaedeutic science, critique, the goal of which is to preserve the purity of metaphysics. Critique differentiates between sensible and intellectual knowledge and protects metaphysics from an intermixing (*contagium*) of the two. Critique forbids the application of sensible concepts to objects of reason (noumena). We must take care not to sensibilize reason (Locke's error) and not to intellectualize the senses (Leibniz's error). No judgment can be genuinely metaphysical which presupposes or requires a knowledge of space or time; consequently the problems which will later appear under the name of the antinomies (infinity of the world; infinite divisibility of substances; etc.) are not genuinely metaphysical problems. The fallaciousness of all putative solutions to these problems is unavoidable until critique eradicates the naive and dogmatic presumption that the limits of the mind are also limits which lie in the essence of things. This dogmatic error is especially consequential, since the human mind cannot intuit noumena but only phenomena, because it intuits only sensibly.

One immediately sees a difficulty which Kant noticed only later in his letter to Herz, in February 1772. It is the problem of how it is possible that concepts, which are not derived from objects, can refer to objects at all. Since all knowledge refers to objects only through intuition, man would have to have an intellectual intuition in order to be able to have any knowledge of intelligible objects. But the full weight of this was not yet recognized by Kant. With his maxim that "the principles proper to sensible knowledge must not be allowed to pass their boundaries and meddle with the intellectual,"[4] he made, without noticing it, his metaphysics as a knowledge of the intelligible world impossible.

But not every "meddling" of the two kinds of principles is forbidden. In mathematics there is a fruitful working together of the two kinds of principles. Moreover, there are subreptitious axioms (*axiomata subrepticia*) which Kant held to be useful, indeed indispensable, in the investigation of nature. Among these are the causal law, the conservation principles, and the maxims which he later considered rules of reflective judgment. These axioms are without exception intellectual and not sensible, even though it appears

4. *The Forms and Principles of the Sensible and the Intelligible Worlds* ("Inaugural Dissertation"), § 24 (Handyside, p. 73).

that they are derived from their objects; we assume them as if they were actually axiomatic, though they are only unprovable (yet indispensable) rules.

A particularly interesting type of subreptitious axioms, the "third sort," arises not in the way of the derivation of intellectual principles from experience, but rather from the circumstance that an application of intellectual knowledge is possible only with the help of sensible "data"; only through their help can it be known whether something is contained under a specific intellectual concept.[5] It is as if we could discover only through experience what lies in an intellectual concept. Thus one comes, for example, to the illicit fundamental principle, "Everything which contingently exists has at some time not existed," from which an empirical criterion of contingency is derived. Thus far one proceeds quite properly,[6] but it is improper to change the subjective principle or criterion of contingency into an objective condition, as if without this empirical addendum there were no contingency. For in ontology one must be able to prove objectively valid judgments without having to take a detour through the world of experience.

In September 1770 Kant sent a copy of his Dissertation to Johann Heinrich Lambert, with whom for some years he had been in correspondence. Lambert praised the work but raised three objections to it. Two of them we can pass over; Kant dealt with them only in the *Critique of Pure Reason*. But one of them must have appeared to him then to be very weighty. Lambert wrote: "It is useful in ontology to make use of concepts borrowed from appearances, because its theory must still be applied to the phenomena."[7] Lambert's criticism did not concern the radical distinction between intellectual and intuitive knowledge—he himself accepted this distinction—but it touched Kant's views concerning the "third sort" of subreptitious axioms. His criticism said briefly: it is by no means illegitimate, rather it is necessary, to use empirical knowledge when

5. Ibid., § 29 (Handyside, p. 81).
6. See *Critique of Pure Reason*, B 290.
7. Lambert to Kant, October 13, 1770 (Ak. X, 103; Zweig, *Correspondence*, pp. 64–65).

one relates pure concepts to objects; empirical concepts must be taken up into ontology, for the ontological theory must finally be applied to phenomena.

This objection by Lambert is important, because it points out the problem of the application of pure concepts to objects; perhaps it even indicates the impossibility of a non-phenomenal objectivity of ontological concepts. But apparently Kant did not at first correctly estimate the importance of this objection. Did he later remember Lambert when he finally came to see the value of this question? When he did, he was no longer in correspondence with Lambert—a thing he long regretted; up until Lambert's death it was his intention to dedicate the *Critique of Pure Reason* to him. Kant wrote nothing about a "suggestion of Lambert" but in my opinion Lambert's detecting this difficulty in the Dissertation is just as important as the "suggestion of Hume" was.

Kant dealt with this difficulty first in the letter to Marcus Herz of February 21, 1772, though without mentioning Lambert's name. After reporting to Herz about his book, "The Limits of Sensibility and Reason," which was to appear shortly, he said, "I was lacking something essential which, in my long metaphysical investigations, I had, like others, not noticed, yet which in fact constituted the key to the whole secret of still obscure metaphysics." He lacked an answer to the general question: "On what grounds rests the relation of what we call a representation in us to the object?"[8] I say the *general* problem, because it is, in Kant's opinion, easy to understand how particular empirical concepts are applied to appearance.

Certainly Lambert's proposal to "borrow" concepts from appearance (phenomena) was alien to Kant's whole attitude in metaphysics; but it was not for that reason entirely ineffective, because Kant had to confess that he had been content, in the Dissertation, to define intellectual concepts only negatively, and without asking how it is possible for "a representation to relate to an object without having been in any manner effected by the object." So he now asks

8. Letter to Herz, February 21, 1772 (Ak. X, 124; Zweig, *Correspondence*, p. 71).

how intellectual representations can agree with things as they are in themselves since "this agreement has not been supported by experience."[9] Kant then sketches the answers to this question given by Plato, Malebranche, and Crusius and he appears ready to give his own answer. But instead of that, he abruptly turns to a new topic and asks the question which will be answered in the metaphysical deduction of the categories in the *Critique.* It must have seemed to him that the metaphysical deduction was sufficient answer to Lambert's question, because he concludes his letter by promising Herz that the book would be finished in three months.

Just as we have sketched an unwritten Dissertation of the year 1768, we can likewise outline a fictive *Critique of Pure Reason* of May 1772. The book would have been in general an expansion of the Inaugural Dissertation of 1770, with the addition of a premature formulation of the metaphysical deduction and with an ontology in which the categories would have played a central role. But "something essential" would still have been lacking. Hindsight tells us that the metaphysical deduction contributes nothing to the solution of Lambert's problem of the relation between pure concept and object, and that Kant's own solution to this problem as given in 1781 destroyed the remaining ontology. Fortunately Kant did not finish the book in three months; instead of three months, it took him nine years to work out the *Critique of Pure Reason* with its answer to Lambert's question. Presumably within the three months which he had seen as sufficient for the completion of his book the "suggestion of Hume" surprised him.

The Hume problem appears at first to have little to do with the Lambert problem. Lambert asked, or gave Kant occasion to ask, how a concept which does not arise from experience can agree with experience or the objects of experience. Hume asked how one concept can stand in necessary relation to another when there is no logically necessary connection between them. That is the meaning of Hume's distinction between "relations of ideas" and "matters of fact." In the former there is a logical relation between two concepts,

9. Ibid.

such that a judgment expressing this relation cannot be false. Hume showed conclusively that between the concept of one event as cause and another as effect there is no such relation. The relation must be found, or sought for, in experience. Correspondingly, but on other grounds, Lambert had taken his stand that ontological concepts must be borrowed from and applied to experience.

Hume's thesis was generalized by Kant. "I sought first whether Hume's objection could not be put into a general form, and soon found that the concept of the connection of cause and effect was by no means the only concept by which the understanding thinks the connection of things a priori, but rather that metaphysics consists altogether of such concepts." [10] In this way Kant reached finally the concept of the synthetic judgment a priori, a concept which had, as it were, been in the air since Locke and Leibniz but had never been precisely formulated.

That it is unavoidable to call upon experience forced Hume to the conclusion that synthetic judgments can be known only a posteriori. This was not Kant's view at all. The appeal to experience requires no surrender of apriority, and Kant had fortunately already shown in the Inaugural Dissertation that the ground of apriority lies in the forms of intuition which are necessary forms of all sensible experience. But consider the other side of the coin: the ground which permits and requires that two concepts be brought into necessary relation to each other is *at the same time* the ground for the impossibility of knowledge of the intelligible world; for the latter would be synthetic knowledge without sensible intuition. The second problem of the Inaugural Dissertation is thus shown to be insoluble, and "the proud name of ontology" must "make way for the modest name of a mere analytic of pure understanding." [11]

What did Lambert have to do with that? Alone, very little; with Hume, very much. It was the genius of Kant again and again to find *one* answer to two different and often opposed questions, [12] and

10. *Prolegomena*, Introduction; Ak. IV, 260 (Beck, p. 8).
11. *Critique of Pure Reason*, A 247 = B 303.
12. See "Kant's Strategy" for evidence that this is a characteristic mode of argument with Kant.

here Kant gave the same answer to Hume's and to Lambert's problem. The regular but not formal logical relation of two concepts *to each other* (Hume's problem) is also the necessary relation of one or more concepts *to objects* of possible experience. Kant determined that the condition of both these relations, the Humean and the Lambertian, is the application of concepts to intuitions, and that when the judgment is a priori the application must be to *necessary* intuitions. Since Kant had recognized the radical independence of sensible intuition from thinking already in 1769, he could now make use of a second, irreducible kind of necessity to supplement the insufficiency of the necessity of formal logic. The axioms arising from the *penuria intellectus* need no longer be regarded as subreptitious; rather, out of this *penuria* there arose one of the principal theses of the critical philosophy: concepts without intuition are empty and have only analytical relationships with one another.

I am inclined to believe that Lambert was not only the first to state one of the central problems of the Kantian philosophy, but that he also gave a clue to its solution. Immediately after writing the passage in which he formulated the problem, he continued: "For in this manner the astronomer begins with the phenomena, derives the theory of the structure of the universe from them, applies the theory in his ephimerides again to the phenomena and to the prediction of phenomena. In metaphysics, where the problem of appearance is of such importance, the method of the astronomer may well be the safest." [13]

Did Kant perhaps recollect this sentence, when he spoke of trying the Copernican hypothesis in his philosophy?

13. Lambert to Kant, October 13, 1770 (Ak. X, 103; Zweig, *Correspondence*, p. 65).

7   *A Prussian Hume and a Scottish Kant*

In a letter to Herder written in 1781, Hamann said of Kant: "He certainly deserves the title, 'a Prussian Hume.'"[1] No one, so far as I know, has had the temerity to state explicitly that Hume deserves the title, "a Scottish Kant." But almost. One trend in contemporary Hume interpretation may finally lead someone to make this claim, or accusation. H. H. Price refers to "a Scottish version of Kant's Copernican Revolution."[2] Robert Paul Wolff finds that Hume's propensities "play a role quite similar to that of the categories in the *Critique of Pure Reason.*"[3] W. H. Walsh says of the Humean imagination that it is "simply the Kantian understanding in disguise."[4]

The traditional notion that Kant and Hume are diametrically opposed, and that whatever merit Kant's philosophy has depends upon his having given a cogent "answer to Hume," does not seem as obvious as it used to. While no one would deny that the great divide

This paper was presented to the Hume Bicentennial Congress at McGill University, September 29, 1976. It is to be published in the Proceedings of that Congress, and I am grateful to the director of the Congress and the editor of the Proceedings, Professor David Fate Norton, for permission to pre-print it here. A part of this paper was presented at the International Hume Congress held at the University of Edinburgh, August 16, 1976.

1. *Hamann Briefwechsel*, ed. Henkel, IV, 293.
2. *Hume's Theory of the External World*, p. 9. See also F. W. Dauer, "Towards a Copernican Reading of Hume," *Nous* 9 (1975), 269–95.
3. "Hume's Theory of Mental Activity," in *Hume*, ed. V. C. Chappell, p. 127.
4. "Hume's Concept of Truth," in *Reason and Reality* (Royal Institute of Philosophy Lectures 1970–71), pp. 99–116, at end.

Studies in the **Critique of Pure Reason**

between naturalism and transcendentalism[5] in the theory of knowledge separates these two thinkers, even that divide is not as clear-cut as it once appeared, and is now rendered somewhat obscure by emphasis upon a pragmatism[6] believed to be pervasive in their constructions of a common world out of private experiences. With growing attention to the role of normative structures in Hume's analysis of experience, and to the possibility of relativizing the hard, fixed categorial lines found in Kant's analysis, it becomes possible to see Kant and Hume as engaged in a common project.[7] I do not wish to go too far and talk as if the differences were less important than the similarities between these two men. But I do wish to make it appear meet, fitting, and seemly to talk about Kant in a gathering called to celebrate the life and work of Hume—something that would, I think, have appeared thirty or forty years ago to be in bad taste.

The problem of causation has traditionally been seen as the bone of contention between Hume and Kant. I shall, on the contrary, argue that it is precisely here that a surprising degree of accommodation between them is possible. To this end, I shall first recount Kant's stand on the conception of causality both before and after Hume awoke him from his dogmatic slumber.[8] I shall then show

5. R. A. Mall, "Humes Prinzipien- und Kants Kategoriensystem," *Kant-Studien* (1971), 319–34; and the same author's "Naturalismus und Kritizismus: Hume und Kant," *Akten des IV. Internationalen Kant-Kongresses* (1974), Part II, pp. 30–41.

6. G. B. Mathur, "Hume, Kant, and Pragmatism," *Journal of the History of Ideas* 16 (1955), 198–208. But see, to the contrary, W. L. Robison, "On the Consequential Claim that Hume is a Pragmatist," *Journal of Critical Analysis* 4 (1974), 141–53.

7. The most comprehensive treatment of the relations between Hume and Kant is to be found in Henri Lauener's *Hume und Kant: Systematische Gegenüberstellung einiger Hauptpunkte ihrer Lehren* (Bern and Munich, 1969); but this well-balanced book does not, in my opinion, break any new ground. See also, Hansgeorg Hoppe, "Kants Antwort auf Hume," *Kant-Studien* 62 (1971), 335–50.

8. The theory of affinity will have to be omitted from this discussion both because of lack of space and because of its perplexing obscurity. Its bearing upon Hume's "pre-established harmony between the course of nature and the succession of our ideas" repays careful study. See Henry E. Allison, "Trans-

that Kant misunderstood Hume's views in the *Treatise*, but that this misunderstanding was a fruitful one. Finally I shall try to show that something in fact needed by Hume but not supplied in the *Treatise* was given by Kant when he attempted to refute the point he erroneously believed to have been argued for by Hume.

Kant's treatment of the problem of causation goes through three distinct phases, which I shall call the pre-Humean, the quasi-Humean, and the post-Humean.[9]

1. In 1755, the year Sulzer translated Hume's *Enquiry Concerning Human Understanding*, Kant was busy criticizing Wolff's derivation of the causal principle from that of sufficient reason, and Wolff's derivation of the latter from the principle of contradiction. But in the work Kant wrote that year, the *Nova dilucidatio*, he attempted to give a rationalistic proof of the principle of efficient causality. This proof is vulnerable to Hume's refutation of all such arguments, which is to be found in the *Treatise*, Book I, Part iii, chapter 3, but Kant was at that time, and perhaps always, ignorant of Hume's refutation.

2. In 1763, in the essay *Versuch, den Begriff der negativen Grössen in die Weltweisheit einzuführen*, Kant gave up his rationalistic arguments to demonstrate the logical necessity of causal judgments. Logical necessity, he says, depends upon identity and contradiction; but any causal judgment may be denied without contradiction, and no statement of identity entails a causal connection

cendental Affinity—Kant's Answer to Hume," *Proceedings of the Third International Kant Congress* (1970), pp. 303–11.

9. It seems hardly possible to formulate an account of Kant's gradually increasing knowledge of Hume which fits *all* the apparent facts. For a long time there has been extensive controversy concerning it. The account given here is a summary of my narrative in *Early German Philosophy*, pp. 424–25, 451–53, 465–67, which, in turn, is in general agreement with Vaihinger, *Kommentar zu Kants Kritik der reinen Vernunft*, I, 344–47. Vaihinger surveys all the polemical literature before his time, and most of his conclusions seem to me not to have been rendered less plausible by significant work done since his time. See L. Robinson, "Contributions à l'histoire de l'évolution philosophique de Kant," *Revue de métaphysique et de morale* 31 (1924), 269–353, esp. 303 ff. See also below, n. 23.

between things not identical: "The rain never follows the wind because of the law of identity."[10] Now admittedly this does sound like Hume, and by this time he had certainly read Sulzer's translation. But one cannot be sure that these new ideas are to be attributed to his reading of Hume, for there was another philosopher nearer home who had definitely influenced Kant and whose thoughts moved in the same direction. This was Christian August Crusius, an anti-Wolffian who had taught (if I may use later Kantian terminology) that the principle of causation, like every specific causal judgment, is synthetic and not analytic; and that the principle of causation, unlike any specific causal judgment, is a priori and not known as a result of induction. While Crusius had given an account of the proclivity of the mind to think causally—not wholly unlike that given later by Thomas Reid—Kant then and always rejected Crusius's explanation because it required, he thought, a belief in a preestablished harmony and permitted a subjective necessity to masquerade as an objective necessity.[11] In 1763, however, Kant had little to say about his own theory of causation, and what he says is obscure and tentative.

Three years later, in the *Träume eines Geistersehers*, Kant writes in an ironic, semi-skeptical manner strongly reminiscent of Hume. He insists that causal connections are not intelligible, that is to say, founded on reason, but appear to us to be intelligible simply because they are made familiar to us through repetitive experience. "That my will is capable of moving my arm is no more comprehensible to me than if someone told me he could stop the moon in its orbit."[12] "The grounds of reason, whether used as an argument for or against the possibility or impossibility of a thing, are absolutely irrelevant. The right of decision must be left to experience [*Erfahrungen*] alone."[13] The ultimate and irreducible causes of things, the *Grund-*

10. Ak. II, 203.

11. Letter to K. L. Reinhold, May 19, 1789 (Zweig, *Correspondence,* p. 144); Reflexionen 4375, 4446 (Ak. XVII, 492, 554).

12. Ak. II, 370 (trans. Manolesco, p. 95). Almost the same example, used for the same purpose, is to be found in Hume's *Enquiry* (ed. Hendel), p. 77: "planets in their orbit."

13. Ak. II, 371 (Manolesco, p. 96).

kräfte, are either unknown or unintelligible to us, and the a posteriori contingency of every causal judgment demands that the way be left open for continual revision of our putative causal knowledge. Kant, in good Humean idiom though citing only Voltaire, appeals to mankind to remain within the limits of experience, since specific causal knowledge is founded on and extends only as far as experience.

While the sentiments in this ironical work resemble those we would expect Hume to express in the face of the fantastic stories of Swedenborg, once again there is no decisive reason to ascribe this essay to Hume's influence on Kant. Such ideas as those I have mentioned were widely accepted in Germany at this time, among natural scientists like Maupertuis and anti-Wolffian philosophers like Crusius and his extensive school, and Berlin enlighteners.[14] The skeptical conclusions which are so prominent a feature of Hume's *Enquiry* are here hardly more than obiter dicta; there is no argument that causal inferences depend upon irrational propensities in the mind and are instinctive. Most of the Humean ideas in this essay were very much in the air in Germany, and it would be difficult or impossible to trace them to one source.[15]

3. The post-Humean phase of Kant's treatment of causation is well known. As I shall repeatedly have to refer to it in later parts of this paper, a brief historical account will suffice at this time. We must consider three events of the years 1770 and 1772.

a. In 1770 Kant published his Inaugural Dissertation, which sharply separated the sensible from the rational faculties in man, distinguished between the sensible or phenomenal world and the intelligible or noumenal world, and formulated the a priori forms of both. The proper method of metaphysics, which is now seen as the

14. Mendelssohn (*Gedanken über die Wahrscheinlichkeit, Ges. Schriften* [1929], I, 156) says that Sulzer's translation of the *Enquiry* is "in everyone's hands."

15. This is the conclusion reached by Giorgio Tonelli, "Die Anfänge von Kants Kritik der Kausalbeziehungen und ihre Voraussetzungen im 18. Jahrhundert," *Kant-Studien* 57 (1966), 417–60. (I am indebted to Professor Tonelli also for a personal communication on how widespread was the knowledge of Hume's works in Germany.)

systematic knowledge of the intelligible world, requires preventing the ascription of the forms of sensible knowledge (space and time) to the objects of pure reason; space and time are the subjective ways things look to human beings, but metaphysics is to deal with things as they are, and most errors in metaphysics arise from the surreptitious application of spatial and temporal predicates to purely intelligible things. Though Kant is copious in his elaboration of the forms of sensibility—so much so that this treatment passes over almost without change into the Transcendental Aesthetic of the *Critique of Pure Reason*—he finds comparatively little to say about pure intelligible forms. What he does say is hardly more than a warmed-over version of some parts of Wolff's ontology, and this little is jettisoned when he comes to write the Dialectic of the *Critique of Pure Reason*, for by then he has realized that there is no synthetic knowledge of what is not spatial and temporal. But this was not his belief in 1770, and he confidently expected to proceed immediately with his metaphysical writings which would expound the principles of pure reason in their application to a purely intelligible world.

Toward the end of the Dissertation, however, he introduces a strangely hybrid form of principle, principles which have a *purely subjective though purely intellectual origin:* "They are commended to us only by the special nature of the intellect, owing to their convenience for its free and extended employment . . . upon conditions under which the intellect seems to itself to make easy and ready use of its insight." They are "principles of convenience" or "rules of judgment, to which we willingly submit and to which we cling as if they were axioms [which they are not], solely for the reason that if we gave them up, scarcely any judgment about a given object would be possible to our intellect."[16] The first of these is the principle of causality according to the law of nature.

b. In his famous letter of February 21, 1772, to Marcus Herz, Kant refers to an objection which had been raised by Lambert[17] to the Inaugural Dissertation's application of theoretical concepts

16. *Forms and Principles of the Sensible and Intelligible Worlds,* § 30.
17. See "Lambert and Hume in Kant's Development from 1769 to 1772."

(presumably including the concept of causation) to purely intelligible objects. He confesses that in writing what he is now engaged upon, the *Critique of Pure Reason*, he noticed that "something essential was lacking" in his account of how purely intelligible concepts which originate a priori in the mind can refer to objects: "If such intellectual conceptions depend on our inner activity, whence comes the agreement that they are supposed to have with objects?"[18] He rejects the answers given by Plato, Malebranche, and Crusius, but does not give his own answer; rather he claims to have found a rule or rules for the discovery of such concepts. To use the later terminology of the *Critique*, he has discovered the root of the Metaphysical Deduction of the Categories, and presumably thought that it could do the work later assigned to the Transcendental Deduction of the Categories,[19] for he expresses confidence that the book will be finished in three months.

c. What led to the extension of the three months to nine years? The third event is more conjectural, but I believe there is sufficient evidence to substantiate it. At Easter time, 1772, there was published a German translation of Beattie's *Essay on the Nature and Immutability of Truth.*[20] Suddenly, through copious quotations, there was opened to Kant many of the riches of Hume's *Treatise of*

18. In Zweig, *Correspondence*, p. 72.
19. See H. J. de Vleeschauwer, *La déduction transcendentale dans l'oeuvre de Kant*, I, 171, 217 ff., for a different interpretation of the order of discovery.
20. Vaihinger (*Kommentar zu Kants Kritik*, I, 347) seems to have been the originator of this hypothesis. It is defended most fully by Robert Paul Wolff, "Kant's Debt to Hume via Beattie," *Journal of the History of Ideas* 21 (1960), 117–23. It is possible that Kant had not hitherto known even of the existence of Hume's *Treatise;* Tetens, whose knowledge of things English (and of the English language) was better than Kant's, referred to Hume and to "the heroic skeptic, the author of the *Treatise of Human Nature*" as if they were two different men (*Ueber die allgemeine spekulativische Philosophie* [1775], ed. Uebele [Berlin, 1913], p. 12). Karl Groos ("Hat Kant Humes Treatise Gelesen?" *Kant-Studien* 5 [1901], 177–81) points to some striking resemblances, partly verbal and partly substantive (dealing with existence as a predicate), between the *Treatise* and Kant's *Einzig möglicher Beweisgrund zu einer Demonstration des Daseins Gottes* (1763), and proffers them as evidence (against Benno Erdmann's "Kant und Hume um 1762," *Archiv für Geschichte*

Human Nature. Kant now realized that Hume had not confined his skeptical attacks to the putative necessity and intelligibility of specific causal judgments—attacks which he himself had participated in—but had raised a serious problem about the causal principle itself. In Beattie's words, "Our opinion of the necessity of a cause to the production of everything which hath a beginning, is by Mr. Hume supposed to arise from observation and experience."[21]

It was this suggestion (*Erinnerung*[22]) of Hume which awoke Kant

---

der Philosophie, I [1887], 62–77, 216–30) that Kant had been influenced by the *Treatise;* but Wolff (p. 122) has located possible common sources for both Hume and Kant.

Upon reading Beattie in 1772, Kant was oddly selective in what he learned, saying that Hume had examined only part of his problem, that concerned with cause and effect (*Prolegomena,* IV, 260). Yet from Beattie he could have learned of the following topics in the *Treatise* absent from the *Enquiry:* the status of material objects and the identity of the self. He might have learned too that Hume was a skeptic about geometry, from a cryptic note in Beattie (p. 162; German trans., 125 n.), but he continued to ascribe to Hume only the mathematical teaching of the *Enquiry* (see *Critique of Practical Reason,* Ak. V, 14 [Beck, p. 14]). In spite of this, there is so striking a resemblance between Kant's explanation of why "A straight line is the shortest distance between two points" is not analytic (*Critique of Pure Reason,* B 16) and Hume's explanation of why it is not a definition (*Treatise,* ed. Selby-Bigge, pp. 49–50) that one can hardly believe that Kant did not know of Hume's argument; yet the passage in question is not in Beattie.

21. Beattie, *Essay on the Nature and Immutability of Truth* (1770), p. 108. German translation (Copenhagen and Leipzig, 1772), p. 85. I do not wish to challenge Beattie's statement that this was Hume's opinion, though it is not, so far as I can see, ever explicitly argued for in the *Treatise* or elsewhere. A reader properly primed by an earlier reading of the *Treatise* might perhaps discern the view in *Enquiry* (ed. Hendel), p. 49, 3 lines from bottom of page, but the *Enquiry* so conflates the two questions formally separated in the *Treatise* that it is never clear (even in the passage just alluded to) that Hume is discussing the causal maxim and not some specific causal generalization. In the letter to John Stewart of 1754 (Greig, *Letters of David Hume,* I, 187), he asserts that the certainty of the falsity of the proposition that anything might arise without a cause proceeds "neither from Intuition nor Demonstration; but from some other Source"—presumably experience. But this remains a presumption based solely on the exclusion of the two alternatives Hume does discuss and is never supported by any positive argument.

22. In my edition of the *Prolegomena* (New York, 1951) I translated *Erinnerung* as if it referred to Kant's recollection of what Hume had said, not to Hume's suggestion or hint, and explained my choice in a footnote. In *Early German Philosophy,* p. 465, n. 104, I wavered; now I wish to renounce that

from his "dogmatic slumber."[23] He was "far from following [Hume] in the concusions he arrived at by regarding, not the whole of his problem, but a part"; he "generalized" Hume's problem and found that "the connection of cause and effect was by no means the only concept by which the understanding thinks the connections of things a priori."[24] Thus was born the fundamental question: "How are synthetic judgments possible a priori?" He finds Hume to be correct in rejecting the possibility of necessary synthetic judgments which go beyond experience, but he thinks Hume was in error in failing to see the difference between a priori in the sense of "going beyond possible experience" and a priori in the sense of "underlying possible experience."[25] As heretofore, he accepts Hume's conclusion that all specific causal judgments are contingent, but under the tutelage of Beattie he states, "Hume was in error in inferring from

---

translation not merely on grammatical grounds (the 1951 reading was strained) but on the grounds that Kant could not, in 1772, have "recollected" what Hume had said.

23. Kant used the metaphor "dogmatic slumber" several times. In *Prolegomena*, §50, he says that the antinomy is "a very powerful agent to arouse philosophy from its dogmatic slumber." Robinson, ("Contributions à l'histoire de l'évolution philosophique," p. 305) has concluded that the allusion to Hume in the Introduction is not meant to be historically accurate, but is an "exposé d'un caractère préconcue et plutôt systématique du rapport de sa doctrine avec celle de Hume." This I find hardly credible, especially since the tone of the Introduction passage, unlike that of §50, is autobiographical. Benno Erdmann, in his edition of the *Prolegomena* (Leipzig, 1878, pp. lxxxv–lxxxvi), argues that the passage in §50 refers to 1769, the year that "brought great light" and prepared the way for the Inaugural Dissertation, which showed that intelligible objects are not spatial (the first consequence of the antinomy); that the allusion to Hume in the Introduction refers to the very different problem which arose after the Dissertation; and that the two passages were allowed to stand in the *Doppelredaktion* that the *Prolegomena* underwent as a result of the Garve-Feder review. According to Erdmann's stratification of the text, §50 was in the original manuscript and the Hume passage in the Introduction was added in the revision.

But in a letter to Garve (September 21, 1798; Zweig, *Correspondence*, p. 252) the autobiographical claim, missing from §50, is supplied when Kant says that the antinomy "is what first aroused me from my dogmatic slumber." This is indeed puzzling. Can it be due to a lapse of memory? The letter is filled with complaints about Kant's declining health and mental abilities.

24. *Prolegomena*, Ak. IV, 260.

25. *Critique of Pure Reason*, A 765 = B 793.

the contingency of our determinations in accordance with the law [of causality] the contingency of the law itself."[26]

Had Beattie not said that Hume treated the causal principle in the same way, and with the same skeptical conclusions,[27] that he had dealt with specific causal laws, there would have been no interruption of Kant's dogmatic slumber. But I shall now attempt to show that Beattie, though he could have documented his statement (he did not) with at most two or three quotations[28] from the *Treatise*, may have misled Kant into thinking that there was an argument to which he needed to reply, not just an "opinion." There is no such argument, and Hume's implicit account of the causal principle is much more like Kant's own than Kant had any reason to suspect. This suggests that we owe the inception of the *Critique of Pure Reason* to a fortunate historical error.

Hume distinguishes two questions concerning necessary connection: (a) "For what reason do we pronounce it *necessary*, that everything whose existence has a beginning, should also have a cause?", and (b) "Why we conclude, that such particular causes must *necessarily* have such particular effects."[29] I shall simplify and restate these by referring to them respectively as the question (a) why every event necessarily has some cause, and (b) why the same cause necessarily has the same effect? Still more briefly, I shall refer to the two principles Hume is investigating as (a) every-event-some-cause, and (b) same-cause-same-effect.

Hume concludes that the principle every-event-some-cause is not known by intuition or reason, and hence that "that opinion must necessarily arise from observation and experience," but I look in vain for an answer to the question Hume now formulates: "How

26. Ibid., A 766 = B 794.

27. Beattie, of course, believed that the principle was known intuitively.

28. I refer to the last paragraphs in *Treatise*, Book I, Part iii, Sections ii and iii (Selby-Bigge, pp. 78, 82). Dr. John Bricke has subsequently called my attention to Section xii (Selby-Bigge, p. 132) as at least marginally appropriate.

29. *Treatise of Human Nature* (ed. Selby-Bigge), p. 78.

experience gives rise to such a principle?". Having asked this question he not only never answers it, he does not even discuss it again.

He finds that it will be "more convenient" to answer the question why same-cause-same-effect and then to "sink" the question why every-event-some-cause in it, in the expectation that "'T will, perhaps, be found in the end, that the same answer will serve both questions."[30] This conjecture leads us to expect a Mill-like argument that the former principle is an induction from cases falling under the latter, an induction from successful inductions, for that is the only way in which the principle every-event-some-cause could possibly arise from observation and experience. But, as we shall see, Hume does not anticipate Mill's argument and, in fact, never answers the first question at all. Though he says "It is universally allowed that nothing exists without a cause of its existence."[31] he also grants that it is easy to conceive "that there is no absolute nor metaphysical necessity, that every beginning of existence should be attended with [a cause]."[32] Question (a), having once been sunk in question (b), never reemerges.

Rather, I shall try to show that the principle every-event-some-cause remains on dry land, ready to rescue the principle same-cause-same-effect when the latter is threatened by recalcitrant experience. Hume availed himself of the principle every-event-some-cause precisely in those cases where the intimate connection he had discovered among regular sequence, contiguity, association, belief, and causation can get no purchase on experience because regular sequence is lacking.

Had the application of the two principles always had the same occasion and outcome, naturally Hume would have preferred to use the second, which he does fully account for. But where they do not, he uses the first to permit the extrapolation of the second beyond

30. Ibid., p. 82.
31. *Enquiry Concerning Human Understanding* (ed. Hendel), p. 104. See also letter to John Stewart, February 1754 (Greiz, *Letters of David Hume*, I, 187).
32. *Treatise*, p. 172.

and even against the teachings of experience, and he gives much the same kind of practical justification for so using it that he had already given for using the principle same-cause-same-effect. Usually Hume warns against giving causal explanations where there is no association of ideas and induction to back them up, thinking that that is the operation of fancy. But there is at least one instance of the proper use of causal explanation which is both counter-associational and practically justified.

I refer to Hume's account of the porter's coming into his room. Hume is sitting in his chamber when on a sudden he hears a noise as of a door opening and a little after sees a porter advance upon him with a letter. "This gives occasion to many new reflexions and reasonings," as follows:

> To consider these phaenomena of the porter and the letter in a certain light, they are contradictions to common experience [in which the sound of a door opening is commonly associated with the sight of its opening], and may be regarded as objections to those maxims, which we form concerning the connexions of causes and effects. I am accustom'd to hear such a sound, and see such an object in motion at the same time. I have not receiv'd in this particular instance both these perceptions. These observations are contrary.... [33]

The conclusion is that

> as all reasoning concerning matters of fact arises only from custom, and custom can only be the effect of repeated perceptions, the extending of custom and reasoning beyond the perceptions can never be the direct and natural effect of the constant repetition and connexion, but must arise from the co-operation of some other principles.[34]

Before considering what these other principles are, we must say something about the role of principles and general rules in Hume's

33. Ibid., p. 196.
34. Ibid., p. 198.

philosophy. [35] Hume often writes, and is usually read, as if belief and causal belief are created in us passively by the mechanism of association. Yet Hume is not content to explain why we believe as we do; he wants to give rules for the correction of our beliefs. These rules, of course, do not have a transcendental origin or sanction, though they function normatively as if they were a priori regulative. What they are is revealed by Hume's contrasting the functions of the imagination whereby we may believe mere coincidences to be causally connected, with "the general and more establish'd properties of the imagination" (which is the understanding[36]) whereby the brute-custom origin of causal beliefs is refined by more cautious inquiry, and superstition is made to give way to science. The human mind is in constant battle with itself[37] —there is a struggle between its instinctive inference to causation from mere association which may be accidental, and its reflective weighing of evidence to achieve a conception of the world less affected by the vagaries of accidental experience. Hume remarks that "reflection on *general rules* keeps us from augmenting our belief upon every increase of the force and vivacity of our ideas."[38]

What is needed in the case of the porter is the inverse of this consideration: A reflexion on the general rule every-event-some-cause keeps us from *reducing* our belief in same-cause-same-effect upon every diminution of force and vivacity of our ideas which occurs when the impression generally associated with an idea is lacking. Regrettably, Hume does not cite this general rule, which cannot have originated in the same way as the generalization which is contradicted by the case of the porter. Rather, he cites explicitly only the general rule that objects intermittently perceived should be

35. See Walsh, "Hume's Concept of Truth"; Thomas K. Hearn, Jr., "'General Rules' in Hume's *Treatise*," *Journal of the History of Philosophy* 8 (1970), 405–22; P. V. Vanterpool, "Hume's Account of General Rules," *Southern Journal of Philosophy* 12 (1974), 481–92.

36. *Treatise*, pp. 267, 440.

37. Ibid., p. 147. Similarly, in moral judgment there is a conflict between immediate sympathy and "general establish'd maxims," pp. 293–94.

38. Ibid., p. 632.

ascribed continued existence when thought governed by this rule will increase the coherence of experience. Presumably he cited only this rule because of his predominant concern in that chapter with the status of unobserved objects.[39] The general rule arises from the following consideration:

> Objects have a certain coherence even as they appear to our senses; but this coherence is much greater and more uniform, if we suppose the objects to have a continu'd existence; and as the mind is once in the train of observing an uniformity among objects, it naturally continues, till it renders the uniformity as compleat as possible.[40]

This gives rise to the theory of double existence, which he says has the backing neither of reason nor of imagination.[41] It does not follow from the standard Humean analysis of causation; it follows rather from Hume's (and the common man's) conviction that if the cause of an event is not found within experience it must be feigned to lie outside it. That is why I said that the first principle, instead of being sunk in the second, is used to rescue the second when experience "contradicts" it.

The description Hume gives of the objects perceived is, in Locke's terminology, in terms of coexistence, not of causation. "Objects have a certain coherence," he says; but the constancy of conjunction of simultaneous properties is not essentially different from the constancy of conjunction of serial properties. In both there is association and consequent belief.

In Hume's observing the porter's entering his room, there is a manifest absence of coherence. He knows that an opening door (as

39. Price (*Hume's Theory*, p. 8) complains about the order in which Hume discusses necessary connection and the existence of objects, which misleads the reader into failing to notice that the discussion of the former requires to be formulated in the light of the latter. Price says it is as confusing as if Kant had put the Analogies before the Transcendental Deduction; I would say, rather, the Second Analogy before the First. (See fourth paragraph from end of this paper.)

40. *Treatise*, p. 198.

41. Ibid., p. 212.

seen) is associated with a particular sound. But here one is present to his senses and the other absent. If coherence and causation were based exclusively on association of impressions, this would be a negative instance. It would lead the pure inductivist to say that the association between the sight and the sound is weaker than it had been, and that the probability of the causal judgment less than it had been. He might even deny that the noise had a cause. Neither Hume nor the common man will draw such a conclusion. Both claim that had they been looking, they would have seen the door open. Why? Because they believe that every event has some cause even if the preceding impression is not the same. "There is nothing existent, either externally or internally, which is not to be consider'd either as a cause or an effect."[42]

The counterfactual claim is supported by *two* principles: every-event-some-cause and same-cause-same-effect. It would be of little use to assert the former without the latter, for to get any practical benefit we must use the latter. But while the first is independent of the second, we cannot maintain the second without the first, since the case before us is counterexample to the second taken alone.

Thus Hume did not "sink" the first question in the second so successfully that the first question need not be raised again. Hume's principle same-cause-same-effect is an induction from his answer to simpler questions about what causes what. But he has no answer to the question about every-event-some-cause, since that is not an induction from the second; rather, it comes into its own where the second breaks down. The principle every-event-some-cause permits us to reinstate the principle same-cause-same-effect in the face of negative instances. We reinstate it for the sake of our need to make our experiential coherence "much greater and more uniform" than the intermittent perceptions we actually have; but it cannot itself be the result of associations of perceptions because it functions precisely where our perceptions are *not* regular enough to support associations, causal beliefs, and the principle same-cause-same-effect.

42. Ibid., p. 75.

This reading of Hume takes at least a small step toward justifying the epithet "the Scottish Kant." It shows that Hume distinguished the a posteriori causal laws induced from the experience of regular sequences from a quite different causal law which is not based on mere association and thus not vulnerable to disconfirmation when the sequence of impressions is not uniform. It is a principle of a higher order which regulates our ascription of causality in the absence of association and even where association and expectation are flouted by the actual course of our impressions. Naturally Hume does not have a theory that one of the conceptions of causation is a priori and the other a posteriori; but a priori is as a priori does, and when a principle is called upon to correct experience, it is functioning in an a priori manner regardless of its origin. It is at least debatable whether Kant's a priori principles have any higher function in spite of their nobler ancestry.

This reading of Hume also throws interesting light on Kant's theory of causation and the true nature of his "answer to Hume." It has often been objected that Kant's Second Analogy does nothing to support the principle same-cause-same-effect.[43] This is true, but it was not Kant's purpose there to support *that* principle; he was concerned only with the principle every-event-some-cause, and did not "sink" this principle in same-cause-same-effect. He says:

> The accepted view is that only through perception and comparison of events repeatedly following in a uniform manner upon preceding appearances are we enabled to discover a rule according to which certain events always follow upon certain appearances, and that this is the way in which we are first led to construct for ourselves the concept of cause. [44]

Kant accepts the first of these tenets. The discovery of what is the cause of what is exactly the same for Kant as for Hume. Kant makes

43. For example, A. O. Lovejoy, "On Kant's Reply to Hume," *Archiv für Geschichte der Philosophie*, 1960, reprinted in M. S. Gram, *Kant: Disputed Questions* (Chicago, 1967), pp. 284–308, at 300–01.
44. *Critique of Pure Reason*, A 195 = B 240–41. What is puzzling about this passage is that Kant calls what he now thinks is Hume's view "the accepted view." *This* view can hardly have been widely accepted in Germany.

no claim that we can discover by reason, or know a priori, the connection of any specific cause with a specific effect and understand its necessity.[45] Even the principle same-cause-same-effect is not known a priori to be true. For Kant, it is a regulative principle,[46] functioning like the principle Hume postulates that unobserved causes must be like observed ones.[47] So far there is little dispute between Kant and Hume. The big difference lies in the second clause of the "accepted belief," namely, that the concept of cause arises in the same manner as the knowledge of what is the cause of some event. Kant insists that the first principle cannot arise in the way the second principle does according to Beattie's reading of Hume, but is rather an a priori condition for the discovery and use of the second.

I shall try to show why Hume did not agree with this, and how Kant supported it. Every reader of Hume is baffled by his repeatedly and arbitrarily shifting back and forth between talking about objects and events and talking about impressions.[48] Sometimes he tries to justify this[49] and sometimes he anticipates Kant in distinguishing between them in a phenomenalistic way.[50] But usually, I think, he is just careless and profits from this carelessness. Because he does not clearly maintain the distinction, in setting up his problem he fails to distinguish between his awareness of a sequence of states in a perceived object and a sequence of mere impressions of a perceived

45. Kant repeatedly asserts that empirical laws cannot be derived from a priori principles of the understanding, yet he believed some of them to be necessary. Those are the ones involved in an overall theory whose principles are derived from the a priori principles of "rational science" or "pure physics." See *Critique of Pure Reason*, A 127–28; A 270 = B 252; B 165; A 216 = B 263. Where the overall theory is lacking (as in chemistry), the principles are only empirical and the laws are only "laws of experience" without any "consciousness of necessity" attaching to them. The body of knowledge containing them should be called "a systematic art" and not a "science." *Metaphysical Foundations of Natural Science*, Ak. IV, 468 (trans. Ellington, p. 4).
46. *Critique of Pure Reason*, A 657 = B 686.
47. *Treatise*, p. 104.
48. Kant is equally at fault; see "A Reading of the Third Paragraph in B," below pp. 141–46.
49. *Treatise*, pp. 67, 118, 218.
50. Ibid., pp. 108, 242.

object. He believes he can see objective events, distinguish them from mental events, feel a "gentle force" among the latter which is absent from the former, and by repeated observation of ordered pairs of objective events come to read the gentle force into them.

But if Hume had rigorously employed the phenomenalistic language to which he is alone entitled, he would not have been able to draw his prima facie distinction between a sequence of impressions and a sequence of perceived objective events, as if the latter were as directly given as the former. He would have seen that the sequence of impressions of a house and the sequence of impressions of a moving ship require rules for interpreting one sequence of impressions as the perception of a stationary permanent object and the other sequence as the perception of a sequence of states or positions of a changing object. Until these rules are made and justified, Hume has no right to use the concept of objective event in classifying some impressions as impressions of events which are observed to occur in ordered pairs, so that same-cause-same-effect could appear to be an empirical generalization from these observations. But Hume does not see that he must justify the use of the concept of objective event before he can establish, even in his own way, the principle same-cause-same-effect. Objective events are not "just given"; as much goes into their construction as Hume properly saw goes into the construction of an identical object intermittently perceived.

Kant's Second Analogy is meant to provide precisely this justification for talk about objective events, and he sees the connection of the two problems by coupling it with the First Analogy, which deals with continued existence. He shows that the concepts of objective event and cause and effect are related to each other necessarily, and not by mere association. Only much later, in an essentially Humean kind of argument, does he deal with the question of the justification of the principle same-cause-same-effect. He is explicitly following a line of argument which I have suggested that Hume actually followed, in contradistinction to the one which Beattie said Hume followed.

Looked at in this way, the charge that "Kant begged Hume's question" and ended up in the same boat with Reid, Oswald, and

Beattie is easily answered. Kant's argument in the Second Analogy does not simply dignify as a priori a principle which Hume, according to Beattie, believed to be a posteriori and therefore uncertain. Rather, it begins with an assumption that Hume never thought of doubting, namely, that we can distinguish between a sequence of impressions of an enduring object and a sequence of impressions which indicates that an objective change is occurring. Hume's answer to how we know same-cause-same-effect could never have been given without this assumption. But Kant raises a question which neither Hume nor any other philosopher before him had seen, namely, how do we distinguish between the two kinds of sequences?

Kant's answer is that any sequence which is taken to represent an objective change of states of affairs, or an event, must be taken as a necessary sequence, and that the concept of a necessary sequence is the concept of causation. Without possessing the concept of causation we could not distinguish between objective events and subjective sequences, and therefore the concept of a causal connection between objective events cannot arise from observation of them, but rather must be presupposed in recognizing them. Given the first principle, every-event-some-cause, which fixes our realm of discourse, we can then, in good Humean fashion, go about finding uniform ordered pairs of events by straightforward observation and induction. Kant does not challenge this; he only argues that his principle, the Second Analogy of Experience, like Hume's principle, every-event-some-cause, is a necessary condition for Hume's second principle, which we know by repeated observation.[51]

I have argued that, once we modify or reject Beattie's interpretation, we can see that such an argument is not wholly unlike Hume's own procedure when faced with the example of the porter, however little inclined Hume would be to use the language of a priori judgments and transcendental principles.

51. The argument given all too dogmatically in this paragraph is based on a fuller treatment I give in "Once More unto the Breach: Kant's Answer to Hume, Again" and in "A Non Sequitur of Numbing Grossness?", this volume. I would modify only one point in the former article: in the last paragraph on p. 133 I accept Beattie's statement at face value, as Kant did, whereas in this paper I give reasons to reject it.

8 Six Short Pieces on the
Second Analogy of Experience

Once More unto the Breach: Kant's Answer to Hume, Again

It is a continuing scandal of philosophical scholarship that after nearly two centuries the question must still be debated: *What* was Kant's answer to Hume? Until there is agreement about this, there is little reason to hope that the philosophical problem of the adequacy of a theory like Kant's to answer questions raised by a theory like Hume's can be solved.

Two recent contributions[1] ascribe to Kant much the same answer. Mrs. Schipper (p. 73) holds that the existence of objectively valid physical science is a fundamental hypothesis of Kant and that this science presupposes the law of causality; hence, she concludes by a magnificent *non sequitur*, "We can have knowledge of such a necessary sequence, since we presuppose it in our laws or 'legislate it to nature'" (p. 74). One is reminded of Lord Russell's acute remark that presupposing has all the advantages over demonstrating that theft has over honest labor.

Reprinted from *Ratio* 9 (1967), 33–37, by kind permission of the editor, Professor Stephan Körner, and the publisher, Basil Blackwood.

1. E. W. Schipper, "Kant's Answer to Hume's Problem," *Kant-Studien* 53 (1961) 68–74; M. E. Williams, "Kant's Reply to Hume," ibid., 55 (1965), 71–78.

The second author criticizes Mrs. Schipper's paper for giving neither "an answer to Hume's problem nor . . . Kant's definitive solution" (p. 71); but seven pages later she concludes that "Kant has shown that the human mind, *if it is to have certain knowledge*, must employ the categories as the a priori presuppositions of Experience" (pp. 77–78, italics added). Of course if we are to say we have certain knowledge, then we must reject the arguments or premises of the skeptic who has striven to show that we do not. There is nothing in the logic of these two papers that Kant would have embraced more gladly than he would have espoused those "who took for granted that which [Hume] doubted, and demonstrated with zeal and often with impudence that which he never thought of doubting."[2]

Professor Wolff's recent book has dealt with the problem of Kant's answer to Hume at great length and with admirable subtlety.[3] Inasmuch as Professor Wolff has paid me the compliment of taking one of my footnotes very seriously and has written an extended criticism of the argument it contained in concentrated, indeed inspissated, form, I should like to comment upon his argument and, at more length and with thanks to his careful analysis, try to make my argument somewhat stronger. Wolff summarizes my argument in the following words:

> A regressive analysis beginning from mathematics and science will not refute Hume, for mathematics and science is [*sic*] precisely what Hume professes to doubt. But if the very same principles (premises) which produce (imply) science and mathematics also imply the distinction between even apparently objective and subjective, etc., etc., then Hume will have been convincingly answered, for not even he can deny them.[4]

Now Wolff's criticism of me is like mine of Schipper and Williams: the regressive method does not prove the truth of the premises even if the truth of the conclusion is assumed. Such an argument merely

2. *Prolegomena*, Ak. IV, 258.
3. Robert Paul Wolff, *Kant's Theory of Mental Activity* (Cambridge, Harvard University Press, 1963).
4. Wolff, *Kant's Theory*, p. 49.

affirms a consequent. Since I was fully alert to the danger of this fallacy, I argued, perhaps too briefly, that conditions *sufficient* to establish the truth of propositions Hume doubted are *necessary* to propositions he accepted. Professor Wolff apparently interpreted me as saying merely that Kant's premises are also Hume's premises, whereas in fact I said:

> The justification of the principles is not merely that they produce the kind of knowledge Hume doubted; rather, they are, Kant argued, the *necessary* conditions also for *any* connected experience in time . . . which any sane man, including Hume, would have to grant.[5]

There is an important logical difference here, for affirming a consequent is valid if the antecedent is a necessary condition.

Let K represent a set of propositions accepted by Kant and doubted or denied by Hume; let H represent a set of propositions Hume (and, incidentally, Kant) accepted; let P stand for propositions sufficient to support K (thus P implies K). Kant's answer to Hume is to show that P is necessary to H and that thus H implies K.

In my footnote, I mentioned propositions necessary for the distinction between erroneous and veridical perception as the crucial assumption Hume had to make in order to support the inductive arguments he needed even for his truncated causal explanations. Now, however, I wish to direct attention to a passage which discusses causation in a way which conforms to the logical pattern just proffered; and though Hume is not mentioned, this passage constitutes, in my opinion, Kant's "answer to Hume." The passage, A 195–96 = B 240–41, occurs in the discussions of the third proof of the Second Analogy, and in order to understand it we must see it in the context of this Analogy.

Kant has been arguing that the apprehension of an objective event, in contradistinction to that of an enduring state of affairs, requires a

5. From my Introduction to *Kant's Prolegomena* (New York, Liberal Arts Press, 1951), p. xix, note. The word "necessary" was not italicized in the original text.

recognition that the representation we call a representation of an event must occur in a fixed position in the order of our representations, for otherwise we would not be able to distinguish the seriality of our representations of enduring states of affairs from the seriality of our representations of an objective sequence of states of affairs, the transition from one to another of which constitutes an event. The order in which I apprehend the representations of events is fixed by the events, whereas the order in which I apprehend representations of enduring states of affairs is fixed by me or by accident. But an order in appearances (objects and events) is one in which one appearance occurs before another or along with it, and this order has a different status from the order of representations, since always one representation occurs before another even when we are representing to ourselves a state of affairs in which one ingredient does not "take place" before another. We are able to decide that a sequence of representations is evidence of a sequence of events only if the order of the representations is such that we believe (rightly or wrongly) that one of the representations must occur before the other. For in that case, we interpret the first representation, call it R_a, as evidence for the event A, and if R_a cannot (we believe) occur after R_b, we think (rightly or wrongly) that B cannot occur before A. Now a condition under which an event B cannot occur before A is that A is a cause of B. Hence the decision that a given representation R_n is a representation of an event is dependent upon the belief (which may be right or wrong) that what R_n represents occurs after what is represented by R_m and could not occur before it. Hence Kant concludes: The experience of something happening is possible only on the assumption that appearances in their succession, that is, appearances as they happen (= events), are determined by the preceding state.[6]

We now come to the application of this analysis to the views of Kant's predecessors, presumably Hume. It is generally assumed, Kant says, (1) that we discover that A is the cause of B by induction from

6. A paraphrase of part of the last sentence in the paragraph beginning on A 195 = B 240.

observations of A's regularly preceding B's; and (2) "that this is the way we are first led to construct for ourselves the concept of cause." Hume argued for both these propositions, and we may call (1) the "*Enquiry*-thesis" and (2) the "*Treatise*-thesis," after the works in which they are most fully and characteristically elaborated.

Kant fully accepts (1). He is in complete agreement with Hume that our knowledge of causal connections between specific events is a posteriori not a priori, synthetic not analytic, inductive not logical, probable not certain. His methods for finding the cause of B are exactly those which Hume prescribed, and the chances of success in this venture, as estimated by Kant and Hume, are very much the same. Kant's first answer to Hume, then, is to agree with him, and to disagree with the rationalists who thought that logical insight into causal connections was possible.

But Kant denies (2). While we can make "logically clear" the conception of the relation of cause to effect only after we have "employed in experience" (as in [1]) the general rule, to wit, that for B to be an event there must have been *some* other event as the condition for its position in a serial, temporal order, "the recognition of the rule, as a condition of the synthetic unity of appearances in time, has been the ground of the experience [of the sequence of A to B] itself."

What does Hume need in order to find that A is the cause of B? For though he challenges the common and the metaphysical interpretation of "cause," he certainly knows how to use it in experience, and he tells us how we do and should use it in order to avoid mistakes that would damage us in practical life.

He needs (a) to know that some impression I is an impression of (or evidence for) an event and not of a state of affairs (like the side of a house); and (b) to find some other impression I′ which regularly precedes I and is likewise the impression of an event.[7] Task (b) is the

7. It is one of the merits of Mrs. Schipper's article that she argues that Hume and Kant are not using "experience" in the same sense; but she carries this point, in my opinion, too far, in arguing that Kant's analysis applies only to scientific and not to "familiar experience." It would have been better for her to argue that Hume has not yet reached "familiar experience" in which he

inductive task, and Kant accedes to Hume's arguments in respect to how it is carried out and what the limitations upon it are. But to accomplish (a), Hume has to be able to decide which of the various impressions are impressions of objective events. He never discussed this problem; no one before Kant even saw that it was a problem. Kant's thesis is that (a) cannot be accomplished unless we accept the rule that representations are to be taken as representations of events only if the representations are already thought to have an order fixed by events which are themselves in a fixed temporal order—even if our thought about the specific order be in fact incorrect. (For the Analogies are regulative principles, not constitutive; they tell us where and when to look for causes and substances, and do not guarantee that we will discover them in specific cases.)

To return now to our logical pattern:

K. "Everything that happens, that is, begins to be, presupposes something upon which it follows by rule" (Kant's Second Analogy).

P. Events can be distinguished from objective enduring states of affairs, even though our apprehension of each is serial (the accomplishment of Hume's task [a]).

H. Among events, we find empirically some pairs of similar ones which tend to be repeated, and we then make the inductive judgment: events like the first members of the pairs are causes of events like the second (the accomplishment of Hume's task [b]).

P implies K, by the arguments of the Second Analogy, which give a sufficient reason for K. H implies P, since if events cannot be distinguished, pairs of events cannot be found, and thus P is a necessary condition of H. Hence: H implies P and P implies K, therefore H implies K. That is Kant's answer to Hume.

---

could distinguish events from enduring states of affairs solely on the basis of the (subjective) association of ideas.

On "Just Seeing" the Ship Move

Professor Jeffrie Murphy, whom I am proud to have had as a student, in his reply to "Once More unto the Breach" has made a counter-accusation to my statement that Hume begged his question by surreptitiously employing a Kantian premise. He argues that Kant begged *his* question by surreptitiously using a Humean premise which he was intent to refute. This ingenious argument requires a fuller examination than I gave it in my "Rejoinder to Professors Murphy and Williams"; and not merely a fuller answer but a rather different one.

Murphy's argument may be put succinctly as follows. Any sequence of impressions may be imagined to occur in reverse order. If the original sequence was one of impressions of events, the reversed sequence is one of imagined impressions of another event which did not take place. If the original sequence was not one of impressions of events, the reversed sequence is one of imagined impressions of a static state of affairs. There is nothing to guide us in the decision as to whether the reversed sequence is to be interpreted as a sequence of imagined impressions of an event which did not take place or of a static state of affairs, *except* a prior decision as to whether the original sequence was evidence of an event. That decision was made independently of the reversibility of the sequence. Hence reversibility-irreversibility is not a criterion for the distinction between state of affairs and event. The Humean concept of event (naive, intuitive) must have been used by Kant, therefore, in setting up his house-ship paradigm.

"Once More unto the Breach" was answered by Professor M. E. Williams and Professor Jeffrie Murphy in *Ratio* 11 (1969), 75–81. I responded to them in "Rejoinder to Professors Murphy and Williams," ibid., 82–87. I am now dissatisfied with my reply to Professor Murphy, and the present paper (previously unpublished, but using four paragraphs of my "Rejoinder") should replace it.

Kant's irreversibility criterion is applied to apprehension, not to imagination. I can *imagine* anything; the question is, what can I *see?* I can *imagine* ship going downstream when I see it going upstream. I *cannot see* it going downstream when it is in fact going upstream. I can *imagine* seeing the roof before the basement and the basement before the roof; and—here is the difference—I can *see* the basement before the roof and the roof before the basement without saying that there are two houses or a growth from basement to roof and a growth downward from roof to basement. If I can see the ship first here and then there, and then there and subsequently here, I do say that there are two things, namely, two events.

It is hard to talk about irreversibility if we do not bring in the imagination. Every sequence is fixed, even the house sequence, because any sequence whatsoever is unique. But, on the other hand, *every* sequence (and not merely the house sequence) is reversible in imagination. Murphy is right, then, in arguing that reversibility in imagination is not criterial.

Though the reversibility of a series of representations in apprehension through imagining a different sequence is perhaps a transparent conception requiring no comment, one must be cautious in speaking of reversibility in apprehension itself. Since a representation is a "fleeting existence," a representation cannot recur, and a sequence of two representations R_1 and R_2 is, strictly speaking, neither repeatable nor reversible. Having once occurred, a pair of representations is over and gone. Since it is no part of Kant's argument or conclusion in the Second Analogy that there are like causes for like effects, it is apparently premature, in all strictness, to speak of repeated sequences and mean members of a class of pairs of similar sequences. Yet we must speak of them in order to make the argument of the Analogy, and the dispute between Murphy and me, intelligible. The following seems to me to be an innocent way of clarifying these concepts.

When we speak of an irreversible sequence we mean the following: any R' not distinguishably different from R_1 except that we are conscious of it at a different time, and any R'' not distinguishably different from R_2 except that we are conscious of it at a different time, are in the same temporal relationship to each other that R_1 and R_2 were. If the sequence $R_1 R_2$ is said to be reversible, we mean that R' and R'' sometimes occur in a different order from that of R_1 and R_2.

In *this* sense, the sequences of representations of the house and the ship are both reversible. But we interpret this reversibility in different ways. The sequences $R_1 R_2$, $R'R''$, and $R''R'$ lead us to say that we are seeing a house whose states are coexistent, by the First and Third Analogies. In the case of the ship, if we have $R_1 R_2$ we say the ship is moving downstream, and if we have $R''R'$ we say the ship is moving upstream. It cannot be doing both at once. The house has a basement and a roof at the same time though we may not be able to see both at the same time and sometimes see roof then basement, and sometimes basement then roof. The question is: what makes the difference in our interpretation of the reversibility in the one case and in the other? The difference is that the ship is moving, and the house is not.

But this leads to the question, central to both Professor Murphy's and my papers: How do we know that the ship is moving? Kant says we do know this,[1] and it is an essential premise in his argument; for it is not a mere consequence of, or a rephrasing of, the sequence of representations, since "the objective relation of appearances that follow upon one another is not to be determined through mere perception."[2] Professor Murphy denies this, asserting that we have the "ability to recognize immediately the difference between one event and another."[3] So far from disputing this right now, I will make another concession (with Kantian authority[4])—that we have the ability to recognize, just as immediately, the difference between seeing successive and seeing coexistent states of an object. (In my original "Rejoinder" I granted the former but not the latter; I now

1. *Critique of Pure Reason*, A 192 = B 221 (Kemp Smith, p. 221, lines 15–16).

2. Ibid., B 234 (Kemp Smith, p. 219, lines 7–8).

3. *Ratio* 11, 77, lines 7–9.

4. *Critique of Pure Reason*, A 190 = B 235 (Kemp Smith, p. 220, lines 16–17).

see that I was wrong in not going even further than Professor Murphy pushed me.)

But so far from this constituting a case of Kant's using Hume's "immediate" perceptions of events, a further inquiry will show that our "ability to recognize immediately" the difference between the ship's going downstream and the ship's going upstream, and the difference between the moving ship and the stationary house, has a conceptual dimension and is not based exclusively upon what we immediately apprehend. Whether acknowledging this conceptual component is compatible with calling the ability an "ability to recognize *immediately*" is a terminological matter of little importance.

For undoubtedly much of what Kant attributed to the understanding and to the rule-governed operations of imagination is generally well taken care of by the nervous system in its integrative functions. Certainly nature has not left us men, and brutes, dependent upon the knowledge of the First and Second Analogies for our ability to tell the difference between a moving ship and a stationary house. Our nervous system enables us to see the difference between a moving ship and a stationary house "immediately." But the trouble is, it does not always enable us, without certain conceptual and methodological precautions and adherence to rules, to do so *correctly*.

The case of a common sensory illusion is instructive. I am in a train in a station between the building and another train. I look out of the right window and see ("just see") the other train begin to move. But having had this kind of experience before, I check my observation by looking out of the left window and observe successive positions (not coexistent states) of the station. But "no one will grant," Kant says, "that the manifold in the house is also in itself successive."[5] Why not? Why do I say my train is moving instead of saying that the building is moving? Because my concept of a house is an (empirical) concept of a thing that does not (normally) move, and my concept of the train is an (empirical) concept of a

5. Ibid.

thing that does (often) move.[6] The "ability to recognize immediately the difference between one event and another" and a fortiori the ability to recognize the difference between an objective change and merely apparent motion of a stationary object depends upon my having concepts of the kinds of things that do or do not ordinarily move. It is this conceptual difference which must be applied to the sequences of representations in order for me to determine whether the observed states are themselves successive or coexistent. Normally the nervous system provides sufficient cues for us to draw this distinction "immediately," but these cues are interpreted in rule-governed ways which Hume ought to have analyzed instead of taking the difference between the two cases as phenomenologically *schlicht gegeben.*

It is this conceptual difference, not the mere difference between reversible and non-reversible series of representations, which Kant tries to show to be dependent on a priori concepts and rules by which we distinguish not between houses and ships (an empirical distinction) but between successive and coexistent states of a thing in general (a categorial distinction). Since I have dealt elsewhere with the way in which the categorial distinction underlies the empirical distinction, and since that part of the argument is not at issue between Professor Murphy and me, I need not pursue the matter any further here.

6. Kant's definition of "object" at A 191 = B 236 (Kemp Smith, p. 220, bottom) is relevant here: the concept of the object (house or ship) is the rule for interpreting the sequence, and the concept of an object in general (an a priori concept) underlies the distinction between two kinds of objects, viz. substances which are permanent and states which change.

A Reading of the Third Paragraph in B

Introduction

One of the most important paragraphs in the *Critique of Pure Reason*, and one absolutely essential for the understanding of the Second Analogy, is also one which causes great difficulty to the reader and, consequently, gives rise to different interpretations of the Analogy itself. In this, the third paragraph in B (equivalent to the first paragraph in A) Kant confirms the epigram that he succeeded in being technical without being precise.

The principal source of the difficulty is that he repeatedly shifts back and forth between using the words "representation," "appearance," and "object" in their empirical sense and using them in their transcendental sense. He identifies two or perhaps three of them (Kemp Smith, p. 219, lines 3 and 2 from bottom; p. 220, lines 1, 5, and 20) despite the fact that the main thrust of the discussion is to distinguish the one from the other and to show their relations. To the extent that they are identified, Kant is writing as a transcendental idealist; to the extent that they are distinguished, he is writing as an empirical realist; and, of course, he holds that transcendental idealism is the only foundation for empirical realism. But if the distinction between the two sets of meanings is not readily apparent to the reader, he will read the passage as a commitment to empirical idealism, and as Van Cleve[1] has shown this makes a proof of the Second Analogy impossible.

Kant poses his problem in the terms of empirical realism, but he solves it in the terms of transcendental idealism, arguing that the

---

This paper, prepared for my seminar students, has not previously been published but seems to have been rather widely circulated.

1. James Van Cleve, "Four Recent Interpretations of Kant's Second Analogy," *Kant-Studien* 64 (1973), 71–87 (at 75–77).

problem is insoluble if the object be interpreted in terms of transcendental realism. Until the very end, the transcendental idealistic theory of the object is held in abeyance; but it infects Kant's terminology[2] almost from the beginning. No wonder readers have had trouble with the paragraph. Since it is explicitly introductory (it is followed by the words, "Let us now proceed to the problem"), the correct interpretation of it must be one which permits it to introduce the arguments which follow. An interpretation which provides a genuine introduction is to be preferred to one which makes the subsequent proofs strained or impossible.

To facilitate what I consider to be the correct interpretation, I provide the following glossary and then, after a few intervening comments, rewrite the passage using this glossary. In the passage as glossed, added words are inserted in square brackets [ ] and changed words are in angle brackets ⟨ ⟩. The unchanged parts are from the Kemp Smith translation.

Glossary

Representation: an actual sensory content of consciousness, which Kant called *perceptio* (A 320 = B 376).

Manifold of representations: all of the representations in a specific apprehension (A 98).

Appearance (in the empirical sense, as in the expression "appearance of a house"): either

a. an optical projection of the empirical object to the eye, as in the expression "the appearance of the (rectangular) house is trapezoidal" (i.e., more idiomatically, "the house appears trapezoidal"); or

b. a part of the empirical object that gives rise to an appearance in sense (a), as "the roof of the house was its only appearance" (more idiomatically, "the only part of the house that appeared was its roof"); or

2. "By transcendental idealism I mean the doctrine that appearances are to be regarded as being, one and all, representations only" (A 369). "Appearances" here means "objects in the empirical sense."

  c. a state or position of an object which appears in sense (a), as "the ship's appearance was under the bridge" (more idiomatically, "the ship made its appearance under the bridge," or "the ship appeared under the bridge.")

Manifold of appearance: either

  a. the appearances (in any of the three senses) which stand in a 1:1 temporal correspondence to a manifold of representations;[3] or

  b. the appearances (in any of the three senses) as they are temporally related in the empirical object and not (necessarily) as they are related to each other in so far as they stand in a 1:1 temporal relationship to the manifold of representations.

Object (in the empirical sense): what is ordinarily called an object, namely, "a thing which is to be found in space" (A 373). It is that whose projections, parts, or states are appearances in the manifold of appearances in sense (b), and also in the manifold of appearances in sense (a) if there is such a manifold as a subset of (b). It is the thing "which prevents our representations from being haphazard and arbitrary" (A 104; see also last sentence in the paragraph). Note: When Kant equates object with appearance, he is using the words in the transcendental, not the empirical, sense. In neither case is the object the thing in itself.

Transcendental object: here, though not necessarily elsewhere, the thing in itself.

---

3. S. F. Barker, "Appearing and Appearances in Kant" (in *Kant Studies Today,* ed. Beck, pp. 274–89) argues that Kant indiscriminately used the "language of appearance" and the "language of appearing," presumably because be believed, like A. J. Ayer but not like Barker, that whatever was said in the one was translatable into the other. If the languages are equivalent, we could dispense with either the manifold of representations (appearances) or the manifold of appearances (what appears). I do not believe this simplification would have an adverse effect upon the interpretation of this paragraph, but it would be so radical a departure from the words in the text that it could hardly be called a gloss. (It is interesting to note that the language of appearing is close to that of the transcendental, and the language of appearance is close to the empirical meaning of "appearance" and "representation.")

Preliminary Comments

The problem of the Analogies is the following: granted that the temporal relation in the manifold of representations and in the manifold of appearances in sense (a) is that of succession, while the temporal relation of appearances in the manifold of appearances in sense (b) is not necessarily that of succession and is in some cases known not to be that of succession, how do we know that the manifold of the appearances in sense (b) is not successive in the case of the house and is successive in the case of the ship?

Kant assumes that the manifold of representations is always successive. This is certainly wrong. When I open my eyes I do not scan the visual field as if my eyes or my attention worked like the electron ejector in a television tube, aiming first at one point and then at an adjacent point. But as a consequence of his sensational atomism, Kant assumes that my apprehension does work in this way. It may be asked: how does this error affect his results?

In general, when a philosopher commits a factual error which makes his solution to a problem more difficult, his mistake is likely to be less damaging than it would have been had it made his solution less difficult. Here Kant's error does not make his problem less difficult, but only makes his preferred solution to it more cumbersome than it need be. But, it might be replied, it is his factual error which generates the problem in the first place. Had he had a more adequate phenomenology of vision the problem which exercises him would not have arisen at all.

This conjecture, however, is incorrect. Whatever be the temporal order of representations in the manifold, it does not determine the temporal order in the manifold of appearances in sense (b). While the connection between the temporal order of the manifold of representations and that of the manifold of appearances in sense (a) is necessarily one of identity (whether the order in question be that of simultaneity or that of succession), the connection between the temporal order of the manifold of appearances in sense (a) and that of the manifold of appearances in sense (b) is contingent and variable. It is the *difference in temporal orders*, and not the putatively *necessary successivity of representations*, which generates the problem of the Analogies.

Gloss

The apprehension of the manifold of appearance [in sense (a)] is always successive. The representations of the parts [or states or appearances in sense (a)] follow upon one another. Whether ⟨the appearances⟩ also follow one another [in the manifold of appearances in sense (b), that is] in the object is a point which calls for further reflection, and which is not decided by the above statement. Everything, every representation even, insofar as we are conscious of it, may be entitled object. But it is a question for deeper inquiry what the word "object" ought to signify in respect of ⟨representations⟩ when these are viewed not insofar as they are (as representations) objects, but only insofar as they stand for (*bezeichnen*) an object. The ⟨representations⟩, insofar as they are objects of consciousness simply in virtue of being representations, are not in any way distinct from their apprehension, that is, from their reception in the synthesis of imagination; and we must therefore agree that the manifold of ⟨representations⟩ is always generated in the mind successively. Now if ⟨objects⟩ were things in themselves, then since we have to deal solely with our representations, we could never determine from the succession of the representations how ⟨the manifold of appearances in sense (b)⟩ may be connected in the object. How things may be in themselves, apart from the ⟨appearances in sense (a)⟩ through which they affect us, is entirely outside our sphere of knowledge. In spite, however, of the fact that ⟨objects⟩ are not things in themselves, and yet are what alone can be given to us to know, in spite also of the fact that their ⟨appearances⟩ are always apprehended successively, I have to show what sort of connection in time belongs to the manifold in the appearances themselves [that is to say, the manifold of appearances in sense (b)]. For instance, the apprehension of the manifold in the appearance [s] of a house which stands before me is successive. The question then arises, whether the manifold [of the appearances in sense (b)] of this house is also in itself successive. This, however, is what no one will grant. Now immediately I raise my concepts of an object to their transcendental meaning, I realize that the house is not a thing in itself, but [in the transcendental, not the empirical sense] only an appearance, that is, a representation, the transcendental object of which is unknown. What, then, am I to understand by the question: how the manifold [of appearances in sense (b)] may be connected in the ⟨object⟩ itself which is yet nothing in itself [that is to say, not a thing in itself]? That which lies in the successive apprehension is here viewed as [mere] representation [in the empirical sense], while ⟨that⟩ which is given to me, notwithstanding that it is nothing [in the transcendental sense] but the sum of these representations, is viewed as their object [in the empirical sense]; and my concept, which I derive from the representation of apprehension [that is to say, the manifold of representations] has to agree with it. Since truth consists in the agreement of knowledge with the object, it will at once be seen that we can here enquire only regarding the formal conditions of empirical truth, and that ⟨the manifold of appearances in sense (b)⟩ in contradistinction to the ⟨manifold of representations and to the manifold appearances in sense (a)⟩ can be represented as an object distinct from them only if it stands under a rule which distinguishes it from every other [manifold of representations in] an apprehension and necessitates some one particular mode of connection of the manifold [of representations]. The object is *that* ⟨in the manifold of appearance in sense (b)⟩ which contains the conditions of this necessary rule of apprehension [of representations].

A Non Sequitur of Numbing Grossness?

In 1906 Lovejoy pointed out what he considered to be "one of the most spectacular examples of the *non-sequitur* which are to be found in the history of philosophy."[1] Nobody took any notice. In 1966, commenting on the very same passage in the *Critique of Pure Reason*, Strawson called it "a *non sequitur* of numbing grossness."[2] This caused a flurry of responses by *echt-Kantianer*, none of which seems to me to be satisfactory. The sudden thrust of the Lovejoy-Strawson argument has not been parried but only muffled in the cloak of the transcendental philosophy as a whole. Believing that the effective refutation of an argument should not be significantly longer or any less clear than the argument itself, I shall try to deal with it in its own terms, in a paper not disproportionately longer or piously Kantian.

The non sequitur which Lovejoy and Strawson claim to find at A 192–93 = B 237–98 is as follows. From the irreversibility of the sequence of perceptions of states of an object, we infer that the states of the object are themselves in a sequence which is irreversible. That surely would be a non sequitur. The question is: is this Kant's inference? I shall try to show that it is not, or at least that perplexing obscurities of his argument allow, if not require, an interpretation which does not contain this non sequitur. Then I shall try to show why Strawson thought Kant's argument did.

First published in *Kant-Studien* 67 (1976), 385–89, under the title, "Is there a Non Sequitur in Kant's Proof of the Causal Principle?", and reprinted by kind permission of the editors, Professors Gerhard Funke and Joachim Kopper.
1. A. O. Lovejoy, *On Kant's Reply to Hume*, Archiv für Geschichte der Philosophie (1906), reprinted in M. S. Gram, ed., *Kant: Disputed Questions* (Chicago, 1967), p. 303.
2. P. F. Strawson, *The Bounds of Sense* (London, 1966), p. 137.

In reconstructing Kant's argument, I shall make use of one or two points Kant makes clear only by additions made in the Second Edition, perhaps because he saw that the first proof in the First Edition was vulnerable to criticism.

I reconstruct the argument as follows:

1. That the state A in the object precedes the state B in the object (that is to say, that the objective event symbolized as [AB] occurs) is a sufficient condition, given perceptual isomorphism,[3] for the irreversibility of the sequence of the perceptual representations of the states A and B. (The sequence of representations is symbolized as $[A_r B_r]$.)

2. But knowledge of $[A_r B_r]$-irreversibly is not a sufficient condition for knowledge that [AB] occurs, and a fortiori not a sufficient condition for knowledge that [AB]-irreversibly occurs. For:

(i) It could be the case that A and B are coexistent but such as to be always perceived in the order $[A_r B_r]$, which is interpreted as $[A_r B_r]$-irreversibly; or

(ii) It could be the case that B precedes A, if perceptual isomorphism fails.

3. In order to know, or to have good reason to believe, that [AB] occurs, given knowledge of $[A_r B_r]$-irreversibly, I must know or have good reason to believe both that:

(i) A and B are opposite states of a substance (B 233), in order to rule out 2 (i); and

(ii) [AB]-irreversibly, in order to rule out 2 (ii).

4. Knowledge of, or a sufficient reason to believe, 3 (i) is sufficient reason to know or justifiably believe that there is an event (a change of states of an object) but not sufficient reason to know or believe that the event is [AB] and not [BA] (B 233).

5. But I know, or have sufficient reason to believe, that [AB] occurs.

3. The term is borrowed from James Van Cleve, "Four Recent Interpretations of Kant's Second Analogy," *Kant-Studien* 64 (1973), 71–87, at p. 81. But I use the term to refer only to the condition that there be no relevant difference in the modes of causal dependence of A_r on A and of B_r on B. See p. 161, below.

6. Therefore I know, or have sufficient reason to believe, that [AB]-irreversibly occurs. (3, [ii]).

7. [AB]-irreversibly is the schema of causation.

8. Therefore to know, or to have sufficient reason to believe, that [AB] occurs, I must know, or have sufficient reason to believe, that A is, or contains, a causal condition of B.

I shall now briefly comment upon several of these steps.

ad 1. Kant says (A 193 = B 238) we must derive (*ableiten*) $[A_rB_r]$ (and perhaps even $[A_rB_r]$-irreversibly) from [AB]. But surely he means merely that $[A_rB_r]$ and $[A_rB_r]$-irreversibly are dependent upon [AB]; any sequence of representations is *given*, not *derived* in any sense of "concluded."

ad 2. The denial of this is the non sequitur ascribed to Kant. But 2 is explicitly stated at B 234: "The *objective relation* of appearances [that is, of A and B] that follow upon one another is not to be determined through mere perception [that is, from the sequential relation of A_r and B_r]." Hence Kant does not claim that $[A_rB_r]$-irreversibly entails [AB].

ad 2 (i). The world might be so constituted that all its parts are coexistent but (for some queer reason) they can be perceived only in an irreversible sequence of representations. To use Kant's example of the house: maybe there is a house so situated that, as I approach it by the only road leading to it, I always see the roof before seeing the windows, and the east side before the west side. Let us suppose this is my reason for (incorrectly) asserting $[A_rB_r]$-irreversibly. But I would be wrong, *ex hypothesi,* in interpreting the putative $[A_rB_r]$-irreversibly as evidence for [AB].

ad 2 (ii). Perceptual isomorphism fails when, for example, I cannot but see an eclipse of the moon before I see the explosion of a nova, even though the nova exploded thousands of years before the eclipse occurred.[4] But unless I know that [AB] and not [BA]

4. Kant talks about the sequence of states in a substance and not the sequence of events. His model of causation is Leibnizian, not Humean. (If one remembers this there is no danger in using examples like the eclipse and the

occurs, I cannot discover the absence of perceptual isomorphism. It is knowledge of a law of nature, for example, a law concerning the necessary sequence of positions of states of the wave-front of a light-ray, which requires me to say that [BA] occurred *in spite of* $[A_rB_r]$-irreversibly. In other words, at least causal laws of nature must be posited in order to know how to interpret $[A_rB_r]$-irreversibly. In order to know the objective order of the two events, "the relation between the two states must be so thought that it is thereby determined as necessary which of them must be placed before, and which after, and that they cannot be placed in the reverse relation" (B 234).

ad 5. Kant says, "I see a ship move down stream." Paton correctly pointed out that this is an independent premise of Kant's argument.[5] [AB] is not an intermediate step in an invalid inference from $[A_rB_r]$-irreversibly to [AB]-irreversibly; *that* line of argument has been ruled out by 2. Still, one may ask whether Kant had a right to this premise; perhaps all he could claim to know was $[A_rB_r]$. If I am correct in seeing the argument here as a response to Hume,[6] however, Kant has a right to any premise which Hume has made use of in his argument against the causal principle. Hume assumed that he knew [AB] because he had, from repetition of cases like [AB], explained how the illusion arises that [AB]-necessarily. Kant's entire argument against Hume at this point and at A 196 = B 241 takes the following form: Hume knows [AB] but has skeptical doubts about [AB]-necessarily. But unless one knows, or has reason to believe, [AB]-irreversibly, then $[A_rB_r]$, and even $[A_rB_r]$-irreversibly, is not good evidence for [AB]. *If* one knows [AB], therefore, he has good reason for asserting what Hume denied, namely [AB]-irreversibly.

ad 7. You will notice that in the previous note, when dealing with Hume I wrote [...]-necessarily, and when dealing with Kant I

---

nova, which more readily fit into a Humean than into a Leibnizian pattern. Kant will extend his model in the Third Analogy; but nothing relevant to the present controversy depends upon the choice of a Leibnizian or Humean model and example.)

5. H. J. Paton, *Kant's Metaphysic of Experience* (London, 1936), II, 240.

6. As I argue in "Once More unto the Breach: Kant's Answer to Hume, Again."

wrote [...]-irreversibly. The reason for this is that while the concept of causal connection is the concept of [AB]-necessarily, the
schema of the concept is [AB]-irreversibly. While Kant's statement
of the schema of causation at A 144 = B 183 does not absolutely
rule out the interpretation of the schema as being $[A_rB_r]$-irrever-
sibly, it is clear that in the Second Analogy he means [AB]-irrever-
sibly, for he says, "The sequence in time is thus the sole empirical
criterion of an effect in its relation to the causality of the cause
which precedes it."

There is nothing in this argument which requires that our knowledge claim that [AB]-irreversibly be true. It is sufficient against
Hume that it must be assumed in justification of Hume's knowledge
claim that [AB] occurs.

I shall now comment upon why I think Strawson has misinter-
preted Kant's argument, especially why I think he has misread part
of A 193 = B 238 (in Kemp Smith, p. 222, lines 2–12).

Van Cleve points out that Strawson has written his criticism from
a "realistic" view.[7] According to that view, A and B and the substance of which they are states are ontologically real, independent of
any construction; they are not mere phenomena "under a law given
them by the understanding." If it is a fact about the world that
[AB] occurs, and if in order to know it we do not have to "constitute" it or ground our knowledge of it except by adducing the
evidence $[A_rB_r]$-irreversibly, then there is no way to go from
$[A_rB_r]$-irreversibly to [AB]-irreversibly. Given this conception of
the object and our knowledge of it, Van Cleve is correct in ratifying
Strawson's accusation, for the Kantian "proof" stops at [AB] and
does not reach [AB]-irreversibly.

But we must notice that Kant was aware of that, and could riposte
on Strawson that, given *that* conception of object, he and Strawson
could not reach even [AB] from $[A_rB_r]$-irreversibly. For, he says
"If appearance [sc. objects and their states] were things in themselves ... we could never determine from the succession of representations how their manifold may be connected *in the object*" (A 190

7. Van Cleve, "Four Recent Interpretations," p. 84.

= B 235, italics added). Now it is reasonable to suppose that Kant would not then immediately employ a concept of object which he had just seen would render his own argument invalid.

And we have to look only to the end of the paragraph from which I have just quoted, which immediately precedes the passages that are in dispute, to find Kant's own definition of object: it is "*that* in the appearance which contains the condition of this necessary rule of apprehension."[8] The rule for constituting (constructing) an object specifies necessary temporal relations. The rule is a priori, even though in any particular case we may not know, and certainly do not know a priori, what the *specific* temporal relation is between *specific* states.

Accordingly, Kant distinguishes two kinds of objects, the possibility of knowledge of which is constituted by the application of one or the other of two rules. They are: permanent stable objects, like the house, and objects undergoing a change, like the ship. Each fits the broad definition of "object" quoted above. The second object is posited on the evidence of $[A_r B_r]$-irreversibly under the (meta-)rule stated in the Second Analogy: "Everything that happens, that is, begins to be, presupposes something upon which it follows according to a rule."

Thus to know [AB] I must employ not merely the evidence $[A_r B_r]$-irreversibly but also the rule that whichever state comes first does so according to a rule by which a changing object is posited. I do not know that some specific A precedes necessarily some specific B; I might even be wrong in thinking A precedes B at all. But if I know [AB] on the evidence $[A_r B_r]$-irreversibly, then I must follow the rule that the earlier state is, or contains, a condition of the later. This meta-rule for the specific empirically founded rule "[AB]-irreversibly" is the condition under which alone I can distinguish between stable objects and changing objects or objective events, since the evidence $[A_r B_r]$-irreversibly does not suffice.

"[AB]-irreversibly" is the rule that Kant obscurely refers to, or

8. Similar definitions at A 104, A 106, and B 137.

meant to refer to, at A 193 = B 238 (Kemp Smith, p. 222, line 11), not "[$A_r B_r$]-irreversibly," for the latter is not a rule but only evidence to be used according to a rule. To infer the former from the latter would indeed be a non sequitur of numbing grossness.

A Parable

Once upon a time a scientist said to his laboratory technician, "I want you to observe this dial carefully, and every thirty seconds please enter its reading on a punch-card. When you have done so for two hours, please bring me the cards."

The technician did so with great care. When the run was finished he inadvertently knocked the pile of cards upon the floor. They were hopelessly disarranged.

He went to the scientist and very humbly told him what had happened, expressing genuine regret that the experiment had been ruined. The scientist chid him for his clumsiness, but said, "All is not lost, however. In fact we can easily put the cards in order," and he began to shift them about.

The technician was amazed; this was the finest card trick he had ever seen, for the scientist quickly rearranged the 240 cards. He asked the master how he had done such a thing.

"Elementary," replied the professor. "Since you were reading a thermometer which was measuring the heat given off by a gram of radium and absorbed by a liter of water, the lowest reading is necessarily the first, and so on."

What the scientist did not know was that someone had removed the radium from the water when the water had begun to boil.

Moral. "The objective succession will therefore consist in that order of the manifold of appearance according to which, *in conformity with a rule*, the apprehension of that which happens follows

This parable was probably suggested to me by some acute remarks by Arthur Melnick, *Kant's Analogies of Experience* (Chicago, 1973), p. 89. It has not been published elsewhere.

It should be read in conjunction with the following article (especially pp. 163–64), in which I argue that we can understand the various Kantian "faculties" by analogy with different scientific instruments, each of which has a specific and different function.

upon the apprehension of that which precedes. . . . This is only another way of saying that I cannot arrange the apprehension otherwise than in this very succession." A 193 = B 239. "The object is *that* in the appearance which contains the condition of this necessary rule of apprehension." A 191 = B 236.

The Second Analogy
and the Principle of Indeterminacy

In classical physics, given a specification of the relevant parameters of an event E_1 and an appropriate law L, it should be possible to predict the parameters of an event E_2, in a force-free field, with unlimited exactitude and certainty. For example, if E_1 is the movement of a body of mass m with velocity v at time t_1 and position p_1, the laws of mechanics tell us when E_2, the passing of this body through p_2, will occur.

In quantum physics this is said to be impossible when dealing with subatomic events. It may be impossible for one or both of two reasons. First, it may be impossible to determine all the parameters of the two events with sufficient exactitude to foretell precisely where event E_2 will occur or to know whether E_2 did occur at the point predicted; the maximum exactitude attainable is precisely determined. Or, second, the law relating E_1 and E_2 may be only probabilistic, so that E_1 and law L are not sufficient conditions for the exact prediction of E_2, even assuming the parameters of E_1 and E_2 could be precisely known.

Kant's theory of causation is designed to give an epistemological defense of the claim sketched in the first paragraph. Just as the development on non-Euclidean geometries has either modified or refuted Kant's theory of mathematical knowledge, it may be thought that the new development in physics known as the principle of indeterminacy forces a major revision in his theory of physical causation, if it does not, indeed, render it wholly indefensible. The purpose of this paper is to examine the relation between Kant's

First published in *Kant-Studien* 57 (1966), 199–205, and reprinted by kind permission of the editors, Professors Gerhard Funke and Joachim Kopper. It was reprinted in *Einheit und Sein: Gottfried Martin zum 65. Geburtstag*, ed. Ingeborg Heidemann and Ernst Konrad Specht (Kölner Universitätsverlag, 1966), pp. 199–205.

theory of causation, which was fitted to the Newtonian physics, and the features of indeterminacy or uncertainty, which are integral parts of modern physics. More specifically, we shall ask whether the principle of indeterminancy, as sketched in the second paragraph, is incompatible with the Second Analogy of Experience, the putatively a priori synthetic judgment that "all alterations take place in conformity with the law of the connection of cause and effect." While there is a clear contradiction between them, we shall find that the Analogy, properly interpreted and supplemented, is required for the establishment of the principle of indeterminacy itself.

In the Second Analogy, Kant is talking of empirical objects like ships and houses, not of the particles of microphysics. But there is every reason to believe that he would gladly extend his principle into the most recondite parts of microphysics, and it would be a poor defense of his principle to say that it was meant to apply only to middle-sized objects. In the range of middle-sized objects the consequences of the principle of uncertainty are so minute as to be unnoticeable; hence, in spite of Kant's Newtonism, it would be entirely possible to draw a line between the region of objects where the Second Analogy is applicable and the region where the principle of indeterminacy is applicable. But since the Analogy was meant to be one of the foundation stones of physics and to be of universal and necessary application, little of the Analogy would be left. It would then appear to be a mere empirical fact that some events are causally related, but not others, when, in fact, the Analogy is meant to be a priori and the principle of indeterminacy is intimately involved in the whole theoretical structure of quantum theory.

Rather than trying to defend the Analogy by limiting its claims, I wish to defend it by showing that it is required in arguments designed to establish the indeterminacy principle itself, and that the limits of the application of the indeterminacy principle vis-à-vis the application of the Analogy are not dependent just upon physical and statistical laws but have an epistemological basis.[1]

---

1. This paper is not meant to provide a general defense of the Second Analogy. My purpose is to show only that the function it served in the

The principle of indeterminacy holds that the most complete knowledge we can have of E_1 is not a sufficient condition for the prediction that E_2 will occur, but that the knowledge of E_1 only gives a probability that E_2 will occur. Hence E_1 could occur without E_2, and E_2 could occur without or before E_1. If the Second Analogy is correct, however, and if E_1 and E_2 could occur one without the other, there is no way in which we could determine which of them occurs first when, in fact, both do occur.

For the Second Analogy argues that since all representations are successive even when they represent simultaneous or permanent states of affairs, there must be something other than the successiveness of the representations that serves as evidence for the successiveness of the respective states of affairs. The event of representation R_1 being succeeded by R_2 is not a sufficient condition for saying that the states of affairs represented, S_1 and S_2, are successive, or that there is an event (the transition from S_1 to S_2) instead of a continuing complex state of affairs in which S_1 and S_2 are ingredients manifested one after the other.

This analysis of the meaning of and conditions for the assertion that an event occurs other than the transition from R_1 to R_2 is the central point in what I consider to be Kant's principal answer to Hume (though Hume is not mentioned) at A 195–96 = B 240–41. There Kant tells us that the Humean theory that the causal principle is abstracted from similar event sequences is incorrect because the distinction between event sequences and mere sequences of representations (which is all Hume has a right to claim to know) itself requires the principle that the *object* of one representation must precede the *object* of the other. But this principle is equivalent to the causal principle itself. Hence in supposing that we observe sequences of events and *then* come to know by generalization that

---

epistemological foundations for the Newtonian theory is involved also in establishing the evidence for the non-Newtonian theory; that is, I propose to show only that the *need* for the Second Analogy is not reduced by the success of the indeterminacy principle, and that the *scope* of the Analogy is not thereby limited.

the earlier event is the cause of the later, Hume put the cart before the horse. We do not know that we are cognizing events except when we know that events are causally related in a way in which simultaneous states of affairs are not causally related.

The difference between Hume and the proponents of the indeterminacy principle is this. Hume supposes that in event sequences E_1-E_2, E_1'-E_2', etc., events like E_1 will always be followed by events like E_2, though he can give no reason why this should be so or how we can know it if it is so. The indeterminist denies this supposition, and hence denies the principle of uniformity and the ideal of perfect predictability. But their resemblances are greater than their differences, for both assume that we can determine the difference between the following cases: (a) the series R_1-R_2 when the R's are representations of events and when their sequence is evidence of the event sequence E_1-E_2; and (b) the series R_1-R_2 when the R's are diverse representations of permanent or simultaneous states of affairs so that the R-series is not evidence for an E-series. Hence both Hume and the indeterminist are committed, if Kant is correct, to the Second Analogy in establishing the occurrence of an event series. That Hume thinks the event series is itself causal and that the modern physicist thinks it is not are secondary to their fundamental agreement that events can be distinguished from continuing states of affairs revealed seriatim.

It would appear also that the differences between Hume and Kant are much less significant than those between Kant and the modern physicist, since the former two in fact agree that the event series is causally deterministic and they dispute only about our way of knowing this (whether it be a posteriori or a priori). It would seem that Kant and the physicist cannot agree at all, since the former holds that events can be recognized as events only if they are causally related, and the latter holds that there are events not causally related but only statistically related that are yet recognizable as events.

The question then arises, how does the physicist know that E_2 temporally follows E_1? More fundamentally, how does he know that his representations R_1 and R_2 are representations of events, if the events in question are not causally related? For if they are events, and if the Second Analogy is correct, they must be causally related.[2] If it is asserted that they are events, and denied that they are causally related, obviously the Second Analogy must be denied.

Let us examine the experimental situation, to be sure idealized and simplified, which would give evidence for the principle of indeterminacy. We set up a clock on which we can read times t_1, t_2, etc., when the hand points to positions C_1, C_2, etc. We call the successive positions of the hands the clock series. Whenever we observe a certain flash of light from another apparatus (be it what it may, but one thinks naturally of a scintillation counter), we set the clock at C_1 and say the flash occurred at t_1. We then find that when the clock is at C_2 and when we say the time is t_2, in some fraction of the cases we see another flash of light. (In classical theory, we should always see another flash at t_2; it is an empirical fact that we do not.) We interpret the flash at t_1 as evidence for a subatomic event E_1 and the flash at t_2 as evidence for another subatomic event E_2, and deny that E_1 is the cause of E_2 because it is not perfectly correlated with it.

The question then is, in the light of the Second Analogy, why do we say E_1 and E_2 are events? The flashes of light are like Kant's representations; they must be successive if they occur at all. For all we know, the flash like that at t_2 could occur before the flash like that at t_1; and if it did, reasoning according to the Second Analogy would show that what were represented by the flashes (namely, the subatomic states of affairs) were not events at all. In that case it is utterly trivial to say that they are not causally related. The indeterminist means to assert far more than that, namely, that they are events not causally related.

2. This is not strictly true, since the Analogy (being regulative, not constitutive) does not tell us *what* events are causally related with each other, nor does it guarantee that a pair of events picked out by induction are in fact a causal pair. But if E_2 is an event, the Analogy tells us that there is *some* other event which is causally related to it, and it tells us how to proceed in finding that other event. For the purpose of simplification in this exposition, I ignore this fact, since the principle of indeterminacy denies that there is any other event E which is related to E_2 as a classical cause.

It is here that the Second Analogy must be called upon by the indeterminist. The clock, as a middle-sized object, must have a fixed order in its readings so that the reading C_1 must occur before the reading C_2, regardless of whether the flashes F_1 and F_2 which are *usually* simultaneous with C_1 and C_2 respectively are *invariably* associated with the clock series. The decision that the subatomic states of affairs we call E_1 and E_2 are events not causally related to each other depends upon a *prior decision* that the states of affairs we call events in the clock series are causally related and hence invariably associated with each other in a fixed order, and upon the *empirical fact* that the F-series is not invariably correlated with the C-series. But we need still another principle (which in some cases is empirical, in others a postulate) to associate the E-series with the F-series.

That an additional principle is needed is easily shown by a simple example. Suppose I have a clock which is set to read C_1 when I see a cannon firing in the distance, and I find that I always hear the explosion when the clock event is C_2. This does not indicate that there is an objective sequence of events: flash of light, then sound of explosion, instead of a complex situation involving simultaneous light and sound (like Kant's house, in contrast to his ship). We need to assert another postulate in order to make sure that the sequence of events simultaneous with successive clock events is evidence for a sequence of events said to be correlated with them. We need, in other words, to postulate a specific connection between the F-series and the E-series, analogous to perceptual isomorphism.

This postulate is: The temporal relation between the clock event C_1 and the state of affairs E_1 giving rise to a report F_1 at C_1 is the same as that between C_2 and E_2 when F_2 is made at C_2.

This postulate is not fulfilled in the example of the sight and sound of the cannon; hence the sequence of F's is not evidence of a sequence of E's in the firing of the cannon. Nor is it fulfilled in the example of the discovery of different reaction times of different astronomical observers. In these examples, we use our knowledge of the states of affairs giving rise to the reports at C_1 and C_2 to determine the *difference* between the temporal relations of the states of affairs and the F_1 and F_2 occurring at C_1 and C_2 respectively. (Thus we use our knowledge of astronomical regularities to measure psychological reaction times, and our knowledge of the nature of explosions and of the speed of light to determine the velocity of sound.)

If the postulate is not fulfilled but we can measure the differences between the time interval F_1-E_1 and the time-interval F_2-E_2, we can generalize the postulate and still use it for establishing the objective order in the E-series; the postulate as stated is merely the limiting case. The complete generalization of the postulate in the special theory of relativity is needed in order to correct errors which arise from neglect of the speed of light in a signal arriving at C that an event E has occurred elsewhere. In its complete generality, however, the postulate is only a postulate, not directly testable empirically, but acceptable as a decision made for the sake of giving an order to the E-series which is independent of the position and movement of the observers with different clocks.

In the experiment on the unobserved subatomic events, we cannot show that our postulate is fulfilled by any independent observation of the date of the members of the E-series, for any attempt to do so again involves us in the correlation of C-series, F-series, and E-series. Hence this postulate (perhaps, however, in a more generalized, but equally a priori form) must be assumed if we are to reason from the sequence of F-events to the sequence of E-events. When we assume the Second Analogy in order to fix the sequence of the C-events and thereby the sequence of F-events, and when we assume the postulate in order then to serialize the objective states of affairs as E-events, it remains a merely empirical question whether the E-events are invariably related to each other or not.

Kant thought that they were, for he had no reason to doubt it in 1781; it is now denied on good empirical grounds. But it is denied only after the Second Analogy has done its work in setting up a temporal order among C-events and after the postulate has done its work in synchronizing E-events with F-events which have already been synchronized empirically with C-events. Therefore I suggest that there are good epistemological grounds for regarding our knowledge of indeterminacy as parasitic upon our knowledge of causal determinacy. Without the causal determinacy of middle-sized objects, as asserted in the Second Analogy, I do not see how we could get the evidence we have for non-causal relations among microscopic objects.

In conclusion, I wish to point out an analogy (in the ordinary, not the Kantian, sense of this word) between some of the "transcendental apparatus" of the Kantian philosophy and the apparatus used in a scientific laboratory. It has often been pointed out how the "forms of intuition" resemble "colored spectacles" in their function of determining the content of our sensibility; this analogy may be of some pedagogic value (but it also has dangers and does not cut very deeply). On the other hand, it may be noticed here how the flashes synchronized with clock readings function like the representations which are the raw data with which Kant begins. They are and must be successive; but what they mean can be inferred to be successive only by means of the Second Analogy and a postulate which involves the formal features of signals. Scientific instruments like clocks and rulers are constructed in order to do things to raw data very much like what forms and categories and schemata do to or with the contents of sensibility in Kant. There is an analogy between instruments which reduce the "rhapsody of sensations" to data in a scientist's notebook and the transcendental synthesis which makes it possible to "spell out the appearances so that they may be read as experience." Since Kant wishes to avoid psychologism, but necessarily uses language borrowed from psychology, he sometimes obscures his arguments and purposes and seems to be describing how we in fact think in the ordinary affairs of life, when what he says is more lucid and defensible if interpreted as an account of what a sophisticated scientist would do in reasoning from his data to the objects of experience he is interested in constructing logically. We do not normally think by rules but, at best, in accordance with them; but when one reasons from clocks and flashes of light to unobserved events occurring somewhere else, knowledge of the construction and function of the instruments used plays a constitutive role in the establishment of empirical facts. The terminology of "forms of intuition" suggests much less about the truths of physical geometry than discussion of the construction of rulers and clocks; discussion of the ways in which successive flashes of light and the movement of a clock hand indicate or fail to indicate successive events generating these flashes provides a lucid and sophisticated account of scientific procedure which is, I think, relatively free from the dubious psychological assumptions (for example, that of the non-simultaneity of representations) which underlie Kant's exposition of the Second Analogy.

I do not propose that such analogies get to the root of Kant's own meaning; after all, something very like his Analogies is required at the next lower level in determining the conditions under which we can see whether the flashes of light and the readings on the clock are simultaneous or not. But if we decide to shift to a protocol language of physics instead of using a phenomenalistic protocol language and build our science on the former rather than on the latter, the rules, forms, and concepts by which Kant moved from the latter to a scientific world picture are, as it were, brought out of the "mind" and put into "instruments" and rules for their use. They thereby become more readily inspectable and corrigible. No complete parallelism between the Kantian movement from representations to objects and the movement outlined here from physicalistic protocol statements to statements about objects can perhaps be maintained. It would be worthwhile, both from the standpoint of a better understanding of Kant and that of a better understanding of the rules of scientific construction, to see where the parallelism obtains and where it breaks down. The present essay is a very preliminary and tentative exploration of this way of freeing the Kantian philosophy of science from its exclusive concern with the problems of Newtonian physics and its apparent dependence upon a psychology of faculties. A full exploration of these possibilities would be the life-work of another Kant.

PART TWO

Varia

9 On the Putative Apriority of Judgments of Taste

Kant says that "we desire that judgments of experience shall always hold good for us and in the same way for everyone else,"[1] and we consider a judgment of experience as "valid and hence necessary."[2] "Necessary," however, does not mean a priori; it means merely universally valid, having a legitimate claim upon the credence of every competent observer: "The objective validity of the judgment of experience means nothing other than its necessary universal validity [*Allgemeingültigkeit*]."[3] "The sun warms the stone" is not an a priori but an empirical judgment; if it is true that the sun does warm the stone, however, then it is necessary for everyone who judges to judge that the sun does warm the stone. What makes this necessary is an a priori judgment, namely the Second Analogy of Experience, applied to observational evidence.

A like argument in the *Critique of Judgment*, however, leads Kant to say of judgments of taste that they are not merely necessary but a priori, "or are held to be such."[4] This is surely wrong, and resembles a like confusion in the first *Critique* (A 104) between the two senses of "necessary," only one of which is equivalent to "a priori." "This

Originally published as "Über die vermeintliche Apriorität der Geschmacksurteile," in *bewusst sein, Gerhard Funke zu eigen*, ed. Alexius J. Bucher, Hermann Drüe, and Thomas M. Seebohm (Bouvier Verlag Herbert Grundmann, Bonn, 1975) and translated and published with their kind permission.
1. *Prolegomena*, §18.
2. Ibid., §19.
3. Ibid., §18 (Ak. IV, 298).
4. *Critique of Judgment*, §36 (Ak. V, 289; Meredith, p. 145).

arabesque is beautiful" is no more a priori than "The sun warms the stone." What is a priori in the latter is the presupposed Analogy of Experience, in the former "the a priori principles of pure *Urteils-kraft* in aesthetic *Urteilen*."[5] What seems to have led Kant astray here is that there is an a priori relation between the judgment of beauty and the claim to universal (that is to say, necessary) validity. "It is an empirical judgment that I perceive and estimate an object with pleasure. It is, however, an apriori judgment that I find it beautiful, *that is* that I may attribute that delight to everyone as necessary."[6] The "that is" (*d.i.*) should be "therefore" (*daher*), and while the whole sentence put into hypothetical form may be a priori, the protasis is not.[7]

It would be odd, in Kant's usage certainly, to admit that an a priori judgment could be wrong. Yet unless there is some standard for assessing a judgment, that is to say, unless the judgment first is "necessary" in contrast to "arbitrary," the judgment cannot be said to be right *or* wrong. The first standard is that of *Allgemeingültigkeit* (universal validity). It is frequently said (though not by Kant)[8] that Theaetetan judgments are incorrigible because they do not make a claim that can be assessed, but they nevertheless may be false (because I can lie or make a verbal error). But an objective judgment of experience makes a claim, whether it be true or false; in fact, it makes the *same* claim whether it be true or false. The conditions of cognitive validity are independent of the truth or falsity of what is claimed.[9] Thus "The sun warms the stone" is objectively valid

5. Ibid., § 36 (Ak. V, 288; Meredith, p. 144).

6. *Critique of Judgment*, § 37 (Ak. V, 289; Meredith, p. 146).

7. If C. I. Lewis's claim (*Analysis of Knowledge and Valuation*, pp. 161–62) is sound that the Second Analogy is analytical of the "concept of objective event," it might be argued that the definition of the beautiful drawn from the Second Moment of Quantity, viz., "The *beautiful* is that which apart from a concept, pleases universally" (*Critique of Judgment*, § 19), makes even the claim by Kant in § 36 that the principles of aesthetic judgment are *synthetic* false.

8. Though he comes near doing so: the senses do not deceive, for the senses do not judge (*Critique of Pure Reason*, A 293–94 = B 350).

9. Gerold Prauss, *Erscheinung bei Kant* (Berlin, 1971), p. 86.

(makes a necessary claim upon our credence and ratification) even though it is not a priori and may, in fact, not be true.

Once we see that Kant's judgments of taste are not comparable to a priori cognitive judgments but to objective empirical cognitive judgments (= objectively valid judgments of experience), we can understand the way in which judgments of taste can be *valid but erroneous* while they could hardly be *a priori but erroneous*.

Critical disputes presuppose the distinction between judgments of agreeableness (like judgments of sensation) and judgments of taste (like judgments of experience), and the a priori ascription of validity to the latter. Disputes about them are only about whether "the correct application of the faculty of taste" has been made.[10] One who makes a judgment of taste is a "suitor for agreement from everyone else" and is "able to count on this agreement" provided the case being judged does fall under the conditions of aesthetic approval.[11] The judgment, "The arabesque is beautiful," is not and does not imply the empirical judgment, "The arabesque is liked by everyone." It does not *postulate* the agreement but *imputes* it (*sinnt nur jedermann diese Einstimmung ein*).[12] Thus "The arabesque is beautiful" is not refuted by "Mr. X does not like it." Nonetheless I may judge "That nude is beautiful," not meaning merely that I (and others) *like* it, and yet make an aesthetic error. How?

The grounds of erroneous judgments of taste are very much like those of erroneous cognitive and moral judgments, all of which are necessary (in the sense defined) and none of which (as singular judgments of specific cases) is a priori.

a. *Cognitive error* arises "from the unobserved influence of sensibility on the understanding, whereby it happens that the subjective grounds of judgment enter into union with the objective grounds and make these latter deviate from their true functions."[13]

b. *Moral error* is possible for "we cannot by any means conclude with certainty that a secret impulse of self-love falsely appearing as

10. *Critique of Judgment*, §8 (Ak. V, 214; Meredith, p. 54).
11. Ibid., §22 (Ak. V, 239; Meredith, p. 85).
12. Ibid., §8 (Ak. V, 216; Meredith, p. 55).
13. *Critique of Pure Reason*, A 295 = B 350–51.

the idea of duty was not actually the true determining ground of the will." [14]

c. *Error in taste* arises from sinning against the conditions of aesthetic validity,[15] especially the condition of the disinterestedness of the pleasure (like the disinterestedness of motive in morality). A "taint" of empirical delight is always present "where charm or emotion have a share in the judgment by which something is to be described as beautiful." [16]

14. *Foundations of the Metaphysics of Morals*, II, second paragraph.
15. *Critique of Judgment*, § 8, end.
16. Ibid., § 14 (Ak. V, 224; Meredith, p. 65).

10 Kant and the Right of Revolution

Kant's enthusiasm for the French Revolution, the American Revolution, and the Irish efforts to throw off the English yoke is well known. It earned him the unenviable epithet of "the old Jacobin"; though he condemned the excesses of the Reign of Terror and the execution of the King and Queen, these events which turned many of his compatriots against the Revolution and all its works did not make Kant modify his adherence to the principles of the Revolution; and it was even believed that he was to go to Paris as advisor to Sieyès.[1]

When, therefore, in 1793 he sent his essay, *On the Saying: "That may be true in theory but it does not hold in practice,"* to the *Berlinische Monatsschrift*, the editor wrote him with obvious relief: "To speak quite openly, it pleased me all the more since it refuted the rumor (which I had suspected from the start) that you had come out in favor of the ever increasingly repulsive French Revolution, in which the actual freedom of reason and morality and all wisdom in statecraft and legislation are being most shamefully trampled under foot."[2] For this essay of Kant's denies the right of revolution, when

A slightly revised version of a paper presented at a symposium on "Kant on Revolution" held at Temple University, December 5, 1969. I am grateful to my fellow symposiasts, Professors Sidney Axinn, Charles Dyke, and John E. Atwell, for criticisms; also to Professors Jeffrie G. Murphy and John B. Christopher for comments on an earlier draft. Reprinted from *The Journal of the History of Ideas* 32 (1971), 411–22, by kind permission of the editor, Professor Philip P. Wiener.

1. An account of this rumor will be found in G. P. Gooch, *Germany and the French Revolution* (London, 1920), pp. 276–77.

2. Biester to Kant, Oct. 5, 1792 (Ak. XI, 456; Zweig, *Correspondence*, pp. 208–09).

the editor had reason to believe that Kant would defend it. But what was a relief to Biester, the editor, has been a paradox to others.

How could a man of Kant's probity sympathize with revolutionists and yet deny the right and justification of revolution? I say a man of Kant's probity; for it has been suggested that Kant's condemnation of revolution in his published works was deceptive, a sop to the censor. Of course we cannot disprove this accusation; but while it is not improbable that Kant was intimidated by the censor, I find it incredible, for Kant's actual response to the censor in 1792 was silence, not deception. In 1766, he had written to Moses Mendelssohn, "Although I am absolutely convinced of many things that I shall never have the courage to say, I shall never say anything I do not believe."[3] I think that was a true in the 1790s as in the 1760s; and therefore, I must try to find some other way to explain the apparent inconsistency in Kant's attitudes.

We can understand Biester's delighted surprise in finding in Kant's essay a denial of the right of revolution. Not only had Kant's reputation as a Jacobin spread to Berlin, but also in his *Idea for a Universal History* published nine years earlier, even before the French Revolution, Kant had spoken the hope that "after many reformative revolutions, a universal cosmopolitical condition . . . will come into being."[4] In fact, one might almost suppose that the conclusion of *Theory and Practice* came as a surprise to Kant himself; for in unpublished notes we find Kant writing that resistance to government may be justified provided some constitutional provision is made—as he believed it was made in England[5]—under which there can be a formal legal finding that the original contract has been broken by

3. Letter to Mendelssohn, April 8, 1766 (Ak. X, 69; Zweig, *Correspondence*, p. 54).

4. Ak. VIII, 28; *Kant on History*, ed. L. W. Beck (Indianapolis, 1963), p. 23. The words translated "reformative revolutions" (*Revolutionen der Umbildung*) do not suggest (as the English words may) that these revolutions were to be bloodless.

5. Reflexionen 8043, 8044; Ak. XIX, 590, 591. But popular violence (*turbas*) is forbidden. In *Über den Gemeinspruch: Das mag in der Theorie richtig sein, taugt aber nicht für die Praxis* (Ak. VIII, 303; *On the Old Saw: That May Be Right in Theory but It Won't Work in Practice*, trans. E. B.

the monarch; and even without such a constitutional provision he
held in certain cases that revolution is justified:

> Force, which does not presuppose a judgment having the validity
> of law [*rechtskräftig Urtheil*] is against the law consequently [the
> people] cannot rebel except in the cases which cannot at all come
> forward in a civil union, e.g., the enforcement of a religion, com-
> pulsion to unnatural sins, assassination, etc., etc.[6]

—and the etceteration is Kant's own. Given what we know of Kant's
theory of natural law and of the justification of positive law by
reference to it—a theory as susceptible to a Lockean as to a Hobbesian development—it is easy to suppose that Kant could have asserted
the right of resistance to a tyrannical government which denied
autonomy to the legislation of the citizens. In fact, one of his
disciples, August Wilhelm Rehberg, in the following issue of the
Berlinische Monatsschrift, replied to Kant and drew precisely this
conclusion from Kantian premises:

> If a system of *a priori* demonstrated positive specifications of
> natural law is applied to the world of men, nothing less than a
> complete dissolution of present civil constitutions would follow.
> For according to such a system, only that constitution is valid
> which accords with the determination of the ideal of reason. In
> this case, no one of the existing constitutions could stand. . . . If
> these constitutions contradict . . . the first requirements of a
> rational constitution, the human race is not only permitted, it is
> required, to destroy these constitutions which are opposed to the

---

Ashton [University of Pennsylvania Press, 1974], p. 71), he approves of the
silence of the "contractual arrangement" made in 1688 with respect to the
right to overthrow a monarch who does not fulfill it.

6. Reflexion 8051; Ak. XIX, 594–95. The passages cited by H. S. Reiss
("Kant and the Right of Rebellion," *Journal of the History of Ideas* 17
[1956], 190–91) as evidence that Kant justified seeking to overthrow government under the saying, "We ought to obey God rather than men" (*Religion
innerhalb der Grenzen der blossen Vernunft*, Ak. VI, 99 n.; trans. Greene and
Hudson, p. 90 n.) do not seem to me to go beyond the justification of passive
disobedience, and not even to go that far when the politico-civil law does not
command anything "in itself evil."

original moral law. The form of the constitution of the state is a matter of indifference, so long as complete equality is established; but to establish this, everything else must be sacrificed.—Thus the theory of revolution is a necessary consequence of the physiocratic system.[7]

Kant spurned Rehberg's essay (without specifically mentioning the putative deduction of the right of rebellion),[8] and his tentative justification of the Glorious Revolution of 1688 remained hidden in his notes. In his published works, there is only one halfhearted commendation for revolution (cited above) and one passage (later than the contribution to Biester's journal) which excuses, if it does not justify, revolution. It occurs in the *Rechtslehre*, where Kant speaks of a people's having "at least some excuse for forcibly [dethroning a monarch] by appealing to the right of necessity [which knows no law]."[9] But otherwise Kant's denial of the right of revolution is as firm and clear as his express sympathy for the French Revolution.

I shall proceed to examine this paradox as follows. I shall first state Kant's jurisprudential objections to the right to revolt; next I shall give a brief summary of those parts of his political theory which provide a context for his understanding of the events of 1789; then I shall discuss the non-jurisprudential ground of his sympathy with the Revolution. In conclusion, I shall draw some comparisons between his views and those of Hegel.

1. Kant's argument against the right of revolution is brief to the point of lucidity. By virtue of the ideal of the social contract, sovereignty is indivisible. A constitution cannot have within it a positive law permitting the abrogation of the constitution; there is a contradiction in the conception of a publicly constituted *Gegenmacht*.[10]

7. *Über das Verhältnis der Theorie zur Praxis* (1793), in *Über Theorie und Praxis*, ed. Dieter Henrich (Suhrkamp, 1967), p. 128.

8. Letter to Biester, April 10, 1794 (Ak. XI, 496–97; not in Zweig).

9. *Rechtslehre* (Part I of *Metaphysik der Sitten*), Ak. VI, 321 n.; cf. 236; *Metaphysical Elements of Justice*, trans. John Ladd (Indianapolis, 1965), p. 87 n.; cf. p. 42.

10. *Über den Gemeinspruch*, Ak. VIII, 303 (Ashton, p. 71).

The constitution cannot contain any article that would allow for some authority in the state that could resist or restrain the chief magistrate in cases in which he violates the constitutional laws. For he who is supposed to restrain the authority of the state must have more power than, or at least as much power as, the person whom he is supposed to restrain ...; in other words, he must be able to command the resistance publicly. But then the latter would be the chief magistrate, not the former; and this supposition contradicts itself.[11]

To permit any opposition to this absolute power (an opposition that might limit that supreme authority) would be to contradict oneself, inasmuch as in that case the power (which may be opposed) would not be the lawful supreme authority that determines what is or is not to be publicly just.[12]

In this argument, we see Kant's formalism *in extremis*. There cannot be a law which permits lawlessness, nor an institution of power that provides for its own forcible dissolution.

It seems to me that no one should be unduly shocked by Kant's argument; and if one is not convinced, it is because one objects to the narrowness of Kant's base, not to the stringency of his proof erected upon it. The revolutionist does not appeal to the terms of the constitution for justification of his efforts to overturn the constitution; at most he appeals to the constitution for reform of administrative practices, or perhaps to the preamble of the constitution with its adumbration of natural, not positive, law as a basis for criticism of the positive law and the constitution which he rejects. In the *Rechtslehre*, which is concerned with the a priori foundation of civil society, Kant could have drawn no other conclusion. Revolution abrogates positive law; therefore positive law and its system condemn revolution. Revolution means a return to nature, which the contract establishing positive law renounces.[13]

11. *Rechtslehre*, Ak. VI, 319 (Ladd, p. 85).
12. Ibid., Ak. VI, 372 (Ladd, pp. 140–41).
13. Ibid., Ak. VI, 355 (Ladd, p. 129).

Up to this point it may appear that Kant is making a point of boring obviousness, namely, that there can be no *legal* right of revolution. Revolution by its very nature is a denial that established legal and constitutional claims are indefeasible; and to tell a revolutionary that he should desist from his revolutionary activity because he is breaking a law would be met with derision.

In *Perpetual Peace*, however, there is another criticism of the putative right of revolution, a criticism which is more deeply rooted in Kant's moral philosophy than in his metaphysics of jurisprudence. The previous argument is, as it were, a legalistic consequence of the categorical imperative in the form which forbids us from acting on maxims which are self-contradictory when universalized. The new argument is derived from the form of the categorical imperative which requires us to treat human beings as end-setting ends in themselves, and it leads to what Kant calls the "transcendental formula of public law": "All actions relating to the right of other men are unjust if their maxim is not consistent with publicity." "The illegitimacy of rebellion," he infers, "is thus clear from the fact that its maxim, if openly acknowledged, would make its own purpose impossible. Therefore [the maxim to revolt on occasion] would have to be kept secret"[14] in order to be effective, and is therefore illegitimate. The maxim to put down revolution, however, passes this test and is likely to be most effective when given the widest publicity.

In place of revolution, Kant favors evolution. The evolution of the state to a more just form and administration, Kant believes, is inevitable only if there is public enlightenment and freedom of the press. The free press is the palladium of human rights.[15] It permits the reform of the state by apprising the rulers of the dissatisfactions of the subjects, and it is to the interests of the rulers themselves that these dissatisfactions be removed, since an irrational legislation—one decided for the people in a way in which the people would not decide for themselves[16] —makes for instability in the government

14. *Zum ewigen Frieden*, Ak. VIII, 381; in *Kant on History*, pp. 129–30.
15. *Über den Gemeinspruch*, Ak. VIII, 304 (Ashton, p. 72).
16. *Rechtslehre*, Ak. VI, 327 (Ladd, p. 95).

and insecurity of the rulers. Reform can be effected only by the sovereign,[17] but it can be undertaken by him with wisdom only if he is made aware of the inequities and inadequacies of his administration.

Until this reform is effected, however, the people must obey. For to disobey is to return to the state of nature and to leave it to chance, or providence, whether the new government yet to be established will be better or worse than the one which is overthrown. Reform means progress, the metamorphosis of the state; revolution means palingenesis[18] of the state, a new beginning of civil society from the state of nature without profit from the steps previously taken on the path away from the state of nature.

That a government may have been established by an act of lawless violence does not impugn its legal authority and validity, nor reduce its claim to allegiance. Kant is willing to believe that all governments began with power, not with contract. But to inquire into the historical origin of a government for the purpose of thereby impugning its authority is itself punishable.[19] This principle of the irrelevancy of historical origin to judicial validity is used to legitimize the government which is, in point of historical fact, established as a result of insurrection.[20] The new government cannot legitimately punish the fallen ruler, since he could, under the previous constitution, have done no (punishable) wrong.[21]

2. I turn now to Kant's theory of government, in which the doctrine of the separation of powers is the most basic principle.

The sovereign (*Beherrscher*) or lawgiver of a people (the head of the state) derives his rightful authority from the united people under the contract.[22] It is as though he held his legislative authority from the perfect lawgiver, God.[23] But his actual authority is in all prob-

---

17. Ibid., Ak. VI, 321–22 (Ladd, p. 88).
18. Ibid., Ak. VI, 339–40 (Ladd, p. 111).
19. Ibid., Ak. VI, 319, 339–40, 372 (Ladd, pp. 84, 11, 140).
20. Ibid., Ak. VI, 323 (Ladd, p. 89).
21. Ibid., Ak. VI, 317, 341 (Ladd, pp. 82, 113–14).
22. Ibid., Ak. VI, 315 (Ladd, p. 80).
23. Ibid., Ak. VI, 319 (Ladd, pp. 84–85).

ability based upon his power, with only a *post facto* justification of it by the ideal of the contract. The sovereign has rights with respect to the subject, but no coercive duties.[24] Hence the sovereign can do no wrong[25] in the sense that nothing he does is punishable: "There is no right of sedition, much less a right of revolution, and least of all a right to lay hands on or to take the life of the chief of state."[26]

The head of the government (*Regent*) is the agent of the sovereign. His commands are not laws but only ordinances and decrees.[27] He is obligated to the sovereign and subject to the laws given by the sovereign. His decrees must be obeyed by the subjects, and even if he proceeds contrary to the law, the citizens must not actively resist him except by exercising their freedom to criticize and petition for reform.[28] But the head of the government may be deposed by the sovereign and the sovereign may modify his administration.[29]

Various abortive forms of government arise when the legislative, judicial, and executive functions of government are confused or lodged in the same moral or physical person. If the same person both makes and executes the laws—if, that is, the sovereign is himself the head of the government or the supreme judge—the system of checks and balances is not in effect, and the government is despotic.[30] A government may be monarchical in form while republican in spirit if the sovereignty resides in the united people, and the person of the sovereign represents the interests and rights of the people.

The ultimate agency of legitimate reform in the government lies in the person of the sovereign, as we have seen; but there are limits even on his right to change the constitution. The sovereign, for example, cannot validly arrange a transformation of one constitution to another (for example, from an aristocracy to a democracy), for these are matters for only the collective will of the people to decide.

24. Ibid., Ak. VI, 319, cf. 241 (Ladd, p. 85, cf. p. 47).
25. Ibid., Ak. VI, 317 (Ladd, p. 82).
26. Ibid., Ak. VI, 320 (Ladd, p. 86).
27. Ibid., Ak. VI, 317 (Ladd, p. 82).
28. Ibid., Ak. VI, 319 (Ladd, p. 85).
29. Ibid., Ak. VI, 317, 321–22 (Ladd, pp. 82, 88).
30. Ibid., Ak. VI, 317, 319 (Ladd, pp. 82, 85).

"Even if the sovereign were to decide to transform himself into a democracy," Kant writes, "he would be doing the people an injustice, because the people themselves might abhor this kind of constitution and might find that one of the other two was more advantageous to them." [31]

When the chief of state allows himself to be represented in a body of deputies of the people, sovereignty *ipso facto* reverts to the collective people; the surrender of sovereignty by the person of the monarch has already occurred, [32] and it cannot be regained at the end of some specified time unless it is freely granted by the body of the people or their deputies. This event, according to Kant, took place on May 5, 1789, when "the sovereignty of the monarch disappeared completely . . . and passed over to the people, to whose legislative will the property of every citizen now became subject." What was not justified was, first, the surrender of his sovereignty by Louis XVI to the Estates General; and, second, the execution of the former monarch—an act which "fills the soul, conscious of the ideas of human justice, with horror." [33]

But the success of the Revolution, in spite of the illegitimacy of its beginning and the crimes which marked its effectuation, "binds the subjects to accept the new order of things as good citizens, and they

31. Ibid., Ak. VI, 340 (Ladd, p. 113).
32. Ibid., Ak. VI, 341 (Ladd, p. 113). The King had plenty of warning against convoking the Estates General, with such admonitions as "Un roi qui subit une Constitution se croit dégradé: un Roi qui propose une Constitution obtient la plus belle gloire qui soit parmi les hommes . . . ." and besides "It is illegal!" (see Jean Egret, *La Pré-révolution française* [Paris, 1961], p. 322, and George Lefebvre, *The Coming of the French Revolution* [New York, 1959], p. 27). But the notion that it was radically "unconstitutional" (like an act of revolution itself) seems to be original with Kant. More study of the polemical literature of the time, however, might reveal earlier sources for this singular idea.
33. *Rechtslehre*, Ak. VI, 321 n. (Ladd, p. 87 n.). There is, however, an inconsistency in Kant's comparing the execution of Louis XVI to an act of state suicide, since it follows from his thesis that Louis was no longer sovereign. He suffered injustice, to be sure, and one can sympathize with Kant's abhorrence of this act without putting it into a special class "more heinous than murder itself," inexplicable except as "the pure Idea of extreme perversity" (Ak. 322 n.; Ladd, p. 88 n.).

cannot refuse to honor and obey the suzerain (*Obrigkeit*) who now possesses authority." [34]

Kant's fervid denial of the right of revolution, therefore, is historically focused not against the Estates General and the successor government, but upon the efforts at counterrevolution and restoration of the Bourbons. Thus he specifically denounces the right claimed by other sovereigns to intervene in French affairs so as to undo the Revolution. [35]

Our exposition has perhaps let it appear that Kant's formalism—the notion that a legal right to rebel is self-contradictory and a moral right to rebel is unjustifiable—makes him oppose all revolutions yet to come, while precisely the same formalism permits him to accept all successful revolutions of the past, especially those of 1688, 1776, and 1789. His enthusiasm for these revolutions, especially that of 1789, is made compatible with his denial of the right of revolution, for "revolution" now means "Restoration." This, however, would seem to me to be time-serving dishonesty which one would not willingly attribute to Kant if a more ingenuous resolution of the original paradox is possible.

But even if one hesitates to apply to Kant the maxim that what matters is "whose ox is being gored," there is a sophistic legalism in his theory of a non-juridical transfer of sovereignty from Louis XVI to the Estates General. He seems to be exculpating the Estates from the charge of rebellion, saying rather that they discharged the duty that legally devolved upon them to "reform" the government. This outcome, to be sure, removes the paradox with which I began this paper: Kant disapproved of revolutions, but what was called the French Revolution was not really a revolution or, if it was a revolution, the only revolutionary was Louis XVI! [36] Surely, however, this is explaining away one paradox by means of a greater one.

3. To remove the paradox requires us to consider things not from a moralistic or legalistic point of view, which is perhaps the one most

---

34. Ibid., Ak. VI, 323 (Ladd, p. 89).
35. *Zum ewigen Frieden*, Ak. VIII, 346 (*Kant On History*, p. 89).
36. Cf. Dieter Henrich, "Einleitung," *Theorie und Praxis*, p. 32.

natural to Kant, but from the standpoint of his teleological conception of history. For from this point of view alone can Kant justify comparing a state before and after a revolution and thus pronounce a moral judgment on a revolution unjustified a priori on grounds of positive law and on the natural law that authority must be obeyed.

In so doing, however, Kant cannot, without being unfaithful to his moral principles, appeal to a utilitarian justification for a revolution. And he does not do so;[37] whether a people is happier before or after a revolution is as irrelevant from the standpoint of the judgment of the philosophy of history as it is from the standpoint of positive or moral law. Progress in history is not measured by the happiness of the people but by the formal criterion of the rule of law and the scope of juridical freedom.

The perfect civic constitution, Kant holds, is republican, for it alone derives from the idea of the original compact which is the norm, if not the historical genesis, of all government:

> The republican constitution is the only enduring political constitution in which the law is autonomous and is not annexed to any particular person. It is the ultimate end of all public law and the only condition under which each person receives his due peremptorily. . . . [Under any other form of government] it must be recognized that only a provisory internal justice and no absolutely juridical state of civil society can exist.[38]

> The republican constitution is with respect to the law the one which is the original basis of every form of civil constitution.[39]

Thus Kant can distinguish between revolutions toward the better and revolutions toward the worse, though *qua* revolution both are to be condemned. Since revolution produces an *interregnum* which is equivalent to the state of nature, revolutions probably have a tendency to end in a worse government than the government which could have been achieved by gradual reform. Political wisdom, there-

37. *Rechtslehre*, Ak. VI, 318 (Ladd, p. 83).
38. Ibid., Ak. VI, 341 (Ladd, pp. 112–13).
39. *Zum ewigen Frieden*, Ak. VIII, 350 (*Kant on History*, p. 94).

fore, stands on the side of reform to make the constitution better accord with the ideal of law; but "when nature herself produces revolutions," political wisdom will use them "as a call of nature for fundamental reforms to produce a lawful constitution founded upon principles of freedom, for only such a constitution is durable."[40]

When nature herself produces revolutions ... ! The *Idea for a Universal History* is like a theodicy, asking "Is is reasonable to assume a purposiveness in all the parts of nature and to deny it to the whole?"[41] Kant answers: "The history of mankind can be seen, in the large, as the realization of Nature's secret plan to bring forth a perfectly constituted state."[42] The unsocial sociability of mankind, the competition among tribes and states which leads to war, and revolutions—all of which are judged, juridically and moralistically, to be evil—are the means nature uses in realizing her "secret plan" for mankind.

That the French Revolution is to be understood at least by analogy to natural teleology is made clear in the *Critique of Judgment*. The organization of nature, Kant tells us, has nothing analogous to any causality known to us, but it throws light on "a complete transformation, recently undertaken, of a great people into a state" where

the word "organization" has frequently, and with much propriety, been used for the constitution of the legal authorities and even of the entire body politic. For in a whole of this kind certainly no member should be a mere means, but should also be an end, and, seeing that he contributes to the possibility of the entire body, should have his position and function in turn defined by the idea of the whole.[43]

40. Ibid., Ak. VIII, 373 n. (*Kant on History*, p. 120 n.).
41. *Idee zu einer allgemeinen Geschichte in weltbürgerlicher Absicht*, Ak. VIII, 25 (*Kant on History*, p. 20).
42. Ibid., Ak. VIII, 27 (*Kant on History*, p. 21).
43. *Critique of Judgment*, Ak. V, 375 n. (*Critique of Teleological Judgment*, trans. J. C. Meredith [Oxford, 1952], p. 23 n.).

But the French Revolution is not to be understood only by analogy to natural teleology; it has a distinctively moral dimension too. In the *Strife of the Faculties*, Kant draws a moral conclusion from the French Revolution. The passionate participation in the good, namely, the disinterested enthusiasm with which the Revolution was greeted, could have no other cause, Kant thinks, than a moral predisposition in the human race to seek what is ideal and purely moral.[44] It gives hope and evidence of the moral progress of mankind. The participants in the Revolution, of course, were not morally disinterested; but the impartial spectators approved, and "such a phenomenon in human history"—Kant is not now speaking of the Revolution, but of the moral enthusiasm it engendered—"*is not to be forgotten*, for it revealed a tendency and faculty in human nature for improvement such as no politician, affecting wisdom, might have conjured out of the course of things hitherto existing, and one which nature and freedom alone, united in the human race in conformity with inner principles of right, could have promised."[45]

4. Kant does not have a categorial scheme adequate to take account of the juxtaposition of the illegality and immorality of a man who makes a revolution and what might be called his higher morality when, through revolutionary activity, he establishes a better stage of political culture as a basis for further moral development. He does not accept the doing of evil that good may result. He does not do so in part because his political ethics reduces to the maxim of my station and its duties except insofar as complaining and striving to reform a government are imprescriptible rights; and in part because his conception of natural law is static.[46] Not only is it static; it is in fact inconsistent, for it includes both the teleology of

44. *Der Streit der Fakultäten*, Ak. VII, 85–86 (*Kant on History*, pp. 144–45).

45. Ibid., Ak. VII, 88 (*Kant on History*, p. 147).

46. Not natural law, of course, in the sense that the study of empirical nature gives rise to it; it is a law of reason. But it functions in the same way as natural law, as a norm and warrant for positive law. See Leonard Krieger, "Kant and the Crisis in Natural Law," *Journal of the History of Ideas* 26 (1965), 191–210, esp. 201, 207.

seeking to bring about the rule of law under a republican constitution (which may, in fact, require not merely efforts at reform but actual violence[47]) and a formalism of obedience to the powers that be. The duty we have to contribute to the progress of mankind is a duty of imperfect obligation, is unenforceable, and leaves elbow-room for its realization. The latter, the duty we have to fulfill the requirements of the established law, is a duty of strict or perfect obligation, and is thus for Kant prior in its claims to the former.[48] As consequences of this priority of duties of perfect over duties of imperfect obligation are those famous cases which have served for generations as a *reductio ad absurdum* of Kantian ethics, for example, the denial of the right to lie in order to save the life of an innocent man. A like consequence is here drawn in Kant's political philosophy. We are to work toward the end of the improvement of mankind by striving to secure a political stage on which the rights of man will be respected and war will be abolished. But in so doing, we are not to overthrow by violence even a tyrannical government which blatantly traduces these rights. for to do this would conflict with a duty of perfect obligation. We are not, therefore, justified in killing a tyrant in order to preserve the lives of thousands or millions of his subjects. The most I can morally do is to expose the abuses of his power and make proposals for his reform, to disobey him if he commands me to do something immoral and to suffer martyrdom if necessary.[49]

A conception of natural law which is evolutionary can profit from an understanding of the inconsistency into which Kant falls in condemning revolution while holding that the enthusiasm for the French Revolution sprang from a moral disposition in mankind. The

47. As certainly the first step from a state of natural savagery to civil society required the exercise of a natural right to violence: "Everyone may use violent means to compel another to enter into a juridical state of society" (*Rechtslehre*, Ak. VI, 312; Ladd, pp. 76–77).

48. *Zum ewigen Frieden*, Ak. VII, 377 (*Kant on History*, p. 124).

49. *Critique of Practical Reason*, Ak. V, 155–56 (trans. L. W. Beck [New York, 1956], 159 f.), on the effort of Henry VIII to suborn a witness against Ann Boleyn.

moral aspirations of mankind are not satisfied by punctilious obedience to the powers that be; they demand that the powers that be should earn our respectful obedience, and they sometimes justify the disobedience to the positive law out of obedience to a "higher law." Both obligations are rational and natural, and it takes deep moral and historical insight to adjudicate their conflict, and this adjudication need not and does not always lead to the same decision. An evolutionary view of morality and of the law of nature draws a distinction between the morality of stable societies, which is necessary to maintain or to gradually improve the status quo, and the historical demands which abrogate static laws and institutions when they fall significantly below the level of moral aspiration; but no rules can be given for this adjudication which will decree an all-or-none answer in periods threatened by, or promised, radical changes.

The agents whose acts are directed against the stable moral order are, descriptively, criminals; but they may be, in Hegel's terms, men whose "words and deeds are the best of the age."[50] If they succeed, their words and ideas will be the ruling words and ideas of the new moral community they will produce—and if they fail, they will (rightly) be hanged as common criminals against the stable ethical order.

Such an evolutionary conception—an evolutionary conception which is meant to justify revolution, if that is what is required for progress—is found in Hegel's dialectic of private morals (*Moralität*), public ethics (*Sittlichkeit*), and the egotism of world-historical individuals whose crimes against the first two are converted, by the cunning of world-reason, into quantum jumps in the moral progress of the community or state:

> The basis of duty is the civil life: the individuals have their assigned business and hence their assigned duties. Their morality consists in acting accordingly. . . . But each individual is also the child of a people at a definite state of its development. . . . A

50. *Die Vernunft in der Geschichte (Einleitung in die Philosophie der Weltgeschichte), Sämmtliche Werke*, ed. G. Lasson (Leipzig, 1930), VIII, 76 (*Reason in History*, trans. R. S. Hartman [Indianapolis, 1953], p. 40).

moral whole [a specific moral community], as such, is limited. It must have above it a higher universality, which makes it disunited with itself. The transition from one spiritual pattern to the next is just this, that the former moral whole is abolished. . . . It is at this point that appear those momentous collisions between existing acknowledged duties, laws, and rights, and those possibilities which are adverse to this system, violate it, and even destroy its foundations and existence. . . . These possibilites now become historical fact; they involve a universal of an order different from that upon which the permanence of a people or a state depends. This universal is an essential phase in the development of the creating Idea, of truth striving and urging towards itself.[51]

Thus arises the conflict between the morally good man who fulfills the duty of his station and the man who breaks down that system—the "world-historical individual" who is impudently judged to be immoral by schoolmasters and valets, "those exquisite discerners of spirits."

But the history of the world moves on a higher level than that proper to morality. . . . Those who, through moral steadfastness and noble sentiment, have resisted the necessary progress of the Spirit stand higher in moral value than those whose crimes have been turned by a higher order into means of carrying on the will behind this order. . . . They stand outside morality. The litany of the private virtues of modesty, humility, love, and charity must not be raised against them. [52]

This is a teleological suspension of the ethical, to adapt Kierkegaard's terminology to a new use.

51. Ibid., 73–75 (Hartman [slightly modified], pp. 38–39). No inferences must be drawn, of course, from this passage concerning Hegel's own view of the right of revolution and, specifically, the French Revolution; much else entered into his judgment on these questions. I have dealt with this topic in detail in "The Reformation, the Revolution, and the Restoration in Hegel's Political Philosophy," *Journal of the History of Philosophy* 14 (1976), 51–61.
52. Ibid., 153, 154 (Hartman, p. 82; trans. slightly modified).

Kant's enthusiasm for the French Revolution is based upon his teleological conception of history, which is a forerunner of Hegel's definition of history as "the progress of the consciousness of freedom." That the final purpose of the world is moral, not eudaemonistic, makes it possible for Kant to have a moral enthusiasm for the Revolution which his formalistic moral system does not justify. Had Kant's approval of the Revolution been eudaemonistic, the inconsistency would have been greater. But some inconsistency remains because Kantian ethics is not adequate to resolve the painful problems of conflicting duties. [53]

53. He even denies that conflicts of duties exist. *Metaphysik der Sitten, Einleitung*, Ak. VI, 224 (Ladd, p. 25).

11 Kant on Education

Kant as Educator

Kant is one of the few philosophers to have both written on education and had actual experience as an educator, experience that was had by neither Locke nor Rousseau. Kant's experience as an educator can be summarized under four headings: his work as a house tutor, his work as a propagandist and money-raiser for the Dessau Philanthropin, his career as a university professor, and his lectures on pedagogy to university students.

1. From 1749 to 1754 (the dates are only approximate, but probably not wrong by more than a year) Kant was *Hauslehrer* in two or three families near Königsberg. From 1749 to 1750 or 51 he instructed the children of Pastor Andersch in Judtschen, from 1751 to 1754 those of Major von Hülsen in Arnsdorf, and perhaps in 1754–55 those of Graf Keyserling in Rautenburg. We know little of these years, since there is only one letter extant that has any bearing on his tutorial duties, and it is only a brief letter of courtesy accompanying a gift of some books to the boys in the Hülsen family. Years later Kant said, "there probably never was a worse tutor than I,"[1] but he must have been satisfactory, for later he was consulted by

This paper is based on two lectures, one given at McMaster University, February 16, 1977, and the other at the University of Tübingen, October 19, 1977. Professor Paul Fritz, who will edit the McMaster symposium papers in a volume to be published in 1978, has kindly given permission to pre-print material which will be in his book.

1. H. Jachmann, *Immanuel Kant geschildert in Briefen an einen Freund*, second letter, second paragraph.

one of his former pupils about the appointment of a tutor to his children; and it is well known that he long continued social relations with the von Keyserling family; the earliest portrait of Kant was painted by the Gräfin von Keyserling, and the Keyserling boys when they came to the University were placed in his care. We do not know what benefits the children gained from Kant's lessons; we can be more confident that Kant learned much from the social intercourse he had with the noble families with which he lived. Kant had been brought up in very straitened financial circumstances and an inelegant social milieu; when he returned to Königsberg about 1755 he was apparently fluent in French, polished in the artificiality of aristocratic conversation, something of a dandy in dress and comportment, and the "galant master" as he was known in the University. How good a tutor to the children Kant was I do not know, but he was an apt pupil of their parents.

2. Johann Bernard Basedow was deeply influenced by Rousseau but in personality as ill adapted as Rousseau for the practical work of being a school administrator (Herder said of him that not only children, but cattle, should not be entrusted to his care).[2] Through his earlier writings and then through the curriculum he instituted Basedow attempted to realize Rousseau's teaching. Teaching was to be through dialogue and play; emphasis was to be displaced from exercising memory to exercising observation and thinking; French and Latin were to be taught by actual use in conversation; character development and mechanical skills were emphasized, and moral education was to be independent of religious instruction though the child was to be brought gradually to recognize the truths of natural religion. Each teacher was encouraged to experiment and to develop his own program and technique of teaching. Basedow's writings on educational reform, subsidized by enlightened despots like Joseph II of Austria and Catherine the Great of Russia, had attracted wide attention, and in 1774 with a grant from Prince Leopold of Dessau (to whom he had been introduced by Goethe) he established his

2. Goethe's sketch of Basedow's character (*Dichtung und Wahrheit*, Box XIV) is unlikely to inspire more confidence in him.

school in Dessau. Two years later, in May 1776, there was a public exhibition through performances by the pupils and public examinations to which many of the leading people of Germany were invited, and attention to the school was attracted throughout Germany. Unfortunately there were more visitors than pupils, for Basedow had succeeding in getting only thirteen children, two of whom were his own. Basedow was removed and was followed by Wolke and Campe, who were more competent administrators.

Kant became an enthusiastic backer of the Philanthropin in 1776. Basedow published an account of his school addressed to parents who wished to send their children to it, and Kant reviewed it in the Königsberg newspaper March 28, 1776.[3] "To every community, to every citizen of the world," he wrote, "it is important to learn about a new institution whereby a wholly new order of human affairs is to be brought about which will produce a wide reform both in private and social life." To help the school Kant volunteered to receive subscriptions to later numbers of the *Philanthropinisches Archiv*. A year later he reviewed the second volume of the reports on the Philanthropin, saying that what was needed was not a gradual reform but a sudden revolution in education, and that for this was required "only one school based on the genuine method of education, guided by enlightened men who will show the learned world what they can do, and who will teach students to follow the same method later in their own schools."[4] Again he urged parents to subscribe by sending their money to him.

On the same day that the first of these reviews was published, Kant wrote to Wolke recommending George Motherby, the six-year-old son of his friend Motherby, describing how perfectly the Philanthropin fitted the educational ideals he and the elder George Motherby held in common;[5] a short time later he wrote Basedow[6] saying that Motherby thought every day lost that his son was not in the Philanthropin, and was about to leave Königsberg to bring him

---

3. *Aufsätze, das Philanthropin betreffend.* Ak. II, 446–52.
4. Ibid., 446, 448 (Ak. X, 191).
5. Letter to Wolke, March 28, 1776 (Ak. X, 194).
6. Letter to Basedow, June 19, 1776 (Ak. X, 234–35).

to Dessau. In 1777 there are many letters concerning the business of raising money for the school, one of which[7] shows, in the words of Kant's biographer Vorländer,[8] almost jesuitical cunning (*beinahe jesuitische Schlauheit*) in Kant's successful efforts to flatter an influential local minister (Crichton), who had been critical of the Philanthropin, into taking over the money-raising effort.

All of Kant's efforts except this last were in vain; the school recovered for a while under new management, but finally closed in 1794. Kant wrote of its demise:

> People imagine, indeed, that experiments in education are unnecessary, and that we can judge by our reason whether anything is good or not. This is a great mistake, and experience teaches us that the results of an experiment are often entirely different from what we expected. Thus we see that, since we must be guided by experiments, no one generation can set forth a complete scheme of education. The only experimental school which had in a measure made a beginning to clear the way was the Dessau Institute. This must be said in its praise, in spite of the many mistakes with which we might reproach it—mistakes which attend all conclusions from experiments—namely, that still more experiments are required. This school was in a certain way the only one in which teachers were free to work out their own methods and plans, and in which teachers were in communication with each other and with all the learned men in Germany.[9]

3. Kant had more experience than any of us have had in the practice of education as a university teacher. For forty-three years, without a sabbatical break, he lectured and held exercises for his students (disputatoria and repetitoria) in an appalling variety of fields including logic, metaphysics, ethics, anthropology, physical

---

7. Letter to Wilhelm Crichton, July 19, 1778.
8. Karl Vorländer, *Immanuel Kant, der Mann und das Werk*, I, 225.
9. *Education* (University of Michigan Press, 1960), pp. 22–23. All subsequent references in the text which cite only a page number are to this edition. For reasons that will become obvious, however, when I have occasion to refer to this book by title I shall call it by its more accurate name, *Pedagogy*.

geography, physics, natural theology, pedagogy, and fortification engineering. His normal teaching load was fourteen hours a week, and he began lecturing at seven o'clock in the morning. His lectures were famous in the University and even brought students from foreign countries to hear them. Johann Gottfried Herder, a student of his in 1762 who later became embittered against him, nevertheless vividly remembered the lectures he had heard:

I have had the good fortune to know a philosopher. He was my teacher. In his prime he had the happy sprightliness of a youth; he continued to have it, I believe, even as a very old man. His broad forehead, built for thinking, was the seat of an imperturbable cheerfulness and joy. Speech, the richest in thought, flowed from his lips. Playfulness, wit, and humor were at his command. His lectures were the most entertaining talks. His mind, which examined Leibniz, Wolff, Baumgarten, Crusius, and Hume, and investigated the laws of nature of Newton, Kepler, and the physicists, comprehended equally the newest works of Rousseau . . . and the latest discoveries in science. He weighed them all, and always came back to the unbiased knowledge of nature and to the moral worth of man. The history of men and peoples, natural history and science, mathematics and observation, were the sources from which he enlivened his lectures and conversation. He was indifferent to nothing worth knowing. No cabal, no sect, no prejudice, no desire for fame could ever tempt him in the slightest away from broadening and illuminating the truth. He incited and gently forced others to think for themselves; despotism was foreign to his mind. This man, whom I name with the greatest gratitude and respect, was Immanuel Kant. [10]

4. I turn now to Kant's activities as a teacher of education. In English-speaking countries the normal source of information on Kant's views on education is a small book entitled *Education* published by the University of Michigan Press from an earlier and undated translation by Annette Churton. There is, in this miserable

10. Quoted from my edition of Kant's *Prolegomena* (Liberal Arts Press, 1951), p. xxii.

volume, no word of identification or explanation, no indication of its provenance. We are not told what it is a translation of, and the added notes are mostly uninstructive. The numbered paragraphs are rearranged, we are told; but we are not told from what they are rearranged. The book is an example of how translations ought not be made and published.

And when one overcomes his initial distaste for a cheap and tawdry piece of presswork and begins to read it, suspicions about its authenticity are aroused. Kant, who was usually meticulous about organization—some say he was overly meticulous, and object to his scholastic architectonic organization—is here presented as a writer either incapable of or careless about good organization. He gives incompatible definitions and classifications, and does not even succeed in making his chapter heads correspond to the contents. Another thing which puzzles the reader is the familiarity of much of the material. There are, to be sure, discussions which have no counterpart in the remainder of Kant's writings; these are usually either quaint or boring, such as discussions of whether children should be rocked in cradles, attended to when they cry, and given the first flow of mothers' milk. One is reminded of Dr. Johnson's angry impatience with Boswell when Boswell asked him what he would do if he were left alone with an infant; Kant discusses these questions *ex officio*, as it were, and without putting his old bachelor's heart into it. But aside from these passages, the rest of the book seems to be made up of paraphrases, quotations, and slight misquotations from Kant's other writings. What is even worse, many of the passages have obvious parallels in Rousseau's *Émile*.

Faced with this mess, the curious reader will soon throw aside this wretched little book and, with curses on the press, on Miss Churton, and perhaps even on Kant himself, will turn to the Akademie edition of Kant's writings to find the original. This is in volume 9 of the Akademie under the title *Immanuel Kant über die Pädagogik*, edited by Friedrich Theodor Rink and first published in 1803. It is not divided into chapters, as the translation is, so that the disorganization of the text is somewhat obscured (as I have said, Miss Churton's chapter headings do not correspond very closely to the contents of the chapters). Nor do we find the paragraphs numbered, nor the total number of paragraphs corresponding to the numbers given in the translation. We do find a foreword by Rink that was not translated and we turn hopefully to it for enlightenment on what kind of book it is we have.

Rink says that the required course in pedagogy at Königsberg was given in turn by several of the professors of philosophy, and that when it was Kant's turn (in 1776–77, 1780, 1783–84, and 1786–87) he used as the basis for his lectures the *Textbook in the Art of Education* by his colleague Bock but "held himself exactly neither to the course of investigations nor to the principles" of that book. "To this circumstance," he says, "we owe the origin of the following remarks (*Bemerkungen*) on pedagogy."[11]

In the light of these introductory statements, it has been commonly believed that we have here a work comparable to the *Lectures on Ethics*, edited by Paul Menzer from a careful collation of several *Kolleghefte* by students in the class, or to the *Lectures on Logic*, which Jäsche compiled by taking Kant's marginal notes in the Meier textbook upon which he lectured.

This assumption has been refuted by an erudite, somewhat pedantic, and mammoth book by Traugott Weisskopf, *Immanuel Kant und die Pädagogik* (1970). I can give only the highlights of this enormous commentary of over seven hundred pages on a text of sixty pages.

First, there is a question about Rink himself. The conclusions are that he was incompetent and dishonorable, and that the trust Kant had in him is to be explained only by reference to Kant's senility and to Rink's pretensions.

Second, the text is based neither on students' *Kolleghefte* nor on any lecture notes of Kant's, for there is no way even distantly to relate the contents either to Bock's text or to the text by Basedow which we know (though Rink does not mention it) was used as the textbook the first time Kant gave the series of lectures on pedagogy. Furthermore there is the reference to the demise of the Philanthro-

11. Ak. IX, 439.

pin, quoted above, which occurred in 1794, years after the last lectures were given.

Third, the compiling done by Rink must have been simply the joining together of at least three piles of Kant's notes without any serious effort to avoid repetition or inconsistencies. These three conjectural and relatively independent collections were made by Kant at different times and for different purposes. (For convenience, I shall refer to chapter headings not present in Rink but introduced later by Miss Churton). Weisskopf identifies these sub-collections as: (a) lecture notes on *Anthropology*, used in the Introduction, chapters 4, 5, and part of 6; (b) a collection of quotations from Rousseau or notes on Rousseau which Kant apparently made from *Emile* in French and not from the German translation, used in chapter 3 and part of chapter 2; and (c) notes for Kant's *Lectures on Ethics*, used in chapter 6.

Weisskopf's fourth contention is that Rink added material of his own, as indicated by differences in style; and collation of Rink's transcriptions of passages we have in Kant's own *Nachlass* and in the published *Anthropology* and *Lectures on Ethics* shows that he modified Kant's own language when he was copying authentic sources.

Weisskopf's conclusion is that the text cannot be regarded as an authentic work of Kant's and should be removed from the corpus. [12] The documentation for the thesis is overwhelming, so much so that there is a high degree of pedantic overkill in Weisskopf's relentless prosecution of Rink. In my opinion Weisskopf has adequately supported his indictment. But I must confess to some doubt about his explanation of the way the Rousseau material got into the book. There are three considerations against it. First, from what we know of Kant's working methods, it seems very unlikely that he transcribed or translated, or even took such copious notes, as this hypothesis requires. Second, there is the absence from Kant's *Nachlass* of any of the notes; most of the Rousseau notes which have survived

12. Traugott Weisskopf, *Immanuel Kant und die Pädagogik* (Basel, 1970), p. 349.

are included in the collection of material which was used in the sixties when he was working on or annotating the *Observations on the Feeling of the Beautiful and the Sublime.* Third, and perhaps most important, is the fact that upon examination of all the passages in Rousseau and Kant which Weisskopf sees as parallel, I do not find as many indisputable cases of parallelism as he does; and the differences between the German translation of *Émile* and the original, and the putative similarities of Kant's material to the latter and dissimilarities to the former, seem to me to be, with perhaps one exception, so subtle and exiguous that I do not believe one can be confident that Kant was reading the original instead of a translation. But I must confess that I have no better explanation of the way the Rousseau material got into the Rink text, unless, of course, Rink put it there on his own authority.

It seems to me, however, that Weisskopf has proved too much for his own purpose. In fact, he has shown very good reason to take *Über die Pädagogik* seriously as a compendium of *echt-kantische* views on education, even if we cannot be confident that we are reading Kant's own words and can be generally confident that we are not reading them in an order and context established by Kant himself. Out of the 175 paragraphs of the German text (which do not correspond to the 113 numbered sections in the translation), Weisskopf has given at least conjectural documentation for all but 31 by citations from other works of Kant, Kant fragments, the hypothetical collection of Rousseau notes, or Bock's textbook (which provides only a very small number). The 31 undocumented paragraphs contain no controversial surprises; they deal mostly with things which neither Kant nor the reader is very interested in. I come to the conclusion that while Weisskopf is on the whole correct in his scholarly and bibliographic research (though some of his parallel passages do not seem to me to be as parallel as they appear to him), the *Pädagogik* is still for the most part a compendium of Kant's views on education, disorganized, but authentic except in the places where the text corresponds only in part to manuscripts in Kant's hand or to his other published works, or where it is interrupted by material not in extant manuscripts or published works and therefore presumably contains interpolations by Rink without Kant's authority. Accordingly, I think one should be warned against using any part of the text of Rink which has no counterpart in authentic Kant works or manuscripts, and when this correspondence *does* exist it is probably better to cite the sources which did not suffer mutilation at Rink's hands; this will be found possible in the case of the most important passages, and one should use other authentic works as a guide to and commentary on the Rink compilation.

While there is no objection to the cautious use of individual paragraphs in the Rink edition or even the Churton translation, especially if one has the Weisskopf at hand as a control, there is no reason to attempt to follow the work or the translation as a whole as if it presented an authentically organized account of Kant's thought on education. Accordingly, I shall find the unifying thought in Kant's educational theory not in the *Pedagogy* but elsewhere.

The Three Stages of Education

In the eighteenth century there was an intimate association of the philosophy of education with the philosophy of history. Lessing's most important work in the philosophy of history is entitled *The Education of the Human Race*, and Rousseau's educational doctrines cannot be understood without knowledge of the philosophy of history he had earlier expounded in the essays on progress in the arts and sciences and on the origin of inequality among men.

Kant's philosophy of history is a much more important base for his educational theory than his epistemology and *Anthropology* is. In the *Pedagogy* he raises the question: "Should we in the education of the individual imitate the course followed by the education of the human race through its successive generations?" (p. 12). It is characteristic of the fragmentary character of this work that the question raised here is never explicitly answered in it. But if we turn to the papers on the philosophy of history we find that we have but little choice as to whether we shall interpret education as a recapitulation of history; the ages of an individual life correspond to the stages in the history of the world. By reading the fuller treatment of the philosophy of history we discover a key to the less well organized treatment of the philosophy of education.

On the *Conjectural Beginning of Human History*, which has some resemblance to the early parts of Lessing's *Education of the Human Race*, Kant interprets Genesis 2-6 as an account of the transition of man from a state of nature, guided by instinct, to a state in which he is guided, at first bunglingly, by the exercise of reason into the enjoyment and suffering of freedom. Prudence supervenes upon instinct, and man is able to foresee and prepare for the future. But the foresight into a future of the vanity of human wishes, labor, and death would have been sufficient to make man "foreswear and decry as a crime the use of reason, which had been the cause of all these ills" had it not been that "he came to understand, however obscurely, that he is the true end of nature, and that nothing can compete with him in this regard."[13] As the true end of nature, his own end must be one which is immune to the vicissitudes and contraints of nature: he is "released from the womb of nature" for a higher destiny in which he is an end in himself. Reason, produced by nature for the attainment of natural ends, creates ends of its own, and man makes the transition from civilization (a stage in the history of nature) to morality.

A like story, without biblical allegory, is told also in the *Idea for a Universal History*. Nature, he says, has willed that all the natural capacities of a creature are destined to evolve completely to their natural end and perfection, but this can be achieved only in the race, not in the individual. In this process, nature has ordained "that man should, by himself, produce everything that goes beyond the mechanical ordering of his existence, and that he should partake of no other happiness or perfection than that which he himself, independently of instinct, has created by his own reason."[14] Nature, using human vice and intelligence, creates civilization, and could do so even with a race of devils, provided only they were intelligent devils. Morality is not a product of nature, but of a new beginning

13. *Conjectural Beginning of Human History*, Ak. VIII, 14 (in *Kant on History*, ed. L. W. Beck [Bobbs-Merrill, 1963], p. 58).
14. *Idea for a Universal History*, Ak. VIII, 19 (Beck, p. 13).

which, nevertheless, presupposes the natural processes leading up to civilization.[15]

With these keys, when we turn back to the *Pedagogy* we can see a pattern of organization which was formerly obscure. Kant divides education, like the history of the world, into three stages. He calls them nurture, discipline, and cultivation. (There are several other bipartite and tripartite divisions in the *Pedagogy*, and they are not all compatible with one another. The one I have chosen works as well as any of the others and is perhaps the one that is most perspicuous and pervasive.)

Nurture deals with the child purely as a part of nature. It is concerned with the feeding and tending of the young child. Kant acts like a Dr. Spock of the eighteenth century, and what he says (taken mostly from Rousseau) is of only antiquarian interest. I mention it only because this stage of education corresponds to the earliest stage in the history of the race, before the exercise of thought was possible or necessary and when all could be left to instinct.

The second stage of education, discipline, is that of the earliest school years. It is the discipline of mind and body under the general rubric of prudence (translated by Miss Churton as "discretion"). The teenage boy is no longer guided by mere nature, but by men who have themselves been educated; there is no *instinct* for education (pp. 6, 13). At this level the child is taught the proper use of his body and mind so that his "animal nature" does not get the better of his "manhood." Kant here speaks of learning games, reading, writing, music, swimming, obedience, and good manners, and of abilities which are valuable for achieving all sorts of ends. At this age the child is no longer like a dog or horse that must be "broken" (p. 20) but must be treated as a free being who has not yet developed full control of his own freedom.

The moral problem is how to unite submission to restraint with the child's capability of freedom; as Rousseau saw, restraint and freedom are antithetic, and yet the former is necessary to the latter. Kant states two principles to guide us through this difficult period:

15. Ibid., Ak. VIII, 27 (Beck, p. 21).

We must allow the child every freedom which does not harm himself or others, and "we must prove to him that restraint is laid on him that he may learn in time to use his liberty aright, and that his mind is being cultivated so that one day he may be free, that is, independent of the help of others" (p. 28). Kant, unlike Rousseau, believes that public education, not education at home, is best for these purposes, since it teaches children how to get along with each other.

This second stage of education corresponds to the second stage in the history of mankind. In it, both the race and the child have left raw nature behind but have not yet attained the level of morality. Historically, Kant calls this stage civilization; in it, outward decorum and the love of honor are a "simulacrum of morality" but civilization without morality is but "glittering misery." [16] (Almost exactly the same thing is repeated in *Pedagogy*, p. 21. Weisskopf, p. 560, finds three other almost identical passages in Kant's other works.) [17]

The third stage of history and education is that of genuine morality. Because Kant makes so sharp a distinction between prudence, even at its highest and most disinterested level, and genuine morality, and because he is in no sense a "naturalist" in his ethical theory, the transition from the discipline of the natural talents and inclinations in civilized maturity to morality is especially difficult for him to deal with in theory, just as it is in fact difficult to manage in practice. Man is not moral by nature (p 108), [18] and morality is not one of the natural dispositions of the child that can be brought to actualization by training. Here he differs from Rousseau, who thinks the "germs" of morality are present for the beginning, as a natural disposition to the good. A moral disposition for Kant is a product of a "revolution in the heart." A moral action is so free that it has no natural antecedents which produce it in the course of empirical, psychological development; [19] a bad environment and evil

16. Ibid., Ak. VIII, 26 (Beck, p. 21).

17. *Immanuel Kant und die Pädagogik*, p. 560.

18. *Anthropology from a Pragmatic Point of View*, Ak. VII, 324 (trans. M. J. Gregor [Nijhoff, 1974], p. 185).

19. *Religion within the Limits of Reason Alone*, Ak. VI, 41 (trans. H. H. Hudson and T. H. Greene [Harper, 1960], p. 36).

companions are absolutely no excuse for immorality even though they may lead us confidently to expect it. The historical transition from a state of doctrinal religion (such as Kant finds in the Old Testament) to the state of moral religion (in the New) cannot, according to him, be explained historically;[20] it is as though a new revelation were responsible for it. Similarly the development of the individual's moral point of view from that of civility and decorum cannot be explained; we can at most, he says in the last sentence of the *Foundations of the Metaphysics of Morals*, explain its inexplicability, that is, show that it is *not* an event occurring under the mechanism of nature.

The teacher, accordingly, cannot make the child moral; only the child himself can do that. Kant states that I have no duty even to try to bring another person to the state of moral perfection; another's moral perfection is not, like his happiness, one of the ends which it is a duty for me to try to achieve.[21] I have a duty to help the child perfect himself only in his *natural* abilities as a part of my duty to promote his happiness.

When Kant is dealing with education, however, he relaxes some of this rigor; he does not even seem to see that his strict moral philosophy has, and can have, no place for moral education. But in both the *Critique of Practical Reason* and the *Pedagogy* Kant seems to take it as self-evident that moral education is both obligatory and possible, and the only question about it is one of proper practice. Only in the *Lectures on Ethics* does he deal with the duty of education as such (including moral education), where he discusses it under the heading "duties arising from differences of age," as a sub-heading under "duties towards particular classes of human beings."[22]

In the *Lectures on Ethics* and in the *Pedagogy* he writes almost as if the *cultivation* of the moral disposition were like the *cultivation* of prudence, even though he still insists upon the great differences

20. Ibid., p. 122 (Hudson and Greene, pp. 112–13).
21. *Doctrine of Virtue*, Part II of *Metaphysics of Morals*, Ak. VI, 385–89 (trans. M. J. Gregor [Harper, 1964], pp. 44–50).
22. *Lectures on Ethics*, trans. L. Infield (Harper, 1963), pp. 247 ff. The point is well discussed by William Frankena, *Three Historical Philosophies of Education* (Scott Foresman, 1965), pp. 109–10.

between morality and prudence. In the *Pedagogy* he writes: "Morality is something so sacred and sublime that we must not degrade it by placing it in the same rank as discipline" (p. 84), though discipline is (normally, at any rate) a precondition of morality:

It cannot be denied that in order to bring either an as yet uneducated or degraded mind into the path of the morally good, some preparatory guidance is needed to attract it by a view to its own advantage or to frighten it by fear of harm. As soon as this machinery, the leading strings, have had some effect, the pure moral motive must be brought to mind.

When a person uncovers the moral law within,

It gives his mind a power, unexpected even by himself, to pull himself loose from all sensuous attachments (so far as they fain would dominate him) and, in the independence of his intelligible nature and in the greatness of soul to which he sees himself called, to find himself richly compensated for the sacrifice he makes.[23]

The child can be brought to this awareness, Kant thinks, by telling him a story of innocence punished (his suggestion is that of Ann Boleyn!) and having the child recognize the difference between what prudence would dictate (agreement with the King in his false accusations) and what morality demands (let justice prevail though the heavens fall), and asking him, in his safety and innocence, which path he would prefer to follow (even though he admits he might not be courageous enough to do so). Through this story and this catechetical exercise, the child discovers within himself a disposition which Kant thinks does not come from nature, and cannot be created by education, but which can best be made salient by the skillful catechism of the teacher who helps the child draw the radical distinction between being prudent and being moral. In the *Metaphysics of Morals* (§52) he gives an example of such a moral cate-

23. *Critique of Practical Reason*, Ak. V, 152 (trans. L. W. Beck [Liberal Arts Press, 1956], p. 156).

chism (not very realistic, we must admit) whereby a child is brought to see that morality is worthiness to be happy, and not happiness itself.

Kant's philosophy of history is, on the whole, a theodicy. He finds the meaning of history to lie in the dominance of morality over nature, and in the achievement of moral goals which he believes are adumbrated in the course of history. Similarly he sees education as a means to enlightenment and eventually to a moral commonwealth, the church invisible or the Kingdom of God on earth. More modestly he writes: "Children ought to be educated not for the present, but for a possibly improved condition of man in the future; that is, in a manner which is adapted to the *idea of humanity* and the whole destiny of man" (p. 14). Education should be for this future, and this future can be attained only through education. "How then is this perfection [of humanity] to be sought? Wherein lies our hope? In education and in nothing else."[24]

This "improved condition of mankind," however, is not the heavenly city of the enlightenment philosophers. It is a moral realm which Kant, continuing the passage just quoted, calls the Kingdom of God on Earth—and precisely this cannot be produced by education. In these brave words from the *Lectures on Ethics* Kant seems to have forgotten for the moment the rather narrow competency in moralizing mankind that he had ascribed to education. Education, like civilization, is a *conditio sine qua non* of moral progress, but it is not its cause. Everywhere in Kant's writings, but chiefly in those of the last period of his activity, one finds a tension between two opposed movements of thought. The one, in which Kant expects and emphasizes the gradual progress toward the good through the historical process, including that of education, is typical enlightenment doctrine. According to the other, Kant teaches that there is a supernatural, superhistorical dimension to morality and the transition to it. In such an eschatology the social institutions of civilization, including that of education, play only a preliminary role; and it is this movement of his thought which principally distinguishes him from other enlightenment philosophers.

24. *Lectures on Ethics*, p. 252.

This tension in his philosophy of history and ethics is reflected also in his philosophy of education. His insights into the strengths and necessity of education, and his insights into its insufficiency and inefficacy, were never reconciled.

12   "Was–Must Be" and "Is-Ought" in Hume

Let me begin by quoting a famous passage from Hume, taking the liberty, which I will attempt to justify later, of changing a few essential words:

> In every system of [philosophy], which I have hitherto met with, I have always remark'd, that the author proceeds for some time in the ordinary way of reasoning, ... when of a sudden I am surpriz'd to find, that instead of the usual copulations of proposition, [*was*, and *was not*], I meet with no proposition that is not connected with [a *must be*, or *cannot be*]. This change is imperceptible; but is, however, of the last consequence. For as this [*must be*, or *cannot be*], expresses some new relation or affirmation, 'tis necessary that it shou'd be observ'd and explain'd; and at the same time that a reason should be given, for what seems altogether inconceivable, how this new relation can be a deduction from others, which are entirely different from it. But as authors do not commonly use this precaution, I shall presume to recommend it to the readers; and am persuaded, that this small attention wou'd subvert all the vulgar systems of [philosophy], and let us see, that the [relation of cause and effect] is not founded merely on the relations of objects, nor is perceiv'd by reason.

This passage might well have appeared in the first book of the *Treatise* as an introduction to Hume's examination of the idea of

This essay was published in *Philosophical Studies* 26 (1974), 219–28, and is reprinted by kind permission of the editor, Professor Keith Lehrer. I am grateful to Professor David C. Yalden-Thomson and Professor Barry Stroud for criticisms of an earlier draft.

causation; in its unmodified form it comes near the beginning of his examination of the idea of "moral distinctions." But the thesis of this paper is that there is a parallelism between Hume's examinations, both in their negative and constructive phases, of these two basic ideas, and that the argument concerning causation, which is both better written[1] and better known, throws light on his argument concerning moral distinctions and serves as a model by which the latter may be understood.

I must first point out the most ambiguous expressions in this famous passage, to wit, "a reason should be given, for *what seems altogether inconceivable*, how this new relation can be a *deduction* from others, which are entirely different from it." "What seems altogether inconceivable" means "what *is* altogether inconceivable" if "deduction" refers to formal entailment; "x and y were contiguous and successive etc." does not entail "x caused y," and "x is productive of happiness" does not entail "x ought to be done." If P stands for a factually descriptive statement, and M stands for a modal proposition containing an *ought* or a *must be*, Hume is saying that P does not *entail M*, and that it should *is* altogether inconceivable. But from P we do in fact *infer M*, and this "*seems* altogether inconceivable and 'tis necessary that [this inference] shou'd be observed and explain'd." In the first book, Hume has observed and explained the inference from "X and Y are constantly conjoined" to "If X occurs, Y must occur," and in Book III he observed and explained this inference from "X is agreeable or useful" to "X ought to be done." The purpose of this paper is to point to the analogies between Hume's accounts of these two inferences.

Fortunately Hume's analysis of the causal inference is so well known that it can be quickly recapitulated.

a. *Causality is not observed by the senses.* We do not observe, as a quality of a preceding event, a power to produce the succeeding event. What cannot be observed in a single pair of events cannot be observed in any repetition of it. There is therefore no impression of

1. This lends credence to Kemp Smith's conjecture that Book III was written before Book I, for why otherwise would Hume have not cited the fuller analysis of a like argument if Book I had already performed it?

causality between events from which the idea of necessary connection could be formed.

b. *Causal knowledge is not derived from reason.* There is no contradiction in asserting the occurrence of one event and denying the occurrence of any other event. The relation of cause and effect is not a "relation of ideas" known to reason.

c. *Therefore* when we assert the cause-effect relation, that is to say, when we assert that there is a necessary connection between two events, we go beyond the testimony of the senses and exceed the powers of reason.

d. *The idea of necessary connection is based on an internal impression.* We assert this necessary connection, when the sequence of pairs of events is constant, that is to say, events like x are constantly precedent to and contiguous with events like y. The *repetition* of like pairs of events must affect the mind in a way that the single occurrence of the pair does not.

By the laws of association, when impressions of x and y have repeatedly been together, the reoccurrence of an x-like impression determines the mind to move to the idea of a y-like event, and the mind has an impression of this constraint which is produced by the repetition.

e. *Belief is an essential ingredient in the idea of necessary connection.* When an impression is associated with an idea, it gives vivacity to the associated idea, and the associated idea with this added vivacity is the belief in the object of that idea. Therefore upon the occurrence of an impression of what we call the cause, the mind expects or believes in the existence or occurrence of what we call the effect. The necessity to move from the impression of x to the belief in y "exists *in us*"[2] and we erroneously feign it to exist in x itself.

f. *The explanation of the causal relation is itself causal*, though it is internal to the mind and not "metaphysical" (112): "The uniting principle among our internal perceptions is as unintelligible as that among external objects, and is not known to us by any other way

---

2. *Treatise of Human Nature* (ed. Selby-Bigge), pp. 165–66. Page references in the text are to this edition of the *Treatise* unless otherwise indicated.

than by experience. . . . It never gives us any insight into the internal structure or operating principle of objects, but only accustoms the mind to pass from one to the other" (169).

g. *The justification of causal inference is pragmatic:* we could not live a single hour without using it. But inasmuch as we would not associate x and y together, and believe that y must occur when x occurs, unless x and y were in fact associated in nature, there is a kind of preestablished harmony between what we believe (when we take due caution) to be causally related and what is, in fact, the regular course of nature;[3] the natural relation of causation supervenes upon the philosophical relation of causation (172).

Underlying this entire analysis are two principles of human nature which Hume does not profess to explain: they are the association of ideas when the originative impressions have been contiguous in space and time, and the mechanism whereby an impression vivifies an associated idea so that we believe in the existence of the object of that idea.

Though the only moral copulas mentioned in the famous passage are *ought* and *ought-not*, Hume's point is more general; in fact, his example of ought and ought-not is a singularly inept one for his purposes, since the most important moral judgments for him are judgments of merit and demerit, not judgments of obligation. But more of this hereafter. In principle, Hume is inquiring how we infer judgments with ethical predicates or ethical force from judgments with only factual predicates and descriptive force, the latter judgments being established by the understanding and the former requiring some other faculty for their establishment.

We can trace Hume's account of how "this new relation" can be a "deduction" from others which are "entirely different from it" by breaking it down into almost exactly the same steps by which he accounted for how judgments of causal necessity arise from judgments of mere constant contiguity.

a. *Moral distinctions are not observed by the senses.* We do not

3. *Enquiry Concerning Human Understanding* (ed. Hendel), p. 67.

observe, as a quality of a state of affairs, anything which requires an ethical term to denote it: "Take any action allow'd to be vicious: willful murder, for instance. Examine it in all lights, and see if you can find any matter of fact, which you call *vice*. In which-ever way you take it, you find only certain passions, motives, volitions, and thoughts. There is no other matter of fact in the case" (468). There is no impression of an object from which the idea of moral value can be formed.

b. *Moral distinctions are not derived from reason* (*Treatise*, Book III, Part i, Section i). Reason cannot discern a relation between ideas "which constitute morality or obligation [so] that we may know wherein they consist, and after what manner we must judge them" (463). For the moral relation is not one of resemblance, contrariety, degrees in quality, or proportions in quantity and number, which are the only relations known by reason. Nor is morality a relation of ideas in the sense of the *Enquiry*, according to which immorality would have to be a contradiction (458, 461 and note, 466). " 'Tis not contrary to reason to prefer the destruction of the world to the scratching of my finger" (416). But even if reason were to discover moral relations, this would not be sufficient for morals: "In order . . . to prove, that the measures of right and wrong are eternal [sc., rational] laws, *obligatory* on every rational mind, 'tis not sufficient to shew the relations upon which they are founded: We must also point out the connexion betwixt the relation and the will; and must prove that this connexion is so necessary, that in every well-disposed mind, it must take place and have its influence . . ." (465). But "we cannot prove *a priori*, that these relations, if they really existed and were perceiv'd, would be universally forcible and obligatory" (466).

c. *Therefore* when we assert a moral distinction, that is to say, when we assert that an act is obligatory or a character has merit, we go beyond the testimony of the senses and the evidence of reason.

d. *Moral distinctions are founded on an inner sentiment or moral sense* (*Treatise*, Book III, Part i, Section ii). As Hume found the source of the idea of the necessity of the connection between cause and effect to exist neither in the objects nor in our senses or reason, but rather in a "uniting principle among our internal perceptions," so also he says that when you assert a moral distinction you "turn your reflexion into your own breast, and find a sentiment of [approbation or] disapprobation, which arises in you, towards [an] action" (469).

> An action, or sentiment, or character is virtuous or vicious; Why? because its view causes a pleasure or uneasiness of a particular kind. . . . To have the sense of virtue, is nothing but to *feel* a satisfaction of a particular kind from the contemplation of a character. That very *feeling* constitutes our praise or admiration. . . . We do not infer a character to be virtuous, because it pleases: But in feeling that it pleases after such a manner, we in effect feel that it is virtuous (471).

Here Hume equates "we feel it pleases after such a manner" with "we feel it is virtuous." The first, at least, is a matter of fact. Hume calls the "sentiment of disapprobation" which we feel upon contemplating a murder a matter of fact, but he misstates its significance as follows: "Here is a matter of fact; but 'tis the object of feeling, not of reason. It lies in yourself, not in the object" (469). What he *should* have said is: "Here is a matter of fact; but 'tis a feeling, not an object of reason, and it lies in yourself, not in the object." Properly stated, then, this passage still leaves open the question of how we move from a statement of a matter of fact, namely a fact *about* our feeling, to the apparently very different judgment which applies a moral predicate to the *object*.

The second judgment, namely, "We in effect feel it is virtuous," is also, as stated, a factual judgment; but Hume did not mean to be moving from one factual judgment to another, both describing the same fact. Rather, I think, "We feel it is virtuous" is for him a pleonastic way of saying "It is virtuous," since the latter statement for him entails and normally *(ceteris paribus)* is entailed by the former. "When you pronounce any action or character to be vicious, you mean nothing, but that from the constitution of your nature you have a feeling or sentiment of blame from the contemplation of it" (469).

We have not yet attended to one of the central features of this transition from a judgment of feeling to a moral judgment. There is, he says repeatedly, a feeling of satisfaction *of a particular kind* which permits this transition to another verbal form which is *constituted* (471) by that satisfaction. It is the *peculiarity* of the satisfaction "of a particular kind" which authorizes us to apply moral predicates; in fact it led us to *invent* the moral predicates in the first place.[4]

e. *Sympathy is to moral predicates what belief is to necessary connection.*

In discussing the peculiarity of the satisfaction felt upon the contemplation of some actions, the peculiarity which leads us to apply ethical predicates to them, Hume introduces his theory of sympathy. Belief and sympathy are both products of association, but his theory of association alone would explain neither the idea of necessary connection nor that of moral distinctions: in each case, something must be added to association (305).

The peculiarity of the feeling of satisfaction which is the matter of fact from which moral distinctions are inferred is this: the satisfaction is disinterested. "'Tis only when a character is considered in general without reference to our particular interest that it causes such feeling or sentiment as denominates it morally good or evil" (472).

Sympathy is the feeling of satisfaction independent of our particular interests. It is the feeling of satisfaction we have when someone else's interests are known to be gratified. It arises in the following way. I observe an action (for example, a gesture) which is associated with the affection of the person who does or who suffers the action. By the well-known mechanism of belief I not only *believe* that he has the affection (the idea of the affection is rendered more vivid by the occurrence of the impression associated with it) but my idea of the affection "acquires such a degree of force and vivacity as to

4. *Enquiry Concerning the Principles of Morals* (ed. Hendel), p. 95. References to the *"Enquiry"* in the text are to this edition.

become the very passion itself (317, 576).[5] The satisfaction of
another person becomes, in a lesser degree, my own satisfaction; but
this sympathetic satisfaction is not contingent upon any antecedent
interest I have in being satisfied by the state of affairs which satisfied
the man I am contemplating. This disinterestedness constitutes the
peculiarity of the satisfaction which calls forth moral judgment:

> We partake of their uneasiness by sympathy; and as everything,
> which gives uneasiness in human actions, *upon the general survey*
> is call'd Vice, and whatever produces satisfaction, *in the same
> manner*, is denominated Virtue; this is the reason why the sense of
> moral good and evil follows upon justice and injustice [which have
> regard to the interest of others generally] . (499, italics added)

f. *The origin of the moral distinctions lies in the peculiarity of the
moral feelings.*

Just as Hume explains causally why our causal inferences are
generally right by saying that there is a preestablished harmony
between the course of nature and the succession of our ideas,[6] he
also shows how our sentiments "of a particular kind" correspond to
the sentiments of others and thus give rise to judgments which
escape from the constraints of first-person statements about matters
of fact concerning the satisfaction of my own interests.

In giving a causal explanation of our causal explanations, Hume
availed himself of two principles of human nature which, being
ultimate, could not be explained. Similarly in his account of the
origin of moral distinctions, he pushes back to entirely contingent
facts about human nature. Human emotions, like all things in the
world, "consider'd in themselves, appear entirely loose and independent of each other" (466). " 'Tis evident our passions, volitions, and
actions are . . . original facts and realities, compleat in themselves,
and implying no reference to other passions, volitions, and actions"
(458). Their connections can be learned only by experience (466),

---

5. Hume compares the mechanism of belief with that of sympathy in the
Treatise, pp. 319–20, 280, and (less explicitly) in the *Enquiry*, p. 60.
6. *Enquiry Concerning Human Understanding*, p. 67.

and Hume goes so far as to assert that he can see "no contradiction in supposing a desire of producing misery annex'd to love, and of happiness to hatred" (368).[7]

But the facts of experience show that we have the sentiment "of a particular kind" only when we sympathize with others; we cannot (psychologically cannot) have this feeling about actions which do not tend to contribute to the well-being and satisfaction of others. The distinction between the generally useful and the generally pernicious "is the same, in all its parts, with the moral distinction" (*Enquiry*, 61) and cannot be otherwise since sympathetic feelings are ingredients in the sentiment "of a particular kind." There is thus, as it were, a kind of preestablished harmony between the course of society and our feelings of disinterested approbation, like the preestablished harmony between the course of nature and our causal knowledge.

  g. *The justification of the ascription or moral predicates is pragmatic and lies in their peculiar function in the social relations of mankind.*

Why do we say "*X* is good" instead of "*X* pleases me" or "*X* pleases me in a particular way"? Why introduce terms for moral distinctions at all, seeing that the descriptive content of the two judgments is the same (just as the purely descriptive content of "*X* and *Y* are regularly conjoined" is the same as that of "*X* causes *Y*")? Hume begins to answer this question in the *Treatise* (522, 584, 603), but his full answer is in the *Enquiry Concerning the Principles of Morals.*

"General language," he there says, "being formed for general use, must be molded on some general views and must affix the epithets of praise or blame in conformity to sentiments which arise from the general interests of the community" (*Enquiry*, 55). One can describe another man as his enemy using morally neutral language to express sentiments arising from his particular circumstance and situation; but "when he bestows on any man the epithets of *vicious* or *odious*

---

7. I have discussed this passage, and what is wrong with it, in *The Actor and the Spectator* (Yale University Press, 1975), pp. 107–09.

or *depraved*, he *then speaks another language* [italics added] in which he expects all his audience to concur with him" (*Enquiry*, 93). "Language ... must invent a peculiar set of terms in order to express those universal sentiments of censure or approbation. ... Virtue and vice then become known" (*Enquiry*, 95).

The language of morals, of ought and ought-not, is the language of the "party of mankind" (*Enquiry*, 96) which we use because we have a sympathetic experience of the satisfaction of others. We speak the language of the disinterested anonymous observer. By it and its principles, "the particular sentiments of self-love [are] frequently controlled and limited" (*Enquiry*, 95).

Moral language and distinctions are therefore necessary for man's social life as the language and thought of causality are necessary for his natural and social life.

We can now give a summary account of Hume's derivation of "ought" from "is." Where X is a voluntary action, the sentence containing "is" is:

a. X is beneficial or immediately pleasing to the generality of mankind.

The sentence containing "ought" is:

b. X ought to be done.

The connection between the two is supplied by two premises which Hume thinks he has established. One is causal (psychological):

1. X produces satisfaction of a particular kind.

The other in linguistic:

2. "X ought to be done" *means nothing but* (469) "There is satisfaction of a particular kind upon contemplating X."

Thus is the transition from "is" to "ought" "observ'd and explain'd." Given the premises, one can infer (indeed deduce) the conclusion that a man with a sound disposition and knowledge of ordinary usage who knows (a) will affirm (b). *This* inference, made by a philosopher, is an inference from facts (a), (1), and (2) to another fact, namely that a moral agent will affirm (b). But for the moral agent in question, (b) itself is not an inference from (a), (1), and (2) nor is it an inference of any kind; it is rather the expression of his feeling of a particular kind upon contemplating X.

The situation is exactly analogous to that in the case of the causal inference. Hume gives two formally distinct definitions of causality (172), one of cause as a relatum in a philosophical relation holding between events *in rerum natura* (corresponding to [a]), and the other a cause as a relatum in a natural relation holding "in the imagination" (corresponding to [b]). Call them (a') and (b'). Given (a') and facts about human nature, the philosopher can infer that a human being will affirm (b'); but (b') is not deduced from (a').

In moral philosophy, the definition of a virtuous act in terms of utility and immediate benefit and the definition in terms of particular satisfaction are likewise independent of each other, though the second is (normally) instantiated only by an X which instantiates the first. What Hume has tried to show in both his analyses is that anything that satisfies the condition of the first of one of these pairs of definitions, given the brute and inscrutable facts about human nature and sufficient information, will satisfy the second in these pairs of definitions respectively, even though the second cannot be deduced from the first.

Index

217